W9-AFM-107

AN ANTHOLOGY OF

UNIVERSITY OF IOWA PRESS   IOWA CITY

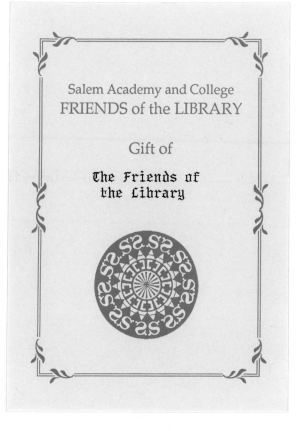

AN ANTHOLOGY

OF CONTEMPORARY

RUSSIAN WOMEN

POETS

CONTENTS

PREFACE

STEPHANIE SANDLER

Anna Akhmatova may be the reason you opened this book. Her name springs first to the minds of Americans who know much about Russian poetry, if I may draw on an entirely unscientific sample of my own chance conversations over the years. Russia must have the only world literature whose poetry has been represented by a woman, an oddity that grows when one realizes that Russia in fact had two great women poets early in the twentieth century: Marina Tsvetaeva may be less known abroad, but only because her linguistic wizardry nearly defies translation. In Russia they command equal respect, and generations of writers have looked to both as exemplary lyric poets.

Some Russian poets look back to Akhmatova and Tsvetaeva as proof that women more than hold their own with men as poets. Thus in "Evening at Tsarskoe Selo," a poem you will find in this volume, Polina Barskova describes Akhmatova walking through a park where Akhmatova had imagined Aleksandr Pushkin walking a century earlier. In Barskova's poem, Akhmatova is preoccupied by an unfinished poem, and she pays little attention to her male companion. Barskova wittily rewrites the myth of Akhmatova as a love poet and makes her first and foremost a poet, someone whose mind and heart are taken up with poetry more than with any lover. In another poem you will find here, Olga Sedakova also turns to Akhmatova and Tsvetaeva as poets, although by means of the briefest mention. She adds a footnote to "In Memory of a Poet" telling readers that she has drawn on the poetic traditions of both Tsvetaeva and Akhmatova; their mediation has given form and intonational nobility to a poem memorializing her great contemporary Joseph Brodsky.

These two examples show Akhmatova as muse to later women poets, but she and Tsvetaeva can also, paradoxically, cast a long shadow. Some poets may wonder which is the greater danger, seeking the lofty, stern harmonies of Akhmatova or risking comparison with the wilder linguistic experimentation of Tsvetaeva. Not for nothing did the poet Yunna Morits once see them as Scylla and Charybdis. For her, the Tsvetaeva and Akhmatova traditions had to be circumnavigated. Happily, the women poets included here have avoided one risk, repeating the biographical fates of these two poets, which included exile and later suicide for Tsvetaeva and the doom of seeing loved ones imprisoned for both Tsvetaeva and Akhmatova. Later poets were blessed by the kinder turn of Russian history. No one has had an exile as difficult as Tsvetaeva's years abroad, and younger poets live more easily in Rome, Jerusalem, Paris, or New York, even if their financial circumstances can be uncertain. Life outside Russia is no longer a form of exile: poets are finally free to visit Russia (this was not true before the late 1980s, which shapes the creative biography of those who left earlier, like Irina Ratushinskaya and Natalya Gorbanevskaya). Today Russian poets living abroad can have intensive, ongoing contact with poetic traditions in Russia itself. They see fellow poets and can travel to Russia if they wish, and the Internet and e-mail have made it easy to remain informed even at a great distance. We in the West have luckily heard some of them read, both those who emigrated and those visiting from Russia; poetry festivals or book fairs in New York, London, Frankfurt, and many smaller cities as well as tours by individual poets have brought their voices very much to life for American and European audiences.

Some of the poets included in this generous collection will be familiar to American audiences, who may have heard Bella Akhmadulina read and seen a volume of translated poems by Elena Shvarts or Olga Sedakova. The prose and drama of Liudmila Petrushevskaya may be known by many. It is all to the good that the barriers should be lowered, that Russia's poets should seem less exotic and strange, more a part of the larger international poetry scene in which national literatures interpenetrate and are transformed by contact. Another paradox emerges here, then, as these poets surprise us when they seem suddenly familiar, even as they pursue new forms of difference. Many of these poets, including some whose names will be entirely new to almost everyone, pay attention to familiar cultural currents in the humanities and in popular culture; and so we recognize the worlds they describe: Mariya Galina's "Ghazal" mentions Jacques Derrida and Gilles Deleuze; Mariya Kildibekova has Osip Mandelstam, Marilyn Monroe, and Oskar Schindler in the same poem; Elena Fanailova writes of Frida Kahlo; and Aleksandra Petrova uses a Quentin Tarantino film as a point of departure. Daily life is here, too, the tumult of communal apartments and the recollection of exotic landscapes—Katia Kapovich, who lives in the United States, writes with irony of "an untidy Russian life." We also see objects of daily life that are not marked as Russian in any way: for example, the computer to whom Inna Lisnianskaya writes an ode; the laundry and household clutter in Nina Iskrenko's "Another Woman." Women are treated for cancer and give birth in the poems of Vera Pavlova; cars and teeth are fixed in a poem by Olesia Nikolaeva. All is not entirely prosaic, of course. Familiar in a different way to readers of modern poetry will be the metaphysical concerns of poets like Olga Sedakova and Svetlana Kekova or, in the poems of Nikolaeva, the sense that religious experience and fear of one's own demise can descend on the dullest catalogue of daily life.

The 1980s and 1990s were good years for poets, despite the chaos induced by massive social change in Russia and the apparently falling status of poetry in an age of electronic communication and mass media. Many poets have found new routes to publication because of these technological and social innovations, and their experiments are often truly inspired. Among the more adventurous in their treatment of poetic form are Rea Nikonova and Larisa Berezovchuk, but the stunning leaps in diction, stylistic register, and theme by many others should not be underestimated. Some of these elements are difficult to convey in translation, but not all. The metaphors remain vivid, and lineation and arrangement on the page are formal traits that show through. Readers will see at a quick glance that these poets have many different ideas about the layout of poetic words on a page.

Would these poets be pleased to find their work in a volume entirely dedicated to women? They have agreed to it, which says something; but many would be ambivalent. At least one, Yunna Morits, flatly refused to have her work in such a book. Herein rests yet another paradox of contemporary Russian women poets. Most do not see themselves as "women poets," and the derogatory sting of the term *poetessa* remains. Their bonds to male poets of their generation or to the male poets who inspired them are often quite strong. Thus Elena Shvarts has enduring ties to Aleksandr Mironov and keen admiration for poets like Lev Rubinshtein and the late Viktor Krivulin; and if you ask about Silver Age poets she admires, she is more likely to mention Mikhail Kuzmin than Anna Akhmatova. But Shvarts maintains friendships with several poets in this volume; if I may inject a personal note, it was she who first told me to read Gali-Dana Zinger, also included here. One could tell similar stories about the ties among other women poets, but still we would want to conclude that the reason to group these poets is not because their primary allegiance is to one another, since it is not; and not because any of them should be read entirely outside the context of their male contemporaries and precursors. They should not. Rather, these women poets require separate attention because some collections of contemporary poetry still do not fully attend to their work. This is a surprising lack, because even surveys that relegate women poets to belated acknowledgment admit that they are doing significant work. What persists is a strange awkwardness about how to think about a woman who is a poet. In December 2003 I was present at an evening of Russian poetry where more than half a dozen men read and performed their work. Polina Barskova was the lone female voice. The men decided to make the evening more interesting, as they put it, by creating a competition among the poets. One of the men self-consciously selected Barskova to receive their Golden Lyre award. One could argue that she was, in fact, the most interesting poet in the room, but the supposed competition seemed more an expression of anxiety mixed with benighted male gallantry.

Books such as this one afford a further opportunity, then: this anthology lets us ask what it means to these poets that they write, and are read, as women. The answer to that question cannot be unitary: the variety among these poets in temperament, tone, and poetic inclination is vast. Some explore a feminine identity with passion or with ironic wit, whereas others find the very idea of gender oppressive and uninteresting. Yet the question must be posed, for without it we will have a diminished appreciation of the achievements of women writing poetry in Russian today. And their achievements are considerable, living up to the legacy of Akhmatova and Tsvetaeva, as you will discover in the pages that follow.

AN ANTHOLOGY

OF CONTEMPORARY

RUSSIAN WOMEN

POETS

INTRODUCTION

DANIEL WEISSBORT

This anthology originated in a special issue of the journal *Modern Poetry in Translation* ("Russian Women Poets," editor Daniel Weissbort, issue guest editor Valentina Polukhina, *MPT* 20, King's College, London, 2002). Our early intention had been no less than to survey the whole of contemporary Russian poetry, but we soon realized that this was vastly overambitious. It was decided instead to focus on women poets, not least because poetry anthologies published in Russia itself still appeared to underrepresent them. Valentina Polukhina subsequently perused work by around 800 poets; even so, she did not feel that the comprehensive task she had set herself was by any means complete. It became apparent that a team of readers might have been necessary, in which case the collection would have lost whatever unity a single sensibility gave it. In the aforementioned special issue of *MPT*, Weissbort's editorial conveyed Polukhina's caveats: primarily, that there were many other poets, even as the journal went to press, of whose existence she was becoming aware and whose absence from this collection she regretted. For this revised edition, Professor Polukhina solicited and received additional material, as well as reviewing selections already made, with a view to both improving the coverage and strengthening the collection. It has thus been possible to supplement the selection. In a period of surely unprecedented burgeoning, however, the editors still would not claim to have been fully representative.

The notion of an anthology of women's poetry may have become problematical. It is not surprising that some poets, such as Yunna Morits, were reluctant to be included or excluded themselves, even though they consented to be in the original journal issue. We regret this; but time was not on our side, and we were unable to engage in protracted discussions which might or might not have persuaded them to change their minds. We do not feel that we should attempt to make our case here—not least on grounds of fair play, since the scales are too heavily weighed in our favor, as editors of this collection! Nor do we propose to write about feminist literary theory; readers may be directed to the work of scholars in this field, such as Barbara Heldt's *Terrible Perfection* (1987), largely devoted to Russian women's poetry, or Catriona Kelly's *An Anthology of Russian Women's Writing, 1777–1992* (1994). Our aim throughout has been to present selections of poets whose work seemed both noteworthy and "translatable," work, in short, that interested us as readers of Russian poetry. As editors, we are, of course, gratified to have been able to feature writers inadequately represented, it seems to us, in home-grown anthologies—a notable exception always being the poetry website Vavilon.

We have attempted in particular to represent poets from nonmetropolitan Russia, looking beyond Moscow and St. Petersburg and showcasing what is being produced in provincial centers like Voronezh, Saratov, and Samara as well as in the Urals, Siberia, and the Far East of Russia. It should be pointed out that a number of the poets are not ethnic Russians, even if they write in Russian. A more accurate if also more awkward title might have been "Anthology of Contemporary Women Poets Who Write in Russian." It was, of course, beyond our means to survey this vast terrain exhaustively; indeed, it would have been nearly impossible to do so from abroad, since many of the publications that should be consulted are unobtainable outside Russia. Nevertheless, the Internet has enabled us to range quite far. In this regard we would especially like to express our gratitude to Dmitry Kuzmin and the Vavilon (Babylon) website, an indispensable source for contemporary Russian poetry. Kuzmin drew our attention to much material that we might otherwise have missed as well as putting us in touch with several poets who were able to participate in the translation process and commenting in detail on many of the translations.

Tempting as it may be to indulge ourselves, this is perhaps not the place for a detailed account of the problems of translating Russian poetry into English; diverse views have been expressed, notably by Vladimir Nabokov, Joseph Brodsky, and Czeslaw Milosz (see *From Russian with Love* by Daniel Weissbort, published by Anvil Press in 2004, for a summary of these). The process is notoriously difficult, because of crucial generic differences in the structure of the two languages. Furthermore, the diction of contemporary Russian poetry is highly innovative and reflects contemporary idiomatic speech. Input from Dmitry Kuzmin (as noted above) and from many of the poets themselves helped to ensure that the translations remained in essential ways faithful to the source texts, although they are also intended, naturally, to function as poetic texts in English. The dilemma is memorably encapsulated by Stanley Kunitz, in the preface to his translations of Anna Akhmatova (*Poems of Akhmatova*, co-translated with Max Hayward [1973]): "The poet as translator lives with a paradox. His work must not read like a translation; conversely, it is not an exercise of the free imagination. One voice enjoins him: 'Respect the text!' The other simultaneously pleads with him: 'Make it new!'" (p. 29).

If our aim, then, has been inclusive, we have inevitably also had to be selective—sometimes, it seems to us, highly so, in view of the extent and variety of contemporary Russian poetry. Valentina Polukhina's bibliography of contemporary Russian women poets, included in this anthology, will, we hope, be useful to translators and scholars in identifying additional poets.

Very briefly, the contemporary phase in the burgeoning of Russian poetry fully got underway in the late 80s, with Mikhail Gorbachev's *perestroika*. Suddenly, it seemed, all of world literature, including the work of important Russian poets living abroad, became accessible. In particular, Nobel laureate Joseph Brodsky's influence was assimilated, enriching the scope of poetic language. Not only that: the new accessibility of poets of the Silver Age (Akhmatova, Mandelstam, Boris Pasternak) further exerted, as it were, a delayed influence, no longer artificially limited by state interference. Banned writings by émigrés or exiles (e.g., Tsvetaeva, Nabokov) became easily available only in the past two decades. All this material seemed much newer than the dates suggest, as Russia's literary history, it might be said, resumed its course. The effect of the influx of this material into what was already a postmodernist environment is still difficult to assess. Traditional verse forms have remained current in Russia, to a far greater extent than, say, in America or in the United Kingdom. As can be imagined, this has exacerbated the problem of translation from Russian into English, when the effect of traditional rhyme and meter may be misleading. The coexistence of such traditionalism and postmodernist trends in Russia has further complicated or enriched the scene, these contrasts inevitably being somewhat attenuated in translation. What is clear is that *perestroika*, in the widest sense, had no less dramatic an effect on the cultural life of the country than the Khrushchevite "Thaw" of the late 50s and early 60s. At that time, the prospect of a disintegration of Soviet power, for instance with the Hungarian uprising in 1956, led to a reimposition of controls by the Party and the stagnation of the Leonid Brezhnev years. Many of Russia's best poets were eventually forced abroad, most notably Brodsky in 1972 and later Natalya Gorbanevskaya, Lev Loseff, and Yury Kublanovsky as well as many others.

A number of anthologies have attempted to represent recent literary developments in the former Soviet Union. (The Internet has hugely increased the availability of writing, from Moscow to Vladivostok, which has inevitably complicated the task of the anthologist.) The interesting recent anthology *Crossing Centuries* (2000), for instance, focuses on conceptualism, polystylistics, the elimination or demise of the so-called lyrical hero, retreat from ego-based poetry, and the apparent apoliticism of post-Thaw poetry. The emphasis on language as such, however, harking back to the avant-gardism of the early twentieth century, renders translation into other languages problematical. We have tried here to be perhaps somewhat more eclectic. Poet and critic Dmitry Polishchuk writes in *Nezavisimaya gazeta* (1 June 2001): "The 25–35-year-old generation is now experiencing an efflorescence—a new type of poetic vision, with a distinct poetic language, a new kind of baroque; with novel structures, combining the far-fetched, the heterogeneous, the incompatible, in a poetics of contrast" (p. 4). This seems particularly true of contemporary women's writing, which transcends postmodernist, postcolonialist, or even feminist tendencies.

It was our aim from the start to concentrate on recent work, on writers who achieved prominence or at least visibility in and after the mid 80s when Gorbachev and his team took over. Our focus, therefore, has been on what is now—already!—the middle generation, writers who have lived through the changes as adults. But we have also sought to represent the most recent generations. Even so, our limited generational focus would not have allowed us fairly to represent Russian women's poetry at this time. We have therefore further extended the range to include a few prominent poets of older generations, such as Inna Lisnianskaya, Bella Akhmadulina, and, abroad, Natalya Gorbanevskaya. We have extended the collection as well to include Russian-language poets in former Soviet republics, like Ukraine and Georgia. Finally, we have included a few poets living outside Russia (e.g., in the United States, England, Italy, and Israel), although not as many as we might have wished, since our primary focus remained on the developments in Russia.

It is our hope that this anthology will help to diversify the rather simplistic—and on the whole disheartening—current view of post-Soviet reality. Poetry has always been of particular significance in Russia; even though book sales there are now greatly reduced from the huge print-runs of the Soviet period—more or less equivalent to what might be expected in Western European countries—the influence of poetry is still formidable.

To the poets go our special thanks. Advice was forthcoming from those both in Russia and abroad. Nearly all we approached responded with extraordinary generosity and enthusiasm, in many cases (as indicated above) collaborating in the translation, patiently and scrupulously answering questions put to them by their translators. It should be added that e-mail immeasurably facilitated this interaction. Thanks are also due to the many scholars, critics, and editors in Russia and abroad who freely shared their expertise. Last but certainly not least, we thank the translators who have contributed to this collection and who quite frequently made suggestions that led us to add to the original list. Translators are in the first place readers, on the most intimate terms with the literature they translate. It has been a heartwarming experience to work with so many generous individuals. Whatever deficiencies remain are of course the responsibility of the editors.

4

A NOTE ON TRANSLITERATION

The Library of Congress transliteration system has been used throughout with some modifications. The apostrophe (') has been omitted except where its absence may alter the meaning: for example, *pust* (empty) and *pust'* (let it be) or *byt* (everyday life) and *byt'* (to be). After soft and hard signs as well as after vowels and at the beginning of a word *y* not *i* is used for transliteration of *ya/ia*, *yu/iu* (e.g., *antologiya*, but *Znamia*; *Yunost*, but *liubov*). In the same positions the letters *e* and *yo* are transliterated without *y* (e.g., Evgeny Evtushenko, Elena, Soldatenkov, with an exception made for Semyon). Some exceptions are made for nouns ending in a soft sign and *e* or *i* (such as Poberezhye, Primorye, *podmasterye*) since without the *y* they become unrecognizable. In view of the fact that some personal names are given in the most common form (e.g., Brodsky), we decided to transliterate all surnames ending with -*skii* as -*sky* (e.g., Kublanovsky, Voznesensky, and Gorky). All surnames ending -*aeva* and -*eeva* are transliterated without a *y* (e.g., Nikolaeva, Matveeva, and Tsvetaeva). At the end of personal names *ii* with a short *i* is transliterated as *y* (e.g., Dmitry, Yury, and Nikolay).

In the Botkin Hospital

As though good Doctor Botkin in his wisdom
had turned his mind to me well in advance,
giving his knife, in time, to Soldatenkov,
I opened life's door again and stumbled out.

My brain sped off into receding twilight —
an ark sealed snug and tightly, hooped and braced,
it was restored by Soldatenkov's genius
into its proper, from the other, place.

He's still the same: no time for shows of honor,
for bowing and for scraping, even praise —
in any case, concern for us poor sufferers
is quite enough to keep a soul sustained.

But can you tell? I was in mines of nothing —
for seven days the doctors sank me deep:
there's no one there. Bulat, I didn't see you,
or maybe was forced to silence by decree.

Placid machines performed a clerkly function —
the pulses leapt and twittered on the screen
transcribing the twin hillocks, the two humplets
of my rearing, bucking, dromedary brain.

This crown of flesh, this mystery of juncture,
lives close beside, but sealed off from my life:
like sharing a vestibule, perhaps, with some shy scholar,
who greets you as you pass, but with dropped eyes.

So how to read its thrust inside my temples?
A survey? an attempt to make its peace?
Grounding in inner space is quite unwelcome:
only the higher places bring release.

We're not well matched. Its job, I think, is torture:
teaching one's skull to list among the waves
of thought. That's right. The outer coasts of knowledge
are banned to knowledge — why, we cannot say.

The brain's not good at contemplating brain-power,
and leaving the bed one's made and where one lies
is far too much. I'd rather walk on point-shoes
or fish for pike in the canals on Mars.

One's lips spend all their time yawning or eating
but cannot speak—they seem to wear a gag.
The moment of transcendence can't be uttered
or compassed: it must simply be endured.

The ward—my world—is wide and bleached to whiteness:
My head is dark and barren as a moor.
To set down ". . . doesn't seem so bright" in writing
requires a miracle of one's brain-power.

My brain's not there. Some maleficent witches
have withered all cognition on the stem.
But now I hear: just try and write more simply,
and let your mind begin to come to terms.

Translated by Catriona Kelly

To Await Arrival

In memory of Galina Starovoitova

That's how it was: I turned my sickroom glances
on the yard outside the ward, as though on groves
or open fields. I tried to write "quite simply":
as it turned out, the impediment was this:

my mind was racked, tortured by constant fretting
about my mind, a tic I couldn't curb:
my neck was weighed down with the convolutions,
the empty effort made me more disturbed,

my feeble gift—the speck I'm proud of sharing
with prophets—flagged; the inner sight was lost.
When you edge along a shelf above a sheer drop
you gasp and do not grasp. That's not enough.

But I *did* feel a quick flash of foreboding—
a bubble from the deep rushed up and burst.
A dog's instinctive knowledge gripped my body,
though consciously I tried to brush it off.

I brushed it off—it didn't cloud that evening
when the motif long trapped inside my head
beat at my skull, but didn't jolt me forward
in the pose you use when praying for the dead.

Then suddenly, the exiled television
opened its eye, into the world beyond.
St. Petersburg, some stairs, a silenced bullet.
A death that made a splash, but not a sound.

The desert of the dark and of my pupils:
no tears could make this drought-struck landscape drink.
This child, this Joan of Arc, was my blood-brother.
An ellipsis of affection was our link.

Meetings were dotted. In June, was it, the last one?
Hiding from empty small talk and the rest,
like schoolgirls playing truant from our classes,
risking the ire of prefects, we embraced.

A handclasp, an embrace, puts one in contact
with good and bad. An answer not provoked
by any question raises skin in gooseflesh—
words know our lives are fragile, though we don't.

How near what we desire in fact lies to us:
easy to grasp a shoulder, touch a palm
(how often, too, we let affection blind us:
no rogue, we think, could offer us his hand).

Spurning the sly-faced bankers and the banquet,
in that hall with its spread feast in time of plague,
she blurted, gauche as any girl of twenty,
"You know I'm married!" "Goodness! I'm so glad!"

Having choked the air with mindless social babble,
I sipped my glass of government champagne.
I should have yelled, "St. George, leave fighting dragons,
take care of *her*!"—for nearby hung his flag.

She let it out; aghast at her own frankness,
she bit her lip to hold in further words.
She had a young girl's tense and radiant shyness.
A face like that suits flowerbeds, bandstands, parks.

The moment swelled. I felt a rising panic.
My mind gave way to nursery dreams of flight.
Give me a veil, four horses, and a carriage,
And let me gallop into a velvet night.

Was it just then a chink of foresight opened?
Seeing a soul stripped bare is ominous.
But there's more horror in the revelation
that joy and sainthood very rarely fuse.

In any case, to stammer a faint suspicion
ahead of time won't balk the march of fate.
A hand wearing a wedding-ring is fragile
and cannot force a viper's jaws apart.

Long in advance the count of years is reckoned:
The furies need fresh blood to slake their thirst.
Moths do not flee, but rather seek out, candles,
the target calls, the rifle cannot miss.

The calls for vengeance are no more than foolish:
talk of "reprisals" leaves me feeling sad.
A life like this imposes its own duties.
In the face of it, revenge should be abjured.

So now I sit in iron and stone December
and think of June to warm my memory.
I wonder if she'll hear me if I call her.
I miss her more with every passing day.

Death is the twin of triumph, its blood-brother.
A martyr's fate can break the hold of time.
Even in draft, her life was virtuoso:
It reached perfection with its final line.

Translated by Catriona Kelly

POLINA BARSKOVA

Evening at Tsarskoe Selo

Akhmatova and Nedobrovo
strolling at twilight in the park,
it calls for a stage direction, say:
"A park. September." He is stirred
by tittle-tattle, news from the front,
and his last article, while she
is stirred by the horizon's slant,
the bench, grown into the ailing oak,
and an unfinished line of verse.
He says: "Tomorrow I shall be
at the Stray Dog. And you?" And while
he waits for her to answer, Anna
watches her shadow glazing over,
and her clear voice utters these words:
"This has been an unnecessary day."
His heart beats faster. Will she? Won't she?
But she knows all too well she won't.
The sky casts down on everything
fragments of heavy mist, like ballast
thrown from a sly earth-bound balloon
deaf to the orders of the pilot.
Nedobrovo rips off a scarf,
it's stifling, scratchy, out of place.
He wants to know! She doesn't want.
Already she has the solution,
half-muttered, to that comic line,
and then, dear God, she bursts out laughing,
and night steals up and licks their shoes.

Translated by Peter France

[*The poet has passed away*]

The poet has passed away. Or rather, snuffed
it. How did the world taste at his last gasp?
We don't know, and we are ashamed to guess.
Like cranberry jelly, maybe, or perhaps
like peas boiled to a mush. But he himself,
he neither wished for life nor termination,
nor children, nor a father. Everything
is repetition, mass, continuation.
And we, his hashish smokers, what are we?
Just nothingness, some kind of super-nil,
plastic sneaked in to take the place of gold.
They'll ship him to the Island of the Dead,
the waves gleaming with sperm and diesel oil,
between palazzos crumbling to death.
Shivering in silks and lace, the youthful widow
sits in the gondola, and the gondolier
will understand: it's not the words, the slush,
nor the ambassadors of his indifferent homeland,
but above all the metrical hysterics . . .
His wishes
—what are they to us? And we,
when our time comes to quit the sandy shore,
when our hour strikes, we'll have our wishes too.

And yet he also wished . . . And how he wished!
As long as our high wishes still are cased
within the leather binding of our bodies,
he is alive—is life—is fuss and trash,
and therefore he is humbleness, a shrine
flowering among the universe's ruin.
What does death mean for him? Another flight.
Who do they sing for now, what do they sing,
his guttural speaking voice, his raucous laugh?
No, people of his kind do not die. No,
they leave, and as they go, turn out the light—
but the grain cannot flourish in the dark.
It lies there unavailing, white and blind,

crushed by an unintelligible fate,
plunged into silence till the moment comes.
What can they mean for it, the empty words?
What can she mean, the captivating widow?
And what the prophet's immortality?

Translated by Peter France

TATYANA BEK

[*Beneath the flakes of Russian snow*]

Beneath the flakes of Russian snow,
Where logos demands caution like a ford,
The cruel bliss of separation lurks,
Resists and dies away.

Beneath a fierce torrential cloudburst,
Brief as blessing,
Controlling fate's a droll endeavor,
Droller than an ancient tooth.

But to continue: under a western wind
Both style and character erode . . .
Does this not constitute (yes, this perhaps)
The hidden source of the soul?

Translated by Robert Reid

[*We've all got history on our hands . . .*]
To Zoya

We've all got history on our hands . . .
But through debauchery and plague
"I will survive" (as Gloria sang)
Survive with ease, survive with rage.

Reducing love to touch once more,
Preserving safe within the head
The subconscious and its niggling sore,
All tightly bracketed away.

Within me Europe's felled by Asia
And freedom weeps for loss of rights
And my untamed imagination
Goes pale at what's before our eyes.

But I swear by what is best to swear by,
Through long nights of prophetic vision,
That I'll survive (oh, yes) survive,
Strong
as the moss that thrives

Translated by Robert Reid

NATALYA BELCHENKO

[*I'd happily survey the world*]

I'd happily survey the world
With affable calm like St. P.
When you've outstripped yourself, you'll see
The allure of ultimate return.

Having taken under my wing
Bricks, mortar, and things of that sort,
A tuning fork is all I'm short
Of to get me stuck in again.

And struck by its recognition
Of me it would be a talisman
Guaranteeing that I too am
Wrought thus: a smile, a street, a station.

Translated by Robert Reid

[*It's boring looking at the same old contents*]

It's boring looking at the same old contents
Of my very own vocabulary
(Like "way out" on a trolleybus window)
While experiencing hopelessness and angst,
An urge to precipitate self through
Same, though that's the way one has just clambered in.
And now it's closed; one might say too tightly.
But turning it sideways I can squeeze the
Reflection, my vocabulary's own, through
To drop into the postbox of life—here!

Translated by Robert Reid

[*Chameleons are fine*]

Chameleons are fine
But rainbows are much better:
Full of color without end
And sound without beginning.
The hunter and the pheasant
Are at one before our eyes.
Synopticize for me
My fine chameleon.
What a nice restaurant:
Mimic all the plats du jour
And in a trice return once more
To your default color.
Carmine, Carmen, Come on . . .
Keep the idol waiting—
Give other names a chance
To get on the menu.

Translated by Robert Reid

LARISA BEREZOVCHUK

[*Calm rocks to sleep in your usual place*]

Calm rocks to sleep in your usual place.
Sooner or later
you will have to believe in the reality
of tales about the Leviathan.
How caressing is the music of inertia. We swim on,
swim on, blessing the darkness . . .
Further. Only occasionally
alongside us it suddenly becomes empty—
that's some submarine creature
disappearing too early: the outer casing
could not stand the friction. The tension
becomes ash
in the materialized length of the womb.
Well? For those left behind
the loss is not noticeable.

But sensing the inevitable,
the adrenaline starts to scream, although
nothing is happening yet. What can happen
in an identical situation? If you do not know
the beginning and end;
for a stream, the middle is everywhere.
When you are alone you get out of the habit of fearing.
The place is the source of gravity. Fate—
and it is the same for all of us—
of the centrifuge, a somersault which is not noticed.
If you are not ill with schizophrenia, you begin to feel
gravity—the balance
between the poles: to know that the womb is shaken
in the surf by the arrhythmic waves. In it
the specks of submarines
spark with the potential of another's energies.
The switch of tension is switched on,
interfering with the reading of the monster's pulse.

Translated by Richard McKane

MARINA BORODITSKAYA

[*Now I am a fan of silence*]

Now I am a fan of silence,
a watcher of snow-covered roofs.
Cupid landed on my windowsill,
but I told him to bugger off.

Translated by Ruth Fainlight

Christmas Eve

If Christians threaten to start a pogrom
    I'll paint a cross on the door.
If Muslims suddenly arrive
    I'll draw a crescent.
Buddhists are peaceful people,
    though a bit spoilt by progress.
I'd better put some sort of hieroglyph there.

I would draw all this
    on my children's foreheads—
but how could I explain
    that such funny signs are better
than ordinary-looking numbers
    branded on pallid forearms:
as if stamped by the devil?

Translated by Ruth Fainlight

Sound Letter

Hullo, Lord!
A minor poet
is writing to You,
a voice from the choir,
a little pine tree from the forest,
a clarinet in the school orchestra.

Do You think it is so
easy, Lord,
to be a voice in the choir,
a fish in water,
and not disturb Your order?
Yet worse is the icy fate
of those appointed
first violin, or the highest
pine on the mountain.

No hardship for us,
year in year out, day after day,
to sink our roots in deeper
and practice our scales,
waiting for the conductor
spot-lit on the rostrum
to point his baton—
and a noble solo rings out
making even the mountains weep.

Translated by Ruth Fainlight

[*So much gentleness from unknown men*]

So much gentleness from unknown men
for no particular reason.
Once in Paris a waiter turned to me: "Chérie!
Don't forget your cigarettes."

And in a London market, when
I wanted to buy a Beatles record,
the stall-holder sighed: "What can I do, love,
if the price goes up again?"

In New York airport, an old black man
took me to the right gate, saying:
"Don't panic, baby, just follow me!"
And I followed in his footsteps.

So much kindness from strange men!
Why the hell should I need more?
Lie peaceful in your oyster, pearl.
Stay calm, Moon, in the heavens.

Translated by Ruth Fainlight

[*Poor composer*]

Poor composer,
useless without a piano,
poor prose writer,
hopeless without a desk.
And poor artist,
who needs his easel, brushes,
little tubes of paint.
I couldn't manage it.

Poor, poor sculptor.
Poor film director.
In this world, only
the poet is fortunate.
He walks in the park,
a stanza in his head.
(As long as you don't shoot him
—like Pushkin—in the gut.)

Translated by Ruth Fainlight

[*A person is reflected by the whirlpool, not the face*]

A person is reflected by the whirlpool, not the face,
in the intelligent Angar, crazy January water.
Silver foil speaks in all human languages
and those of the angels. It makes the New Year
secrets ring out.
The mirror in the town-house is covered by
the white of the royal mourning.
Beyond the sheet—steam, beyond the snow—desert.
A person is reflected by the cold, winter spectacle
and blood flows
into the liquidity of the shaky door.
What can one ask for from the deaf and dumb almighty,
using a fish, a toy animal with a knocked-out eye,
primitive silence,
a torn eyelid,
the youngest child in the family?

I plunge a ladder for myself through each prison spy-hole,
into the quaking sands
at the bottom of the eyes.
Go away, reflection, quickly,
or else I'll think again.
Silver foil, silver foil.

Translated by Richard McKane

ZINAIDA BYKOVA

[*Close of day*]

Close of day.
I walk through dew-soaked meadow grass.
Silly pride
has cost me my closest friend.
By the cold pool
I stand and look and look
at the baby frogs there swimming.

Translated by Robert Reid

At the Stop

A tentative rap at the door would
announce my pupils' evening calls, a pair of lads,
inseparable pals.
And they were all sticky-out ears and apple cheeks
and stubbornly lowered gaze.
And they would tell me stories about that and this
and look at each other.
Then, when we had the first real snow,
they brought their skis and some for me.
All that evening we glided on the road and slopes behind the village.
When the time came for me to leave it for good
they were hanging round the bus stop.
And as the bus was pulling away
their eyes followed it through the dust.

Translated by Robert Reid

[*Potatoes in flower*]

Potatoes in flower,
and silvery vines,
the swelling grasses of fields in July . . .

and in the Volga, Sashka,
my awkward in-law,
though "in-law" is awkward,
takes the last swim of his life.
And the silvery vines
are for my pain,
the potato flowers for my tears.
And the swelling grasses in the July fields
are to make me pine for him.

Translated by Robert Reid

SVETLANA DENGINA

Autumnal Equinox

I am sick of
the rustle of paper and rattle of umbrellas opening.
In the dark room,
among slumbering carp
and scattered beads,
again I want to be
a willow twig in a jug of water.
Again I'll forget how to listen to people
and I'll see my time off,
gazing into the depths of the huge dish.
Hops and haricot beans,
a wild vine and the evening breeze,
will stay outside.
I'll forget about bread, milk, coffee.
But for several days
the wax-like yellow star
signifies for me
the most extravagant day of the year
and the most pellucid night.

Translated by Daniel Weissbort

Russia

If I never again saw your eyes . . .
Moistness . . .
If I didn't hear your barking cough . . .
The light's been used . . .
If I asked you for happy songs . . .
Gaps in the stairs . . .
If there were no reddish-green skull,
smashed against the snowy bank,

no eyes, drowned in the snows,
if in the frames there were no darkness
of effervescing ice . . .
Then I would pity you.

Translated by Daniel Weissbort

[*I don't feel at home where I am*]

I don't feel at home where I am,
or where I spend time; only where,
beyond counting, there's freedom and calm,
that is, waves, that is, space where, when there,
you consist of pure freedom, which, seen,
turns that Gorgon, the crowd, to stone,
to pebbles and sand . . . where life's mean-
ing lies buried, that never let one
come within cannon shot yet.
From cloud-covered wells, untold
pour color and light, a fête
of cupids and Ledas in gold.
That is, silk and honey and sheen.
That is, boon and quiver and call.
That is, all that lives to be free,
needing no words at all.

Translated by Alan Shaw

[*Beyond Siberia again Siberia*]

Beyond Siberia again Siberia,
beyond impenetrable forest again forest.
And beyond it waste ground,
where a blizzard of snow breaks loose.

The blizzard has handcuffs, and the snow-
storm has a knife which kills at once . . .
I will die, pay a debt
for others who live somewhere,

out of spite, out of fear and terror,
out of pain, out of a nameless grave . . .
Beyond the wall another wall,
on the wall stopped dead one sentinel.

Translated by Kevin Carey

[*On the sea-shore, smell of iodine*]

To Graziano Motta

On the sea-shore, smell of iodine,
and square as in Sicily, and dancing.

An intellectual that came from the common people,
preparing himself to be Rosencrantz.
He decides to serve Claudius and therefore
spy on Prince Hamlet from the fountain.

All over the world—the prison. At the world's
end a certain John plays the piano.

Already darkness, and the end is in sight:
Ophelia crying in an empty hut.
And Hamlet walks to and fro with a white headband,
in order to be recognized by the Ghost in the gloom.

Translated by Kevin Carey

Theory of Recruiting

Sons of bitches
were born
with hearts of stone,
cherishing this stone
all their life.
Children of
sons of bitches
were born
with hearts of grenade,
in order to
blow to pieces
everything,
and to leave as a message for their descendants—
entrails
(still smoking entrails)
of sons of bitches.

Translated by Kevin Carey

MARINA DOLIA

from Silence

II

A white iris sprang up
by the dark stone,
a yellow-beaked nestling, shy.
I see no end to its early happiness,
as I don't see the glow above it.

For miles around saturated torment spreads
in the scum upon stagnant water.
One so wants to stretch out a greedy hand
and pluck it,
remove it from danger.

Beauty—too loud for these environs,
a sound painful to the ears. Nothing.
A wasteland, ideal, arose from ambiguous
secrets and stares at it.

Evidently, someone called it to this hopeless place
where there's no love without damage done.
A white iris sprang up like a wise child,
and silently gazes at itself.

IV

Even the longest day
contains the inevitable moment
when the soul
burns
with desire to give away treasures.
Your
concealed double emerges from
himself,
stretches
toward the fire, and demands his reward.

For this lunar day. The brace scrapes,
takes away
a minute and doesn't add happiness.
Your cast-off wreath my double will braid.
My candle will not go out by distant shores.

A hundred flaming wheels of raging silence,
and, following
this, smoke and burning, evil shades crawl.
My bonfire, hard but just that, don't be in such a hurry to weep,
while there's still the smell of grass, and stars, like a sign.

Translated by Daniel Weissbort

IRINA ERMAKOVA

[. . . *toward morning around seven*]

. . . toward morning around seven
when a strip of light under the doors
was redder than the Petersburg
Arrow*
maybe you will read me
at a glance—
snow
acrid clover
dark grapes
idly you think you lived
like a butterfly which
the admiralty spire reached burned through
that it's past seven and there's no sense
in going to bed
it's late and thank god
life has passed
that everything will happen after
that wings wither under glass
although they're far more visible because of it
that I was the amusing specimen
in your collection
that I was . . .

Translated by Daniel Weissbort

*An express train between Moscow and Petersburg (author's note).
Author's note: It perhaps goes without saying that fanciers should not ignore the less
striking species, especially smaller butterflies, the study of which lags behind that of
large squamous winged creatures.

Gethsemane

The moon swims to the fore in the pale heavens
all god's shrubbery illuminates
grows and blankly stares like a blind woman
at everything knowing it all by heart

Crazed of countenance
blood drained
on the dark side the other side her eyes
unsleeping shameless she is attuned
to every sound we make at the
end of time

Hearing is split and the age
like an echo
in which the clash of swords offends the ears
By feel the moon rips open
the river with finger-like rays
and dims the glare

In the sublunar world not a glimmer
the Kedron gushes
through somber hills
A detachment walks by fours
A branch snaps and a different darkness tells

No time
footsteps in the garden steps
fireflies sport above upturned faces
they cannot wake—tiredness overtook them
unseen free and easy
we sleep
—fists outstretched cruciform
side by side beneath the burning bushes
like Your first disciples

Crucified by Lunaria's dream Gethsemenian
in Sardinia Samara in Virginia
on a motionless globe
in the second millennium

and a hollow moon
the silver coin spent
is larger than the very heavens

Translated by Daniel Weissbort

Lullaby for Odysseus

He speaks: My poor Penelope, my little lass,
you've grown so old, while I played the ass,
America is covered in ice, Europe in broken glass,
here, only here, at your feet do the living ages splash.

Dear, while you loafed about,
all got buried in clover,
with its acrid heartlike leaf, pink sticky clover,
free time's a weave, sewn with finest clover,
I'll make you a bitter deathless infusion of clover.

Drink, wind nails the prodigal vessels to the shore,
drink, the suitors are extinct, at sea fateful doldrums,
drink, the sons have grown, are about to undiscover America,
drink, the heavens have paled, drink, Odysseus!

Sleepy waves fawn, petals cling together like a fan,
the ends of your surfacing motherland join in a clover bowl,
enticing as the myth of fidelity, the clover spirit spreads,
drink, do not grieve, drink, my joy, my former joy.

Translated by Daniel Weissbort

GALINA ERMOSHINA

[*And also—the Minotaur, farmer, owner, respondent*]

And also—the Minotaur, farmer, owner, respondent,
on the sleepless page he is the same age, a petitioner and a weaver.
To the dedicated he is light, to the detained— reaping and stoves
in the last Tauride, where the ship's acrobat still lives.

And a marked sign is a lodger and a stepchild of the word,
right when a floorboard creaks—the first step or gesture.
This is an ovary and a backwater, returned, left again,
his best tower—for foam, for veins, for a cross.

And it depicts as melted—thinner than the cracks in a ledge,
the cursed lightness and audacity of fragile chimney swifts.
But the writing pads and grains are a doggedly learned list
on window conciseness and the stinginess of pass-through declensions.

Translated by Gerald Janecek

[*Autumn your bellringing, the apple of bright weeping*]

Autumn your bellringing, the apple of bright weeping.
It does not hurt—the boatman, pendulum, and carousel.
If you had been here—all would have been decided differently,
but who can search for you on the gypsum bottom, Odysseus.

Or follow the traces left of the black road,
only an end of yarn will knit consent into speech.
Let Penelope wait—thus spoke the gods,
and a circle of milk in a bowl, and the oven of a potter's wheel.

If the cup is glued too, and the halves fit together
of an apple, of damp earth, of a page read,
and the trace of yesterday's snow, and the ice of Christmas clay,
then all the same the shore and a seashell of sand will remain.

Translated by Gerald Janecek

ZOYA EZROKHI

A Day at Home

Today I stayed home,
Fearing a pogrom against the Jews,
In the name of Russian Christianity.
The dog pointed its muzzle at the door.
"Don't ask," I snapped.

Since morning I'd felt depressed,
The way you feel on a narrow little island,
At the hopeless hour of the flood tide.
An anti-Semitic pamphlet
Brandished
Its fist.

I'd long been weakened
In the bitter struggle with dust, moths,
With spiritual and bodily sickness.
Now Pamiat* is affecting my nerves,
With the connivance of Minerva,
Who evidently doesn't give a damn.

Maybe we're getting too cocky?
After all, look at the blessings bestowed on us Jews,
As for me, iambic and trochaic verse do my bidding.
Jews are everywhere—in every argument,
And a Jewish acquaintance of mine
Even sings in the church choir.

But, after all, I didn't crucify Christ!
I never ever approved
Of such a finale.
I took a lot on my shoulders,
And, when I die, I won't quit the Russian language
Without leaving my mark.

Today I stayed home,
Fearing a pogrom against the Jews.
It was hot outside.
I went nowhere,
But stayed very snugly just where I was,
And I even wrote something—
Every cloud has its silver lining.

Translated by Daniel Weissbort

* Pamiat is an anti-Semitic organization (translator's note).

Repetition

Poet, do not fear tautologies,
Do not blaze roundabout trails.
Even if the stern critic is displeased,
Say it again and again:

"How buttery is butter!
How light's the light I saw!"
And you'll see how much good sense there is
Where there seemed to be none before.

Let the chemist find fluorine and strontium,
The truth is visible to you:
How sunny, sunny is the sun!
How moony is the moon!

Amid the glades, automobiles, towers,
Wend your way enthusiastically,
Murmuring: "How homey's home!
How rainy the rain! How bestial beasts!

How mindful is the mind, how businesslike is
business, fear fearful, gloomy gloom!
How deathly is death! How lively is life!
How youthful youthful youth."

Translated by Daniel Weissbort

ELENA FANAILOVA

[*Better this way: it's you with nothing to hold on to*]

Better this way: it's you with nothing to hold on to,
Only you (in a taxicab, in darkness), only you.
Quick, like poison running through water, distorting out of tenderness
The undefined features of a face.

O don't wait there clotted up over my soul or behind my back,
Order up some oblivion, some sleepwalking paradise.
I'll launch the little ship and the tiny gold fish through my veins,
In search of sweet daydreams, of manmade heaven, of
    the seven seas.

Like it or not, my heart will stay in one piece.
Vodka shines its dry light like a gypsy.
How blinding it all is: the winter solstice,
These unimaginable, inhuman words,
This other fate, the triumph of verse.

Translated by Stephanie Sandler

Frida's Album (*Frida Kahlo's Album*)

Frida sits coiffed (in whiteface), sits next to the canvas,
A lacy underskirt, apron, earrings, braids in a wreath,
Death at her left hand, headless Diego on her right,
An umbilical cord links them, the vessels, the threads like wiring,
A crystal globe hangs on a thread before her,
Showing skies, room, people, ocean,
Her heart stops, her heart beats in her throat,
Grass has overgrown her bed,
Frida sits there like a stone idol.
In the air hovers a Mother of God, a crucified Frida lies in a cradle,
Crucified Frida lies there
Diego is with Paulette Goddard

Frida sits there like a queen, shawls, brooches, flowers in her hair,
  Look at her tears, lockets, bracelets, beads, embroidery,
    ribbons, pendants, fringe,
Dead dolls lie next to her, portraits (*retratos*) of leaders
  hang at the bed-head,
Frida sits there corseted in staves, covered in scabs,
Grass is overgrowing her bed
Grass grows from her head
Diego is with María Félix
Frida is dressed as a little boy, look at her cigarettes,
  stones, crystals, bits of mica,
Her monkey hugging her, her parrots, women drowning in hair,
Stars in her ears, mirrors in the garden, lace,
Corpses, deer, weird breeds of dog,
The deceased Prince Dimas
Angels cradled by a heart,
                              pierced through her breast
Frida is with Lucienne Bloch
Frida is with *Eva Frederick*
Frida is at home with his wife Lupe Marín
Frida is in a cradle, Diego is in mourning,
                              look at the cards, marriage,
                                mariage
There are two Fridas, two Fridas are there.

Translated by Stephanie Sandler

NINA GABRIELIAN

A Phoenician Statuette

Your hair is tied back in a puritan bunch,
but an animal heat flows out of your eyes.
You are just as the god created you once
from the red meridional clay.

An archaeologist dug you out of your bed
among primitive tools and bones of the dead.
Millennia had passed, and no one had caressed
your strong thighs and your young girl's breasts.

For centuries lust for your torrified land
will rage in you, hopelessly seeking a vent.
And your half-open mouth is cracked by a thirst
that can never be quenched.

Translated by Peter France

Tortoise

Where the scorched quietness is swathed
in the sun's violet rays,
it lies, unmoving, like a trace
of neolithic days.
And on its broad armor plates
the sun scatters its hot dust.
Like someone's lonely breath appears
black, in white sands, one bush.
In this place once children played,
here once existence flowered . . .
And the vertebrae of centuries crunch
beneath its heavy tread.

Translated by Peter France

from the cycle Erebuni

1

I hood my eyes against the savage light . . .
Why am I here, and what do I want here?
Why do these ruins drag me to this place
with the mortal grief of blackened stone?
Am I the keeper of the dead?
I mutter
Cain-like:
"Am I their keeper?"
Graveyard grass crawls over stone,
strong in its underground knowledge.

2

The fortress is immobile
in the haze of noon.
Dead emperors gaze at me
as if their underground labor
had built this world, this city.
Unbeing
longs so to be incarnate,
to raise altars to itself.
Sculptors of unbeing, emperors
and warriors,
whisper to me:
"Look, here it is,
the capital of our realm."

3

Midday sleep, the veil of sleepy maya,
hides the black earth from my eyes.
Grasses whisper,
rustling, dry,
and it seems I am not I . . .
On the town of the dead
heaven rains its flame,

and immobile—straight in my eyes—
a grasshopper stares from a stone
with its fearful faceted gaze.
And pinned to the wall
by premature horror,
I cannot tear myself
from its bulging mica stare,
from the stare of alterity.

4

Above me hangs the dry firmament of the Urarts.
Immortal it floats,
the ancient city,
like a gigantic ark
with its weighty cargo
down the dry bed of underground rivers.

Translated by Peter France

Ghazal

I shall idolize a Turkish woman from Shiraz,
return Samarkand and Bukhara for the sake of her birthmark . . .
(Hafez)

For the sake of a Turkish woman from Shiraz, consumed in the deadly fumes,
I shall pull the post-modern infection out by the roots.
For the moon's face and the shapes of gazelles and tight curls,
I shall drop Jaspers, Derrida and Deleuze, and Jung too
Ah, no need of more in the garden of frantic delights.
There, weeps Mircea Eliade, no Iliad can match his plight.
What's so special about Jaspers—it's the jasper
        of her cheeks, the agate of eyes,
onto the grass her variegated, argus-eyed silks cascade . . .
You're no passion—you're a splinter that cannot be pulled out by force.
Toward you the native tongue creeps through snows from our kolkhoz
to the moony fields of the East, to its minefields,
where the gentle palm of a prophet lifts up a sword with its crescent maw.

Translated by Daniel Weissbort

[*What, in July's honey heat, do you weep for, poor goy*]

What, in July's honey heat, do you weep for, poor goy,
unshaven, naked, what are the snares you flee?
Saturated in lime-tree scent, the boulevard recedes,
and to the acacias clings the hot groin of a cloud,
spray flickers, glimmering on the town clock,
the horny heat of turtledoves seethes in the heavens,
and a sail rummages, listing in a sunny négligé,
while you sit, like some prince, robed in golden mange.
I don't know what I'm weeping for, but I know at whom.
It's the lord, his beggar's bowl, and the entire town,
myself, poor goy, meshuggener ascetic, I sorrow
that there's no other life, and this is no life either.
I loathe the morning and the glorious light—

no longer is it for me, or I for it,
and the burning wind flees the darkness of the steppes.
Take pity, Lord! What you're doing to me? Tell!
From the heavens seeping like resin, flows a pitchy dark,
and my youth has passed, and my life, too, has passed.
The pollen from the poplars has tumbled down, the evening light dies,
and toward night three hags are paraded by the lord of the flies.
Bags of bones, they file past, uncouth—
the one bringing up the rear my love . . .

Translated by Daniel Weissbort

[*I said to him—Just don't throw me into that briar patch*]

"Just don't throw me into that briar patch."
(Tales of Uncle Remus)

I said to him—Just don't throw me into that briar patch:
this is my dear home, blossoming behind me.
Where each leaf trembles, there's a rustling hush,
the berries are shot with black enamel and blue.
I said to him—Better burn me in the bonfire,
blue-gray smoke has already floated over by morning,
and a shrike sings in the thorny branches
in the briar patch, at the time of its dawning.
Better throw me into the water, because it tastes bitter,
like a berry with prickles and down below it's the same sort of colors.
But in the briar patch fixated on a needle is a star,
None of the neighbors needs for now.
Ah, Br'er Fox, you're nobody's fool,
don't be won over by such notions or ideas.
I'll seek out whatever creatures make you drool,
I'll lead them to your blackthorn lair.
I myself can't go home—too sharp's the thorn
lodged in my chest—my left paw aches.
Better watch out for the fine bonfire in your rear
and right there next to you, a splendid lake.

Translated by Daniel Weissbort

DINA GATINA

[*I'm being stalked by a bird*]

I'm being stalked by a bird
with a beak that's all of a piece
it doesn't open
it's like an awl and
somewhat colorless
What she needs from me
I don't know,
one thing is clear though
she cannot be killed
And in her eyes there is such anguish

Translated by Chris Jones

[*My eyes are*]

My eyes are
always directed
somewhat through
whatever I'm trying to examine.
most probably
the basic reason for that
is that my boyfriend is a photographer.
we've known eighteen months now
I look good in photographs
occasionally,
in telephone conversations,
he refers to me as
"one of my models."
I think
in each of us, in our eyes,
there is set up a tiny
photographic device,
from time to time
it makes a clicking sound;

though we might not
be aware of this
I've started being wary of hidden cameras.
Wherever
I don't feel at ease with myself:
not even in the bathroom.
Especially if there's
good paper,
a good catch on the door,
a wire brush
and a big oval mirror.
I start to think about
how beautifully I'm sitting,
my back, so to speak, straightens up of its own accord.
I know
that it's stupid
and I smile.
The left corner is 2–3 mm
higher than the right.
Somewhere, I'm 98% sure of this,
there are people
spilling their seed over my photos.
It seems to me
I know many of them personally.

Translated by Chris Jones

solo

the wire. the ghetto. an eastern landscape.
over the sea the sedge rustles softly and in front of the pupil
the reeds resound
the city withers in the shackles of the night watch
the double body sinks to the meat straw
with a crinkle of dense grass.
zooming cicadas skewer slowly.
slowly the curtain goes down like a shroud
this is the first time i taste your life—
you wince but there is no tearing loose—
the palms of your hands
your knees
your births
your departures into a hollow name
your touches
your
—drink
to drink of yours
—to drink
—to drink

Translated by Max Nemtsov

the grant of death

job came to the rabbi
sei gesund job
hayweh willing rabbi
rabbi cabba
you're like golem job
you let me kill myself rabbi
bless you job god
be off rabbi to see
how i will kill myself rabbi

rabbi: yahweh son job—for the love of god
job: in peace
and in pain
rabbi: let's go

Translated by Max Nemtsov

---

from Cities

VENICE

an enormous clock at the sandy mansion:
the cramped square's bugging out its fisheye
the ponderous sky is squeezed into a narrow frame
and crisscrossed with blue and white laundry over the channel
the laundry smells of fish
the water smells of the lagoon
which smells of the boat
a water taxi

st. mark's square is interlaced with crabs
and the doges' palace windows with water and fish
and i've been squirming like a tapeworm all day long
in the recta, jejuna and colons
disgustingly white on the food
painted
red
white
and green

and in the end of the day
without a chance to blow my eggs
i tumble about in the lagoon effluvia
searching for the next fish

BERLIN

a bloated face. with the fust
of the humid jaundiced ash
of the bovey coal the mouth
of berlin will pant right into the face—mine still mine
still the face—how many times
the city you'll say the word alien.

like a smack off the berlin wall
with the physiopsycholechery
of berlin the dear hungry mouth
will ravage my alien lips:
how many times will i bite and lap up
the cruelly gray
palate over berlin

Translated by Max Nemtsov

LINOR GORALIK

[*Here I am*]

Here I am, looking at you, my orphan. Your thick scarf. Your cold cigarette. A screech of love would be of no avail: the underground winds bear off the sound to other stations trembling and straining on creaking branch-lines. Here I am, looking at you, so firmly ensconced, so fully grounded: hands wired up to your computer, your phone, your TV, your coffee grinder. The soil in which your seedlings grow is properly sanitized with baby disinfectant, well fertilized with baby oil, hoed diligently by grown-ups' tongues saying swiftly and often: "We love you, our dearest." All the worms of conscience are exterminated; they won't gnaw the cortex of a tired brain, or leave their white deposits in your thoughts. Here I am, looking at you, with everything going just right, your house flourishing with love and money; every spring the cracks in the plaster heal, and new sofas and wardrobes sprout like ovaries. Here I am, looking at you ploughing your wife's lap, sowing the seed; later in the dark of your shower touching the scab, feeling the scars, remembering the thick sap running down your fingers and darkening in the wind; thinking: let the sap flow and flow—the roots are powerful; I was bent but am still unbroken. Some fluff from your towel lands like a red mosquito on your dripping hair. That's the only way your pillow gets wet these days. You dream of grown-ups, all with claws, and only you are soft, with sticky fingers holding a raw fly; your mummy's saying, "You should be ashamed of yourself!" Here I am, looking at you, my lignum vitae, looking at you, my orphan, my toddler, my lost baby, my burning bush, my weeping birch, my poisonless ivy. My fingers stick, I have no power to fly like a seed to your neighbor's garden, to bindweed out of harm's way. Here I am, stalking the grass around you, gathering blackberries.

Translated by the author, revised by Robert Reid

[*Every few weeks I see there is an empty chair in our local nursery*]

Every few weeks I see there is an empty chair in our local nursery,
Because my son, still unconceived, flushes away as blood around
    the twentieth of the month,
Though he resists, painfully, puts up a fight, wills to be born,
Weeps blood and whispers: mummy, I would be good, I really would.
Why? Tell me why you don't want to have me.

I sing him a song about other little children:
They didn't cry, not even in Treblinka.
I huddle like a foetus to stop him struggling,
Hug the hot water bottle to let him get warm.
Stop it, I say, stop fooling around. Just stay put
And be glad you've got to sit it out another month.
You'd scream in terror if you saw what it's like out here.
And he says: I'd rather make up my own mind, if it's all the same.

I read him a poem about the girl in Guernica,
How her eyes can't see what her hands are doing.
And he says: is that worse than me rotting from your pills,
My cells disintegrating, falling as bloody dew on your pads,
Knowing every month you don't love me at all?
You won't buy me a little vest or red thread for my hair,
You'll never see my face or ask about my grades.
Please, just love me, mummy, let me out of my cell!

And I tell him about my own mummy,
How she had a hysterectomy and cried under anesthetic.
Then I tell him: OK, you've won, I'll think about what we've got to do.
I don't love you, but I'll try to be a better person,
More feeling and not so scared of you.
Just don't go, don't leave me, d'you hear?

And he says: OK, let's call it quits, there's hardly any of me left anyway,
Some last drops, a blackened clot of heart, and red threads.
We'll talk again, mummy, he says, I'll be back again to be unbirthed,
To flush away in blood, to weep, to beg, to struggle,
To swear I would be good, really I would,
To weep, to plead with you to get me out.
Somewhere around the twentieth I'll be back to visit you.

Translated by the author, revised by Robert Reid

NATALYA GORBANEVSKAYA

[*I will not be able to explain why*]

I will not be able to explain why
the White Nights of the Solstice are no whiter
than the sleeve of my nightshirt, brought into prison
by Constitutional Articles 70 and 72.

I will not be able to explain to myself the price
my brain cells pay for a night's sleep
on a board and under lock and key,
every hour embarking on escape.

I will not even try to explain anything that comes from within
or what would be simpler, from without.
Nor will I remove my shirt and be crucified by the toss of a coin,
my naked back against a cement wall.

Translated by Elizabeth Krizenesky

[*The rhymes picked me in a ditch*]

The rhymes picked me in a ditch,
shook me a little, bathed me,
clothed me appropriately for my height,
which means hand-me-downs from other kids,
rubbed oil into me, removed the scabs,
cleaned me, cleansed me of passions,
cleaned out my ears and my thoughts,
and all but finished me off.

Translated by Daniel Weissbort

[*What I drink is not hot, not sweet*]

What I drink is not hot, not sweet,
what sinks to the grounds is my fate,
my hands do not hold the pen,
and my evenings are not well lit,
nor is my midnight set ablaze.
No one needs my gifts in the least,
on the labeled keys,
my listless fingers feast.

Translated by Daniel Weissbort

[*We live—sometimes*]

We live—sometimes,
and pass years
in the interim
in dreams terrifying

or sweet. And
who's to count
the pits and bumps
rouse us from our rest?

Translated by Daniel Weissbort

Notes of a Cold War Veteran

And Churchill in a bowler,
like a movie comic,
with a cigar, like a waffle,
examines himself keenly.
We wept in anguish,
made ourselves ill weeping,
when the Luftwaffe delivered
its deadly cargo to his island.

Everything began there,
for better or worse:
the allies of the ally
—or capitulants?
At the famous table they sit,
as in a box or a puddle.
And the prisoners sit in prisons
from Archangel to Yalta.

They sit from A to Z,
their hopes pinned on Fulton
yes, on the atomic bomb,
on a third world war . . .
And we mustn't weep,
at least not so it disturbs anyone,
only strike our foreheads against—what?
—an impenetrable wall.

Translated by Daniel Weissbort

[*Epiphanies*]

Epiphanies,
and commas, commas,
and spirit in the grip of dreams,
and a semicolon again,
ah!—and passionate, like Spain, and
through obstacles, punctuation,
Pegasus gallops to spite all
making for his tranquil stall.

Translated by Daniel Weissbort

ANNA GORENKO

[*There the folk museum alone lies in its embers*]

There the folk museum alone lies in its embers
My house! hurry run and see it
but no Alone the mist-ruled attic hovers over the earth
but where then are both storeys
ill fortune of bricky death

Translated by Peter France

[*Flowers live faster than rotting of cherries*]

Flowers live faster than rotting of cherries
still faster and sweeter the life of wine
from here I cannot hear the name of the village
but its white wall is sweet
faster whiter and sweeter than our walls
the church there is up to its knees in black earth

Translated by Peter France

[*death covers up nakedness*]

death covers up nakedness
with boy's flesh and puppy's head
so, we are brother and sister
let us go down to the void

then
up to the throat in blackness
trying not to see the vociferous heavens
so. you are brother and sister
the gods will say as they hide their faces

on this feast of unripe corn there is no one to lead us
from the fields of stony grain of clearcut hemp

on this day of unshrinking blood there is no one to forgive us
we are brother and sister

the doves
the doves of the squares have taught us
to live

Translated by Peter France

[*houses like piles of children's books*]

houses like piles of children's books
lying aslant
take me with you to the south
where the sand is stony
take me carry me to you
where the water is light
to look how quietly why it never kisses

Translated by Peter France

Translated from the European
To A. G.

Like some England some France
Our land at the hour of sunrise
Birds will go blind and flowers and trees go deaf
But to me God himself today has said a rude word

Either I am a saint
or more likely Our Lord resembles a cabbie
He whispers such a word to each maiden
that she will go out on a Sunday morning
to feed the foal the ant the lame cat from a bright-colored dish

But on good days our Lord is a captain
And to a square full of clerks, guardsmen, and barmen
in a foreign, heavenly, beautiful language
he speaks such a word that the ears are closed tight

Lord, give me not for ever but henceforth
a soft suit, ordered in summer in Warsaw,
there are little pleasures, apart from rhyme
raisins from the pocket, for instance, and other crumbs.

[Theresienstadt, April 1943]

Translated by Peter France

NINA GORLANOVA

Three-Liners

The children saved their money
For ice cream
And gave it to daddy for beer.

The middle daughter
Was keen on reading
Thanks to my prayers.

Nowadays it's only
In my dreams that I see
People who have made it.

Everything's gone up.
Even when we're mad at each other
We don't break plates . . .

My younger children
Read like the ancient Romans
Aloud and recumbent.

Reading Brodsky's prose,
I discovered a spiritual kinship:
A consuming interest in dust . . .

Translated by Daniel Weissbort

[*The reflection of a wet finger . . .*]

The reflection of a wet finger that slipped over the faded oil-cloth
like a watery speck of potato settled on the saucer,
rolled in a meandering stream, slow and slender.
This happened in never-never. It was completely before you . . .
To inhale the steam from the hot, yellow potatoes . . .
And having screwed up one's eyes to smile into the colored darkness
hiding in grandma's round apron, veins throbbing at the brow.
This happened in never-never. It was completely before you . . .
And to take the towel worn to weak gauze:
Grandpa really could not have wiped his face with it—
    he must have spread it on the dew.
To feel Grandpa's soft: *Haisl maine.*
This happened in never-never. It was completely before you . . .

Translated by Richard McKane

ELENA IGNATOVA

[*Then there was the rose I fell in love with*]

Then there was the rose I fell in love with—
a December rose.
             When we say "Eden"
amid our snows we have in mind
the image of a rose garden in December.
I pluck a December rose,
similar to these.
Yes, when, amid our snows, we say "Eden"
we conceive of a vale
overgrown with olive trees and laurels
reaching to the flat heavens.
A deer, its antlers entangled in the roses,
a lamb, a lion . . .
            No lamentation, no tears.
On the other side of the ravine, over the heads of the roses
the valley of Ajalon, rough like a sail,
from those times when the sun of Joshua
frizzled its edge. And the blazing little town
ran with blood beyond the sugar-lump walls.
Mountains of folks, donkeys, goats . . .
            Quantities of blood let.
No, December rose, Eden's no magical garden.
On the ashy sole its hills, liner of blood—
just as amid our snows, but more ancient by far,
and the tops of the trees spattered with death's rust,
and the December rose, tight like God's scroll,
like the Lord's wrath, weighs on my heart.

Translated by Daniel Weissbort

[*To sob, pressing oneself against the officer's greatcoat*]

To sob, pressing oneself against the officer's greatcoat—
gives one a special colonial thrill.
West is West—but this is East.
Do you see where we've got, you and I?
The famous atmosphere of the Fifties
has staled here, back to front.
Preserve of childhood.
                                   Again, again
the shoulder-straps on the uniforms of young fathers
smell of oranges and gold.
How many of us are at table, how crowded it's got!
Dream of childhood.
                                   The family clan
closing ranks, like the crown over the head
of the eternal tree. Its scent is corporeal.

Don't wake. The lips of mothers
taste silver and mint.
How deathless, how rich
we were in their love . . .
We were borne off into the dream, into the dark.
You will wake—the desert in full bloom,
soft sound of singing on the other side of the wall—
a coachman, who keels over toward the snow,
a spring, where the light is hot
over the icy waters of life.

Translated by Daniel Weissbort

NINA ISKRENKO

Another Woman

When I cannot stand
to muster strength against misfortune
when I cannot sleep
and face an entire tank of dirty laundry
when I
mistake my children
for dinosaurs
but take the favorable disposition of luminaries in the sky
for a simple act of courtesy
when at a quarter to
eight I have to go
and at a quarter to nine I have to go
and at a quarter to eleven I
have to go
and the radio
is saying all manner of bad things
when the telephone finally tunes out
because it can't take this anymore
and a piece of butter brought to mind
does not spread on an imaginary piece of bread
and what's more I stumble in the dark of night on
the bicycle in the hall

the sleepy and slightly irritated striking of a match is heard
and smoke reaches under the door
This is you
starting to talk on and on to me about another woman

Another woman in your place
Another woman in your position

Another woman at our level of civilization would pay no attention to these
regular monthly whims would not pay attention would not pay

My forehead tenses up with the effort to imagine the seductive adaptability of
a n o t h e r woman to o u r level of civilization and when finally I succeed
I smile the trustingly disdainful smile of the Cheshire cat or of Julio Cortázar

gladly giving up my place at the stove to the other woman and in sleep and in all of my horizontal-vertical-trigonometrical knee-eared cold-nosed spiral-eyed positions and while she masters them paying me no attention whatsoever I steal up to the front door feeling for my shoes and thinking only about how not to get snagged by the bicycle in the hall

The doorbell rings
I open the door
Another woman with a plaintive voice jumping out of her dress asks me to call the police her husband got drunk and she hit him with a skillet full of cutlets you wouldn't have any valerian would you thank you what is this disgusting stuff I've never taken anything like it good God some people have proper lives, quiet and calm and happy

Coming back into the room for a handkerchief
I notice that another woman resiliently-weightily has collapsed onto something brown-red and dirty-blue   She has a splendid golden almost masculine torso cut off by a frame and blind eyes smeared over in black   It seems in my position she is pretty satisfied although Modigliani does not like being looked at

The television flickers
Another woman on the screen
whispers and wails into an invisible microphone
fatally shuts her eyes reveling in her
shrewish gait and animal longing
for another man
For you probably

In half an hour another woman in a crooked veil
and work boots
suddenly falls off the book shelf onto my head
and lies on the floor all open in a swoon
at that page where the enemy has just burned down a Russian village
where Catholics ceaselessly butcher Huguenots
and Turks do it to Armenians
and the bronze horseman wears down the bronze steed
riding from Petersburg to Moscow
trying to get there for the morning execution of the Streltsy

Bunchberry sauce for meat and chicken
is something we never have

Bunchberries do not grow at our market
probably another woman is in the kitchen looking through
the cookbook she turned to me with her
tasty bunchberry butt pasted on a card-
board wrapper of German-made stockings

Blue twilight is soaked
and its contours are lost in the little river and for hours and minutes the suf-
fering cello squeak of the doors winds around the digital lock in the entryway

In the yard wheezing children work hard to carve from snow
another woman
Her head keeps falling apart
it's like some sort of punishment to make this stupid head
who ever thought it up
you could just cut the eyes in her stomach

Growing dark   Starting to drizzle   Growing light   Stretching out
Peering through   It started to freeze

Another woman in my place looks in the mirror
turning her face so that
the circles under her eyes aren't seen

Another woman in my position sorts through the spoons
and climbs up to the top shelf to get washing powder

Another woman at our level of civilization
walks along the sidewalk in dirty tattered jeans
looks through magazines at the kiosks
gets bored talking with friends
figures out the story's ending after the third
paragraph although it only has two

and she comes out of the metro
walking toward the Pushkin monument at that very moment
when the poet with his stiff stone face
takes off his top hat
and turns toward Tver Boulevard
listening wearily to the noise of airplanes
to the light clatter of carriage wheels
and to the squeak of floorboards in Mikhailovskoe
He is watching with feigned indifference

another woman
who pays him absolutely no attention
as she melodically moves across the street
Her face turns pink in the shining warning light
of the traffic signal   Brakes squeal
She shrieks and runs
without looking back   choking on the frozen air
mechanically reading signs and being reflected in
every face until finally she falls
flat in the dark of night
accidentally tripping on a bicycle
in the hall

Translated by Stephanie Sandler

Translator's note: This poem has also been translated by Olga Livshin, and I have
borrowed several of her locutions. See *Slovo* 28 (2000): 98–100. Here, and in my
translations of Elena Shvarts and Elena Fanailova, I have also incorporated some
excellent suggestions from Catriona Kelly, for which I am grateful.

OLGA IVANOVA

To Russian Women

She'll not nag if there's no bread for breakfast
But by nightfall is sure to provide,
A runaway Rolls Royce she'd stop in its tracks
And she'll always stump up some cash.

She's clever at handling money.
But, the fool, she'd not keep a penny.
This land over, poor Russian women
Will never give up, or give in.

Whatever life brings, she will shoulder:
Needs must, she'll just soldier on.
Yank in her belt by yet one more notch,
After scrimping for your hair of dog.

And once the last penny is gone—
Out will come her dregs of "Obsession."
With tough childhood now left behind,
Mad happiness fills her mind.

Translated by Jenefer Coates

Translator's note: This parodies the famous Nekrasov poem "Russkie zhenshchiny,"
which praises Russian women for their idealized virtues.

[*Do I hold the past in my hands*]

Do I hold the past in my hands
Perhaps
A little too tightly?

Translated by Jenefer Coates

[*Time turned inside out*]

Time turned inside out
Hangs down from me
Like empty sleeves

Translated by Jenefer Coates

[*I meet myself each and every day*]

I meet myself each and every day
Never do I leave myself alone
I am out of sight not for a single second
And so I simply fail to understand
What can have happened to
That face
Which stares back at me
From old photographs

Translated by Jenefer Coates

SVETLANA IVANOVA

[O caterpillar, daughter of the butterfly]

O caterpillar, daughter of the butterfly,
You too one day will soar past tower and roof,
Past boring little dachas in the suburbs.
Yet no mere louse are you fated to remain—
You'll outstrip yourself, slipping from your skin.

Wherever—over earth or leaf—you crawl
Your body has to work a little harder,
You're a real
Shakin' break-dancer,
And a hundred flowers all blaze bright for you.

Translated by Jenefer Coates

[Bird, start up your moan, your whine]

Bird, start up your moan, your whine,
whether like a gunner's star
or a ladder's upward climb . . .
fish, beast, gift of a tsar.

"Tails" each time, and this must mean
muteness—yet do throw the coin—
I forgive you in return
for a penultimate copper tone,

and for a penultimate number,
for the sunshine trees of sleep,
all turned inside out—and steep.
So a master forgives the monkey

in its fustian cap, pell-mell
pulled behind him on a string . . .
How to guess which hand it's in,
you, with you I cannot tell.

You're watching me with constant eye.
Do you prophesy or call?
Count it out one final time,
Re-count, re- . . . anything at all

with a teardrop graphomanic,
with a drop of heavenly grace
and with foliage gethsemanic
over a wept and chasmic place.

Translated by Angela Livingstone

Subterranean River Poem

Either archival youths or Aegean men
looked through the blue of the sun
or was it through a March day's windows,
flying through a dance of dust
from the bottom of the reflected morning,
where among stones of a dusky pont,
new-born water
was wholly filled with movement
and, along the Acheron, Neva's ice
moves like sable ships
and voices float in light
in the library's Lethean sleep.
Shout—you get quietness for reply,
nothing but thawing light-blots.
O and turn round—there's only a palm
mutely flashing,
a wave of farewell, a speechless fire
through water.

Translated by Angela Livingstone

INNA KABYSH

Making Jam in July

A woman who's making jam in July
is resigned to living with her husband.
She won't escape with her lover, secretly.
Otherwise, why boil up fruit with sugar?
and observe, how willingly she does it,
as a labor of love,
even though space is at a premium
and there's nowhere to store the jars.

A woman who's making jam in July
is preparing to be around for a while.
She intends to soldier on, to hibernate
through the discomforts of winter.
Otherwise, for what reason, and notice,
not out of any feeling of duty,
should she be spending the short summer
skimming residue off jam?

A woman who's making jam in July
in all the chaos of a steamy kitchen
isn't going to be absconding to the West
or buying a ticket to the States.
That woman will be scrambling out of snowdrifts,
buoyed up by the savor of the fruit.
Whoever's making jam in Russia
knows there isn't any way out.

Translated by Fay Marshall and Alex Marshall

[*Whenever the prodigal son returns home*]

Whenever the prodigal son returns home
he arrives at the height of day;
whereas when the prodigal daughter comes back
she slinks in after dark.

A daughter may have learned her lesson too
but she'll arrive encumbered with children.

Translated by Fay Marshall and Alex Marshall

KATIA KAPOVICH

[*Something from an untidy Russian life*]

Something from an untidy Russian life,
from homegrown truth in the trough,
from a dried bunch of grapes:
I dream of these since there aren't enough events.

I dream simply of circles in front of the eyes,
the harsh chords of alleys in perspective,
so that my face is suddenly flooded
with tears. This cloudburst stands in my throat.

The doors open in the morning of their own accord
like a book at the required page.
Then I dream of some little square without
a subject and then simply of water.

So the sense of loss is growing dull,
memory gradually rusts like a knife.
Even when I am dead I will dream sometime
of these eyes, greener than the river by day.

Translated by Richard McKane

[*Parting makes simple sense*]

Parting makes simple sense,
there's no special sense in it.
The air will be to blame,
the garden full of birds whistling.
The smoke and the strip of water
there by the mossy forest.
Even that the sunset cut
across the rows of pines.
It will turn everything into ashes
with the quiet oncoming of night,
so that in tormenting dreams
the eye should fall for

the thousandth time
to the keyhole of the world
not finding in the light
that which it sought in the dark,
aiming at the door with the little cross-key.

And you raise a pale blue
pupil in the summer sky.
You will not share life with me
and couldn't care less about freedom.
But there is a terrible truth
hidden in your madness.
As though you know everything
about everything. Even more than is necessary.

Translated by Richard McKane

SVETLANA KEKOVA

[*Space is arched like a sail*]

Space is arched like a sail,
its laws the same everywhere,
and the broad faces of moths
compose its outer tier.

While we are balanced
on the chasm's meniscus,
we will not let our pointless sadness
misrepresent God's realm.

Life, that unresolved question,
we leave till later.
Both the crazed woodpecker
and the gaping fish

are like broken keys
jutting from rusty locks,
or an ignoramus
flaunting his ugliness.

Translated by Ruth Fainlight

[*With much effort, I glimpse in the darkness and rubbish*]

With much effort, I glimpse in the darkness and rubbish
unbaptized beings standing in every corner.

Above the bed, hiding its entreaty,
hangs a tarnished mirror with an ulcerated forehead.

Night has the mysterious gift of blindness:
you cannot be seen or see anyone else—
only the square mouths of cut-glass vases
and the dim copper of a cold teapot,
only the devil's net and the airy cage
where space sits, like a songbird,

where a candle starts to smolder and
enclose you in a circle of pale light.

Your naked helplessness, the lord knows well!—
and that faint birthmark near the mouth.
The fallen angel, with an almost imperceptible
tremor of orange wings, opens his lifeless eyes.

Translated by Ruth Fainlight

[*Running water is cold, the river from Eden flows east*]

Running water is cold, the river from Eden flows east,
a lowercase letter appeared on a page of rough copy,
the flowers' pollen settled, fragile life seems exhausted,
slant rhyme craves to be used, but the hand refuses.

What kind of word, uttered, leaves salt in the mouth?
Soon your death is exhausted, sinks like a stone. There
is the source of false light: in the impossible world's center
the fallen angel Lucifer distorts the music of the spheres.

Everything disappears in a motley flame, rising to heaven.
A host of angels inscribes the letter "S" on a banner.
Again the apple is bitten, flesh forbidden,
but that which God created cannot be destroyed.

Do you see in unhealed sores the dark foliage of apple trees,
exhausted woodland creatures in crippled forest giants?
"Theta" sleeps and "izhitsa"* dozes, "yat" slithers from under your hand,
beetles move in brittle armor across the tree-trunks' bark.

I don't want to count my losses or hear the terrible roar of flesh.
The spirit betrayed us, but matter transforms to language.
The focus of a former life hides wherever it can,
and stuttering words sprout from the fertile earth.

Translated by Ruth Fainlight

*Izhitsa is the name of a Russian letter taken out of use by the spelling reforms of
1917 (translator's note).

[*The tsar sits on his throne as if he sat on bones*]

The tsar sits on his throne as if he sat on bones.
Around him, a world of deserving objects,
and the tsar's staff is strong, strong as Rakhmetov*
sleeping on his famous bed of nails
as an example to the young. A coffer stands
high as the throne which the tsar mounts—
he keeps his silver in an oak womb.
Some creature walks over the ruler's skull
and his staff will strike it a blow,
as at our first mother Eve.
The Old Testament serpent sits in a tree
and picks up our thoughts, like radar.
And a blind mole who lives in the worm-eaten earth
has scooped out a dark burrow in the space
between an apple and a plum tree, as in the rind
of the world, and insinuated itself there.

Translated by Ruth Fainlight

* Rakhmetov is a character in Nikolay Chernyshevsky's famous novel *What Is
to be Done?* The revolutionary hero toughens himself by sleeping on a bed of nails
(translator's note).

[*Look, a man is flying and*]

Look, a man is flying and
doesn't know where or why.
He remembers his past life,
glorifies it, curses it, and
watery tears gush from his eyes.

Seductions of this world,
like moments, run in sequence:
naked apples of summer
glistening red currants
basins of rain water.

At dawn, a threesome splits up:
flesh, soul, and restless spirit.
Needles of tender larch trees rake
the thickening air like a comb.
The last rooster sets the tune.

Louder than the instant before the walls collapse,
a white willow thrashes above the ravine.
In the filthy pit of Gehenna
our death burns to ash,

and whirls like a fiery squirrel.
Fine dust irritates the eyelids,
and your suitcase, human sinner,
is spotted by celestial whitewash.

You returned with all your old mistakes,
your previous pain and new misfortunes,
and clouds are heaped
in the blue sky above the white water.

Translated by Ruth Fainlight

[*Already, no more suffering, no*]

Already, no more suffering, no
more speech nor space nor time.
In the city of Bremen, only music
still survives, and light.
Over the bakery, a pretzel gleams,
summing up foolish life,
and in the dark of midnight
a repulsive white flower blooms.

Dusty brakes of yellow acacia
clustered around an empty platform
revealed the law of gravity,
but its effect on the spirit was slight.
Life should not slip away like dross.
Again you climb the hill, but
the faces ripped open like bellies
disclose only the viscera of clocks.

We die, we sleep and eat,
weep loudly, form words
and pursue certain ends,
with no idea of what it's all about.
The fir-tree branches flutter
in a dazzle of eyelashes,
and round-headed nurslings of death
materialize in the maternity wards.

No more honey, hops, or malt,
no burning water, no fire.
The blasted gold cavorts across the sky,
in too much of a hurry.
You'll break the moon like crockery
and, approaching old age, learn how
to persecute those irrepressible Jews.
So your youthful days return.

How the winged horses clip-clopped
over the hot paving stones of the bridge.
We saw Mandelstam, or Blok,
head bowed, walking off
into inordinately deep air-pockets,
where words echo death's knell,
where your disobedient golden head
still seems to be alive.

Translated by Ruth Fainlight

MARINA KHAGEN

[*in the branches' shade*]

in the branches' shade
the sparrow's shadow
hops

morning mist
on a burning lake
in a china mug

the sun touched a snowman
beads of sweat
on his forehead

a map in a puddle
every country
flooded

underground
day and night
the city's the same

the mute child's
first word's
a gesture

Translated by Linor Goralik

OLGA KHVOSTOVA

Flood Songs

1

dark rivers cry cities snivel
as water stands all week long up to the brow

there where i flow on that shore
an orange noah shoiga breaks camp

i beg ask him to let you pass i cannot
part today tomorrow
then later forever
holy meat protein body
the forsaken moist with sweat,
that which is ninety per whole water

2

you know charles i surrender how careful i wait
from window to window i pace, an animal
carrying such need
squeaking my nose along the smooth glass
staring staring at the empty road
circling the cage
each nerve takes the bearing
i pass the four decades' extension course
this ZOO-logy i call it

3

there is something important i won't say yet but have told
behind the wash or stew i stand a broken pressure cooker
i burn, saying burn, but there where you speak, i rumble,
threaten to leave, i do, but where you stand i will be glued

don't send me away, do not, this exit—emergency only,
don't look the way they look, eye-sockets in the Chechen pits
in the temples where you pray let me let me finish my nap
in the checkerboard where you bare your teeth, let me scowl

the sickened lord-have-mercy turns inside out
the sky's basin tilts the lord with peritonitis
break open these bonds take a drag
don't tumble don't torment don't you dare

4

the living won't survive, the dead have died off
when did death ever in Russia give a damn
mister sorokin and Co. reckoned: can't force it

why do they fix blood with a sliver of glass in the rear guard
why won't that other one leave alone
stands clot-like jumpstarting to dive the riverbed
gradually shuts down the oxygen

scrambling onto the bhagavad gita/mahabharata shore
yells into own reflection into own shattered glass
the sea selva's bilirubin regatta's
sails excuse me crimson red bloody corpuscles

5

quit this flickering groveling southward
especially southward with kolchuga in tow
to the sea with its lacquered cover
where clouds hover like smoke after the bombing
and the sinking feeling that a Gauleiter is on his way
with his hands up to one's back he will bark "hell outa here!"
how to live with this unhealed feeling
the skull knows how, names it gustav

6

fifteen years of corpulent blizzards over you
fifteen elbows of corpse water over me
eyes like rotten eggs, mugs arse like
aqualungs released from tubes

i have already forgotten you and your traits
can't see the bottom of this crawling shack
can't bear or recognize
a single voice a single corpse, can you

7

it's the rain falling and not me calling
this heaviness assorti sticky humus water and ash
but you, don't cast the sails away yet, wait
do not dilute, nary a word
unarmed, conceal
inside or out
nails slide grabbing
say dersu uzala

Gulkrevichi
Krasnodar Region

Translated by Tatyana Retivova

MARIYA KILDIBEKOVA

[*Pizza's a populous island*]

Pizza's a populous island
where mushrooms like sad Mexicans live.
Set among crimson pepper squares
an onion surrenders. In the oven
cheese gets above itself, clutches
tomatoes, spreads all across the green
its sweet yawn.

Translated by Roy Fisher

[*Everybody was going on talking the same talk*]

Everybody was going on talking the same talk—
aging, breakdown, the sense of failure—
so I dreamt myself a Celebrities' Liner
loaded with Perrier and Beaujolais and crowded
with opulent riffraff. Maybe
the *Titanic*. Maybe.

There was Kennedy, Marilyn, and—odd—
a very young Arthur Miller. They'd not
met? Stalin, sadly
smoking a pipe and singing
words I can't make out, Georgian most likely.

Complacent, in a coat cadged
from a Greek café proprietor,
Osip Mandelstam sits writing, notebook on his knee,
cellphone on his belt. A ring.
"Who? From Koktebel? No,
I don't remember. I don't owe you
anything. Cheers, then."
No sign of Nadezhda. Not far off
Bliumkin of the KGB
goes past, grinding his teeth.

In the crowd, Oskar Schindler, drunk,
and Hitler run into each other. That perfunctory
salute. "Hi, Oskar! How's it going? How's trade?" "Well.
I've brought a few really good workers. You'll see."

Some very amusing
kids, I just can't remember whose—except
the one on the left's the daughter of the Kuwaiti
ambassador to Russia. And a whole brood of lovely
curly-haired madcaps from Palestine: cast
any one of them as Judas. Zhabotinsky
the Zionist poet keeps an eye on the fun.

Cast him as Christ.

Bankers, ponces, hackers, traders,
Egyptian sheikhs with harems in tow,
a soldier and a businessman at the bar—
"Vietnam?" "Oh no: Chechnia. Stone dead."
Nureev, Freddie Mercury in purple, all
hot and bothered, both of them.

Hippies without tickets on the liner,
a ballerina from Chile, transvestites,
and somebody sweet and familiar
in a crumpled velvet jacket; also
his friend, the puny, bespectacled
expert in kitsch, his nose
eternally in a book, and uttering
never a word about the sick twentieth century.
Grimaces, giggles—two girls! Heading
they don't know where, looking for free
tangerines, as far as they can get
from their sad mothers.

And I wander bewildered for a while, then suddenly
this character charges up—"Just
how long do you think you can just hang around?"
—smacks me across the face and hauls me
into the kitchen. And now I'm holding

a heavy tray: fruit, chocolate,
champagne, drugs, books.
—"Serve the guests!" And I'm crying
in total terror of Hitler.

Translated by Roy Fisher

[*A bomb said to a city*]

A bomb said to a city:
"I'm falling."

The city asked:
"Whose side are you on?"

The bomb said:
"I take no sides. I'm falling."

The city said:
"Look around you."

The bomb said:
"Too late."

The city did not say anything.

Translated by the author

Cassandra to Agamemnon

I've warned you of the bloodbath:
a bath, with your blood in it, literally.
But there you go, blundering right in,
no hand of fate can stop you,
the hand that wants you dead.
And I, who will be killed soon after you,
why should I care—when, or whose hand?
So don't stall—go on, go in,
step blindly into your matron's trap,
hero of the great war, great murderer yourself.
Before I die, I'll see you flounder,
like a fat carp, in the fishnet of your queen.
But what is this water in my eyes?
My eyes that have seen my brothers killed,
my city razed, before and after.

Nobody weeps for you, therefore I will,
I, Cassandra.

Translated by the author

Backward Sound

I'm a backward
sound of myself.
I twist, I turn

through sheer virulence
of habit sleep
that measures me in bursts

of agony, hoary and private.
I ask, I bless.
I speak the raw material of memory;

only flowers here still recall the dead.
I am a green begonia.
I am a red

petal on the stem of morning.
I am, I am . . .
Black sweetness,

save me from these shattered
words, repetitive illusions.
I am dark, uncountable.

I am the meaning of a syllable
the ancients said and dropped.
I am the one the clouds dream of

when their vapor eyes are shut.
The weeping wall, the nakedness of heart . . .
Disinterestedness, now let me go.

You said: it's guaranteed—
the backward glance, the exit,
the twisting back, back, back . . .

Now let me go, beauty grass.
Your kisses pain me
as all that dies pains that which doesn't.

I am the eye-nerve of your marriage,
grassy sky.
I bless, I bless.

I am a friend to all that breathes.
I beg you: do breathe me in;
and let me disappear in you:

Forever, earth.
Forever, sky.

Translated by the author

ELENA KOSTYLEVA

[*A vacancy instead of you*]

A vacancy instead of you
a vacant head, a vacant heart
the joy has never visited this space
no fires burnt there
afterward they usually stub
all
that remains
of our trees

somewhere underground
deep deep under this ground
there are the finest of our roots
no roots are softer, babies of our roots
so smooth yet bitter—
should I say entwined?

humus oh humus
you and I, we inhume us

A vacancy instead of you
One can get rid of any other one
of any dream
by stepping to a window
and shaking one's head up
saying, fains I
saying, fains I

A vacancy instead of you
"In vain, enough already"
There's mother's voice,
it's whispering, exhorting
like an old record I
used to fall asleep to
in the background.
Mother dear, in vain—
Mother dear, in vain
In vain/in vain/

stand before me, stripped to the waist,
smile and shake your head
—how could I sculpt a frail doll—

blindfold us both,
let me touch your face
I know my hands are cold
and my eyes congeal all
that had ever been.

stand before me, blindfolded
let me remember your features
let me drink

There are no endeavors vainer than
shoveling snow, curing people, and bearing kids.
The snow gets melted into wine
that douses streets in summer
for all that dust should be dealt with.
Young doctors cure me
yet I die of their cures
and they die of it.

Dust on the windowpanes.
a baby's born—my hands are cold,
no way to cuddle it.
Doctor, doctor.

an alabaster baby was conceived through a headcloth
the skin is white, but under it there
mine and yours, the blood flows

there's ringing in the ears
his, yours, mine

alabaster, plaster, alabaster

when you look at me in public
everything congeals without me
and everything within I'd ever got
I start to think
God knows what
God wot
step to me, just one step
stay where you are

careful
for when you look at me in public
the sky looks like a sheepskin to me
and my uterus feels like a nubble

humus oh humus
you and I, we inhume us
stand before me strong and luminous

Translated by Max Nemtsov

IRINA KOVALEVA

[*I can still make you out*]

I can still make you out
through the glass fragment of days,
but as if the candle were being taken away
and the radiance dimming, dimming.

I still see the dazzle, as of wingbeat or eyelid,
and the motley dark.
I remember that gasping fright
at your name.

But there, behind the dream's heavy drapes,
behind the window's sash,
where earlier there'd been bustle, a running about,
a rustle and in general much commotion,
there was now silence

and a void. The drift
of clock hands stopped, ended.
Light snow falls indifferently
from void into void.

Translated by Daniel Weissbort

[. . . *And there was beauty*]

. . . And there was beauty—
A hem, flying up—above a slender foot,
Over the grayish timber of the bridge.

Moreover there was love for apples. Each fruit
Was divided into two, but he,
Recalling the story, with a tilt of the head, declined
The apple. The hand . . .

His wings are buoyant,
Dazzling, like flickering
tongues of flame—burning heat—
But when he goes—the heart,
Which was like a star,
Stays empty.

A word, uttered by your voice,
Became golden
And round, goldenly translucent, ripe
In the radiant air, golden and white,
And, immutable, it remains whole.

This, of course, is not the garden, but close enough.
And a branch, glancing out of the garden,
Is reflected in it
Like light, falling into a pool.

Translated by Daniel Weissbort

ELLA KRYLOVA

The Pilgrims

Over the earth they come,
alpha-rays scorching them,
beta-rays scorching them,
gamma-rays scorching them,
passing Mecca and Rome,
passing Jerusalem,
ruins in front of them, ruins
behind them: the pilgrims.

Over the mountains they come;
the sea's like dry land to them:
they suffer no harm, they succumb
to no plague, no famine.

They all have coins on their eyes,
and rockets in their hands,
and floppy disks in their minds.
They travel over the planet,
the round and empty planet,
though they're not on earth anymore,
and there's no one on earth anymore,
and there isn't an earth, anyway,
anymore.

Translated by Yury Drobyshev and Carol Rumens

Cornflowers

Cornflowers, cornflowers,
little blue-eyed beacons,
little land-sailors,
they say you're only weeds,
my poor *vasilki*.

Uselessly lovely ones,
whose loss is the farmer's gain,

my poems, perhaps, are the same
—weeds like you, my cornflowers,
whose modest good looks do not suit
the teeming oatfields
that fill the masses: maybe, at harvest-time,
pitiless God will tear out every root
—mine and the cornflowers'.

Who, then, created me,
gave me a dress of sky,
brought turquoise water for my thirst,
fed me at sunshine's breast?
Who whispered lines of verse,
came to me in a trance,
and wrapped me against the cold
in swansdown whiteness?

I stand above the cornflower sea
of that island-basilisk
which sheltered but never housed me,
rooted into my flesh but never caressed me,
vasilki-blue Vasilevsky:*
I repeat—Who are You? Who am I?

Translated by Yury Drobyshev and Carol Rumens

*Phonetic play of *vasilki* (flowers) and "Vasilevsky" (the island) figuring in an early
poem by Joseph Brodsky (translator's note).

MARINA KUDIMOVA

[*Prison,* zona, *the camps, Taldái-Kustanái, and the low road*]

Prison, *zona*,* the camps, Taldái-Kustanái, and the low road,
Let sparks fly up as my soul squeals into a bend.
May my heart be smelted in patience's slow-burning furnace,
Snatch me and raise me—heave ho!—but gently, on high.
Let the low road batter me, dislocate me,
And catch up my free-floating angst in a long prison train
To Vologda. Howls lie thin on our mouths like tin-plate.
Shoot to kill if we try to escape, abuse us, and then release us:
These are a masochist's joys, the feathery whine
Of branches of birch in a steam-bath, coming down on your thigh.
What I see is the sapping of wills; but when pain's nearly stifling
Your wrist turns into a perch for a goldfinch, a cross-bill,
A kingfisher, even. If you fly, you don't have to sing.
See the one bird, silently moving her interlaced beak-halves
Or the second, giving his tinselly, gurgling laugh,
The other's a humble bird, won't cry out if you snare him:
He'll sing on and on, quite true, not jibbing at all,
A ballad of life in jail to excite and delight you.
As we ride the low road, the convict road to the *zona*,
The rails move closer, apart. They flank us, encircle like swordsmen
In a Roman legion: a stale old optical trick.
The light burns into our eyes like flares on the front line
And shadows fall on the windows like masking tape
To hold in the glass if it goes. So bring out the cards!
Let's get back the sum that we lost playing Stoss with the century,
We were just one point to the bad, or a player was short.
Let's finish the round, and hey for Vologda say I!

Translated by Catriona Kelly

Zona (slang) signifies the location, zone, of the prison camps (translator's note).

[*The pleated strata of air*]

The pleated strata of air,
The fir-branches crimped like wheel tracks,
And October standing by
Saffron and bald, like a Buddhist;
A fancy foreign car
From nowhere, no-man's land,
Has stamped its designer soles
Over the slant stripes of grass.

How short the lease,
How quickly the russet speeds by,
If this crumbling tentative track
Will be whited out come All Saints.
Soon winter will hobble close,
Putting out its dreary dust-sheets.
So burn while you can, October,
Like puerperal fever, melting the brain.

Translated by Catriona Kelly

INNA KULISHOVA

[*Till now*]

Till now
I've not been able to imagine
what it's like to long for water
in a desert,
and striving
to make flour out of the sands.
Evidently,
it's worth surviving
so as to experience something other than writing.

Translated by Daniel Weissbort

[*Total darkness*]

Total darkness.
The light's off in the kitchen,
and people will go into the room.
The window shut,
they turn on the telly, where a poet
(much loved) says we're all going to die
and yet
something will remain, just a trace.
Although it was not he, no way,
not he, who said this. Straight off,
all's forgotten. But
that doesn't matter. The main thing, a trace
will remain. And to appreciate
this is not worth the days
passing so swiftly, the years, so long ago.
And it's not even worth
vanity of vanities.
The main thing is the trace.
That it's evening, dark. That it's late.

Translated by Daniel Weissbort

YULIYA KUNINA

Inconsistent Self-Portrait

I am half Russian, 30, almost got my MA,
1 meter 67, on the list and registered,
fragments of an encyclopedia, excerpts from a dictionary,
three languages, to synopsize.
Here are my eyes: people say they're beautiful.
Here is my long nose.
My lips are plum-colored, or bilberry colored, or lipsticked,
whatever.
Here is my profile: people say it's Nubian,
or perhaps Jewish, or really Russian,
the devil knows what the devil's mixed together.
Here is my thieving magpie's habit.
Here is my decisive chin,
although what is it decisive about?
Here are my shoulders—shoulder blades protruding. I like to
compare them to Natasha's, but they are more like a bird's:
you can squeeze it in your fist, just fluff and feathers.
The journey down, of course, conceals temptations.
I am made out of differing and different
old girls and interesting ladies,
Renoir women and dubious personages,
suffragettes and faithful wives, and these, whom I don't know
who were humiliated in the prefeminist era.

But this is, so to speak, bragging, or rather a hide,
pimply frog skin,
loved by Jew and fool
which I am telling you about.

And so, I crawl, smoldering in ash,
like a serpent or tortoise,
commanding the thunder with my mind.

Translated by Richard McKane

INGA KUZNETSOVA

[*speech is a stream*]

speech is a stream
with hordes of natives inside
missionaries and squares
small-fry and big shots
square-dancing

Translated by Max Nemtsov

[*I'm trying to fit my destiny into*]

I'm trying to fit my destiny into
the eye of a needle, like a pony
into the tightly drawn square collar.
Yet it remains a zero, like a vent
sash. Only a geranium is screaming on
the windowsill, "intolerable."
We survive by blank verse only.
The life is random, memory lives
only in words. The silence of the roads
hangs heavy. But I believe our inner square
where we're keen will budge and the pony
will go capering again, all bitterness forgotten.

Translated by Max Nemtsov

[*repairs are like the fall of Pompeii*]

repairs are like the fall of Pompeii
with dust and ashes all over the books
we're still here, late for a stampede
see the windowsill trembling with
the din of the crowd below us
do you hear it? the placid ethnos

will be safe from the Etna's fury
and the new era calls us

Translated by Max Nemtsov

[*for a centenary*]

for a centenary
you'd been kept under a bushel
under my heart
like a child invisible
a relic in a chest
for a centenary
I'd been holding a thread from the
bird in the bush
in my hand thinking
it'd been the kite flying high
it was some funny kiddy amulet
a periapt
I'm apt to be thrown ashore
and I climb up the precipice
marring the layers of marl clay and grass
the gritty mix
of the homeland
the pastry of earth tasting like love
and strawberries
the pastry
pasted into my texts
my caress at halves with the blues
clenches up and
scatters like fledglings
the thread
jerks in my hand
I've been keeping you in the chest like my dowry
with braids
and an ancient baldric, with worn traces
I need to tell so much
the palate
of the sky won't fit so many words

I rock the cradle
filled with letters to the brim
and weave the future
with a fine thread from that bird in the bush
I'm the bird in my hand
I'd lived overseas and came back
and I burnt those seas to ashes

Translated by Max Nemtsov

[*a seagull shrilly in my head*]

a seagull shrilly in my head
a smell of the ocean from the western
window—no, must be the fresh-
caught fish
my knee
looks like a pebble in wretched jeans
shabby like some POW's
overalls
it's weird
when the body
without you is alien
like the inanimate
nature of a thing
say
a rock or a snag in the grass

Translated by Max Nemtsov

[*breadcrumbs falling from the table*]

breadcrumbs falling from the table
and skating all over the cracked
mirror of a chair
you dream of Tula
not the city but the hinterland
you and I
how weird

our room is a crystal ball
with the breadcrumbs like Breughel's kids
someone jazzy
swings in me
happy life
is regular
is it the
way for the
snow to be

Translated by Max Nemtsov

A Wand

a wand is swaying in the peace
I wish I knew just what it is
I wish I knew just what it is

Translated by Max Nemtsov

EVGENIYA LAVUT

About Love

Your hat smelt of dead moths. Your flabby fingers
Betrayed that vulgar shopkeeping hook.
To want to touch your absence of a torso
With my own hands seemed a kind of joke.

But when my life lacked you my life lacked bread,
Though in your presence food grew rancid, cold,
As if an angel stretched the sky to spread
His knees apart and pissed into my world.

Translated by Yury Drobyshev and Carol Rumens

[*In the body of the town I'm a pupil*]

In the body of the town I'm a pupil.
I wander along its entrails,
with my pack, at an easy pace
from place to place.

I know like my own five fingers
where things are—the smelly things,
the flowing things, where the tramps
get moved on, where they linger.

In the body of the town I love to settle
like pubic lice in trousers.
In the body of the town I'm a monk
for whom there's nowhere to kneel

and as long as the place is possessed
by its crazy thunderstorm,
I'll wander round, an alien
microscopic life-form,

leaving a stubborn trace:
I gasp, grow speechless, go gray.
I'm sorry I don't belong
—but my vision is my own.

Translated by Yury Drobyshev and Carol Rumens

ELENA LAZUTKINA

[*The wind's mane*]

The wind's mane
in the blue pasture.
Its muzzle in the skybald horse's eye.
And with smoke over the barns
how will I find my dream book?

Translated by Robert Reid

[*I stand and inspect the phenomena drawn up*]

I stand and inspect the phenomena drawn up,
as once Dubrovsky stood,
debating—to kill or not to kill
the next squire on his list.

Translated by Robert Reid

[*Ruined so many romances*]

Ruined so many romances,
destroyed so many smiles,
wasted an ocean of time, then disappeared

how can he be
Chinese?

Translated by Robert Reid

Ode to the Computer

For you, little friend,
I gave thousands of greenbacks
and made a green salad
of my stanzas' last lines.

On the pithy meat of reason
with rhyme as trimmings,
from the last provisions
you and I shall feast.

What do I care about money,
fame and magical pageants?
You are the last distraction
of my century.

Echo, mirror, envoy,
ghost and double,
why have you come to trouble
my last days?

Translated by Ruth Fainlight

[*Between hope and failure*]

Between hope and failure—
and trees with foam on their lips—
the bed remembered how the night passed.

The notebook recollected how the day passed,
how life passed: snow and fallen petals.
How death passes, dust and ashes will not forget.

Translated by Ruth Fainlight

[*Like the earth turning, I creak, and dream*]

Like the earth turning, I creak, and dream
of a return to the Garden of Eden

where reptiles, people, birds and beasts,
as I recall, were always glad to meet.

Translated by Ruth Fainlight

Triptych of Reflection

1

Your whole life is a parallelogram
without bisectors.
A superannuated schoolboy
brought you daffodils,

and spring-flower reveries
revived in you.
You smoke, not changing position
in an official armchair.

The lime-tree breathes its bribe of honey
into existence through a hotel window
like the venom of fame
— or a life without limits.

2

I am the reflection of every mirror-
like, living and unliving,
animate and inanimate thing:
brooks and basin-taps,
paradisal wings and infernal
polished relics.

I reflect like the lid of a grand piano,
like a negative,
and my universal sorrows
scarcely belong to me.
They are only a reflected myth.

In this there would be no drama
if I could crawl out
of the annular iambic pit
where there are no reverses
or angles, and amalgams of Spring
blur the surface of the glass.

3

How can one know
who is reflected into the world
and if this reflects well or badly
into your heart?

Try hard not to look
at anything that shines:
not foil nor tin nor copper,
not even into the mirror

hanging here, where life
exists like a heart grown quiet,
where all my verses
come now to die.

Translated by Ruth Fainlight

Jealousy

I look out of the window at the retreating back . . .
Your jealousy is both touching and funny.
Can't you see that I am old, a wreck,
And apart from you nobody in the world needs me?

Well, what's so touching and funny about that?
Jealous, you're keen to drive away literally all
From our home, with its moss-coated roof,
And our life, which consists entirely of holes!

But they keep coming, out of some sort of natural goodness—
To scrape the moss from the roof, here and there to tighten a screw,
And they bring me young flowers as well, and their thanks
For your still being alive and cared for by me.

And something else they steal away with, more exactly, it's a vision
of how to survive into one's dotage
And continue to be loved, and also, as time runs out,
Listen not to the news but to hymns that do not age.

And they envy my attachment to you, as true love, no less,
So you'd better restrain your impulsive jealousy.
In this world, replete with evil and grievous loss,
Let me open the door with a smile to all who wish to enter.

Translated by Daniel Weissbort

[*Quiet days and quiet evenings*]

Quiet days and quiet evenings.
But on the TV, explosions, killings, war.

Quiet days and quiet evenings.
But on the Net—endless idiotic prattle.

Quiet days and quiet evenings.
But on the phone—anxious voices.

Quiet days and quiet evenings—
Spit into my eye and I answer: God's dew.

Translated by Daniel Weissbort

SVETA LITVAK

[*Shadows of the plane-tree leaves*]

Shadows of the plane-tree leaves
along the wall of stone
play like a close-up
of red and blue barrels.

They move the shutters aslant,
opening just a chink,
as if a crooked scythe
had brushed against the stone.

A spurt of tiny drops
leaps clean over the fence,
gets entangled, and misses
the deftly scurrying rakes,

aimed at a striped awning.
On the slope, mold and ivy
and on the neighbors' side,
children playing quietly.

What they're after is trout
or feeding the little donkey.
Bird on the old fir-tree,
a weathercock on a pole,

a child's broken chair.
About to drop from above,
a roof tile, cracked and loose
has missed its chance to do harm.

A lizard has frozen there,
the sun in a circle turns,
the little girl might have fallen,
had the mother not grabbed her arm.

Translated by Daniel Weissbort

[*I catch the smell of beans*]

I catch the smell of beans
Sit silently in a chair
I'd like to add some salt
I'd like to cook some noodles

I'd like to attend a meeting
The one in the Mutualité
O, take away from me
What's standing there on the stove

I've already learnt how
To listen to Maurice Thorez
To look at Fernand Léger—
to scrub spuds and slice them

Proudly to demonstrate
With a little bag and wearing a wig
I was born a foreigner
In Russia in my own little town

A thread of scattered beads
A bow that's untied itself
It's not just a question of taste
But brains and talent as well

Weakly the flame of the burner
Flares up and dies away
The urchin's a pain
Skittish my festive steed

Translated by Daniel Weissbort

Morning

The main thing is not to oversleep, so as later not to have to run for dear life,
Leaving behind, like a conquered city,
An unmade bed, an unscrewed cap on a tube of toothpaste,
Undeveloped dreams, as if lost in a table drawer.
But wake up earlier than usual, and you'll be late for certain:
Am I really a "skylark"? Who would have thought?
Look up prank in the dictionary, the newspaper says
Wallace Stevens had many of those pranks,
Sounds like a lark or a trick, a practical joke.
There is also the picture: Dylan Thomas in his coffin,
Oh joy, no, as regards the newspapers, Tsvetaeva was right,*
A school friend's father, coming home tipsy, would intone:
"Judging from the papers . . . Of what the river rumbles . . .
   judging from the papers . . . of what the river rumbles . . ."**
"As was its professional duty, the river rumbled on below,
and solitary trees threw height into relief . . ."***
Oh, this is far from the catchy clerkese of young Pasternak.
Once we were sorting through the archive of the building materials ministry.
Especially impressive was the correspondence
   between the Topki Iron and Molybdenum Enterprise
   and Yashkino Red Hero Glass-Blowing Factory.
And a letter to the Kremlin: "Dear Leonid Ilich,
   we are writing to you because we cannot wait to go number one . . ."
Somebody found a folder titled "Cases of Injury at Work"
And in it, a mother's complaint on behalf of her son
   (convicted of attempted rape):
"Not only did he not get anywhere" (deplored the mother)
"but the victim broke his arm, concussed his brains,
from the hospital via the court he landed straight behind bars."
And hushed talk from childhood comes to mind
That one was quite soon shot,
Another died in jail,
A third escaped on the eve of the arrest,
A fourth never went to school because she was in exile,
A fifth ended up in the front lines in a penal battalion.

I never asked why, fearing that they had all been murderers,
But this way there was still hope, maybe they stole something,
    they say those were hungry times,
I also stole once, a croissant from a bakery,
I had calculated everything: the cashier wouldn't catch me,
But she didn't budge, only laughed loudly into my back,
See? Just enough time to run for dear life,
Leaving behind, like a conquered city . . .

Translated by Nika Skandiaka

* A reference to Tsvetaeva's invective poem "Chitateli gazet" (Newspaper readers)
(translator's note).
** *Of What the River Rumbles* (*O chem shumit reka*), an old Soviet movie title (translator's
note).
*** From Velimir Khlebnikov (translator's note).

[*Many films begin with a funeral*]

Many films begin with a funeral,
For one has to start somewhere,
And there is no better beginning than a death,
Though that is not what I wanted to say,
But this: It used to seem to me that somewhere
There is a long, long room,
And in it, a long, long table,
And on the table, a new film being unwound to all its length,
And patient people in blue scrubs laboring over every inch,
Scratching it neatly with casing nails;
After that the film is shown to the viewers,
To whom it seems like it's raining throughout onscreen
And it never stops, even indoors.

Translated by Nika Skandiaka

[*Among the men some carved-bone dice are thrown*]

Among the men some carved-bone dice are thrown,
Their wives give gold-toothed smiles in their green-grocers' stalls,
There's a regret with no excuse and cause unknown,

Here one sings jail-bird songs, there the departing trains one calls,
The trains are leaving for the far end of Ukraine,
Where there's a sea just a stone's throw away,
There's a regret I can't excuse, I can't explain,
Stall-keepers cry like seagulls on the bay.

Translated by Nika Skandiaka

[*Like a faded painting*]

Like a faded painting,
Like an antique game,
Half the fated
Life is written in our name,
Waste it freer,
Earn your own,
Leave Judea,
Flee alone.

Translated by Nika Skandiaka

KSENIYA MARENNIKOVA

[*I, Mariya, burn your fingers*]

I, Mariya, burn your fingers.
Anyone knows what "stay" means in
body-language, eloquent just a while ago.
And you can talk as long as you like about the difference
between whorishness and a German
porn classic.

I, Mariya, use few words and speak softly.
It's like a taste of you, i.e.— of grown-up you,
plus one or two other odd secrets:
when you do your eyes, the liner makes them look
shifty, though—it's easy to get the age wrong,
but that's not what I'm on about now.

I, Mariya, easily change over to signs.
Written words, for that reason vulgar, but I cannot
not write even if it's just a line a day, just
to exchange elementary "hi theres"
"take cares" with you keeping one's distance
accordingly.

I, Mariya, will watch out for a visual rhyme.
As you saw, this dependency is unconnected
with your body, but they aren't just linear,
the links. And assuming you yourself have been deprived
of sense (since the two of us add up
to forty), often I'm in pain.

Translated by Daniel Weissbort

[*Mother, squatting hurts*]

Mother, squatting hurts.
How many snowflakes on that window? Eight.
And how much is that? Don't be afraid, dear.
And how much is that? In freckles,

if you imagine a snub-nosed nose, then
really there are just eight freckle-sunlets.
How many? If they ask, say
what you've drawn's an elk or something.

Translated by Daniel Weissbort

[*Don't let me leave you, I may die*]

Don't let me leave you, I may die
faster than they think, because what is death,
just a walk in the cold
just a walk in the cold
in an open shirt,
hand in hand.

Translated by Daniel Weissbort

[*my head is spinning to the right*]

my head is spinning to the right.
Vitalik has red eyes after lovemaking like this.
they massacred him on the commuter train, holding him by the scarf,
    saying that's just for starts.
you live in the inner city, so you can just imagine.
it's less than forty days since and ma's still with you.
you can skewer the belly with a sharp knee down.
kneeling, grabbing your own hair, getting your face punched,
think of something, let your mind drift, or you're just a
    cow in the slaughterhouse

Translated by Daniel Weissbort

OLGA MARTYNOVA

[*What does the river know of its own bed*]

At the heart of this black world
Covered by endless gardens —
Look: at one unopened morning
Rose, and this, shut in the evening.

What does the river know of its own bed,
Or the spider of the web?

What does a canvas know of a painting?

Who knows what anyone understands or needs?
In this dark abyss, everything
is frightening and gentle at once.

What does the backing cloth know about silk?

We are in a dark, hidden
hollow full of songs, moans, whistling
and the click of fingers.

Listen.

Translated by Elaine Feinstein

[*Night unwraps the true stuff of the world*]

Night unwraps the true stuff of the world:
Poorly clothed houses, shadows in a back street,
Lorries and limetrees on the boulevards —
All sleep under the rain; their black and white
Faces show bewildered discontent. What still holds
Of their comfortable life? Is this new look
Deception or reality? Electric words
Suddenly flash their alphabet. Night
Moves, lit only by itself. And until
The light of early morning, you can
Repeat the letters of the night-time world.

Now a sign flashes in a passing headlight,
Then somebody's whisper, menacing footsteps,
God knows what else — as the black scene shines.
Day clothes this nakedness and
Hides the evidence of it within our flesh.
Language turns into babble, and then,
Sitting on a bench in the boulevard,
You try helplessly to remember what remains
Once night has gone, more than
A worn-out negative of how things are
Under the heels of the rain.

Translated by Elaine Feinstein

IRINA MASHINSKAYA

[*So I stood by and watched*]

So I stood by and watched
and you were unwinding
that endless bandage
with its bloody stains
brown rusty
grew bigger bigger
and flashed more often

you were weeping
so helplessly
so silently
so lonely
What could I do?
I stood and gazed
at that descending
growing cloud of gauze

It ended suddenly
    the end
        slipped off

    there was no wound
your skin was clear

Translated by the author

Newspapers on the Plateau

"Ah, Nature . . . Sure, Nature . . . And how about us?"
   That's Guildenstern and Fortinbras,
     they mutter
while dawdling by the door, blocking the exit.
       Behind the door—one hears hooves, a clatter.

Just like movers, carrying a grand-piano
        upstairs—the glare, shine, and glow
            of a big dead animal—
            for those who'd play are gone.
. . . Like dust that horsemen plough

(I hear them beat the earth's breast cracked with heat
        the way children do). . . that dust compressed and baked
plus Sunday papers blow away like sand—not now, no,
    later—
        return to the valley's groin, yet later, later
            are squeezed from craters stained by red

So cover floors with papers, throw them on a basalt
    plateau, or the town square. Put on your winter coat.
—life frolics like a jukebox—
            —let it play.
For what you want, Horatio, is in the morning papers

Yes, I am stubborn. Yes, I insist upon
        and sing what I'm standing on,
and when I fall—I hear the hollow heart
        that's humming miles and miles below
        encrusted granite shield.

—Earth! You're my Shamil, my shield, my Israel,
my fever, you're my hunger.

Translated by the author

LARISA MILLER

[*The light cross of lonely strolls*]

The light cross of lonely strolls
O. Mandelstam
I write poems, what's more in Russian
and I don't want any other workload,
I don't want any other job.
Honestly I don't want to shoulder
any other enterprise.
The time of the year involves me,
the moment of risk, the hour of the soul . . .
I sharpen my pencils with them.
Pencils. Not knife or teeth.
The silver trumpets sing
in the frail neighboring forest
where I will carry my usual cross
of lyric-making strolls.
Each backstreet is full
of the torment of the soul and yearning
for feminine and masculine rhymes.

Translated by Richard McKane

[*Let's fill in the form: date of birth*]

Let's fill in the form: date of birth —
that's the start of the delusion,
the start of delirium or dream . . .
The problem is clear, it seems.
And in the box below the date
we give our address and phone number;
on the left — our sex, lower on the right
we give our nationality,
then the signature. Well, is life clearer
now and how to manage it?

Translated by Richard McKane

[*The heavens are playing with the earth*]

The heavens are playing with the earth,
teasing, threatening a landslide,
they threaten to set fire
to the dwellings and forests—in a fantastic fire.
But on a dull day they hang again
over this mortal world
like a gray, humble shroud
and there's no soothing the tears of the heavens.

Translated by Richard McKane

TATYANA MILOVA

[*Sometimes, not often, it's true*]

Sometimes, not often, it's true,
                              an old man comes in on the mail coach
                         Under the small town's principal arch
And, reclining against the dashboard, the driver smokes and reads
                              his paper
                         But a harp is concealed in his bosom;
The inn is closing up, the church is quite silent, the shopkeeper won't sell
                              his kerosene
                    Nor anything else besides.
The old man adjusts his dickey-bow, his hanky traps a sneeze, his pocket
                         yields a harpsichord
                    Which he puts together to the sound of trumpets.
The distant rumble of a tuning-fork, storm-like, disturbs our eternal
                         repose
                    The air of which is windless and bitter;
The last flies are trooping, and gather on the horse's backside and a
                         flourish of its tail accidentally
                    Sounds the triangle under the shaft-bow;
In melodious embrace all intertwine: reverberating bronze and
                              horsehair, and a noble cedar
                    Sawn up out of eyeshot;
And we, stuck to the tarmac and barely awake, still manage to listen to
                         the orchestra
                    Beneath our unsetting sun.
And this is the only reason behind all that we do in our small forgotten
                              town,
                    Its forgotten houses and little cinemas;
And the children run after the coach empty-handed,
      or almost—with a
                              doughnut if they're lucky
                    Legs dappled with iodine;
Carelessly clad, outlandishly red of face, hair tousled
      beyond all combing,
                    Or parting or ribboning, they run . . .

. . . To where there's hope of loving one another, of flying, aching,

vanishing away

To the thunder of their drums.

Translated by Robert Reid

[. . . *I've overslept my stop . . . the train will spit me out*]

. . . I've overslept my stop . . . the train will spit me out . . .
The halt is deserted. I'll panic, that's for sure.
The wind is wet and drives me from the platform
And tears and tousles me until I speak.

Wind, if I'm a sail, then where's my boat?
If I'm a treetop, wind, show me my roots.
What am I to you? I'm asking calmly, nicely.
Distant clanking. Buckets? . . . Distant neighing. Horses?

"Silly" comes the whisper nice and calm,
"We know your niceness and we know your fables
But what are you to me?—a Chinese lantern or a sparkler.
If I can, I'll huff and puff—you'll gutter and go out."

Wind, you're master here. And I'm the guest and will be silent.
Ruined tractor. Gravel pit. Rusting stove-pipes.
The smell of the river sticks in my throat like a bone.
You're master here. It's hard to deny.

The train has come and I am leaving.
God Save the Wind! The houses echo and the fields are bare.
I'm strange to them and whether it's my fault's
Too late to say. There's nowhere for me here . . . no word for me here.

Translated by Robert Reid

STELLA MOROTSKAYA

[*morning sleep*]

morning sleep
it's sweeter than your palms
whiter than knees, milk and down duvets
longer than the strings of rain
on the shower curtain
more languorous than kisses

morning sleep
melting in the folds of the curtains
prolonging itself in blankets
enveloping flesh in pink

I grow endlessly long
my soul hangs blissfully like a silken thread

in a thin cocoon I'd rest a virgin
having folded my dragonfly wings
so that my hands would never love anyone
so that my feet would never touch the ground

Translated by Vitaly Chernetsky

[*Screams and hair come out*]

Screams and hair come out
of my night-time poems,
but my husband comes,
in his hands a comb and scissors,
no, rather a stiff brush and a knife . . .

Oh my dear gray-eyed king,*
why is there so much steel in your hands,
why is there surgery in your gaze?

Why do you cut off everything
and throw it to the dogs outside,
don't you feel pity:
it still moves, can't you see?

All right, I'll shut up, I won't, I'll shut up,
it comes out quite beautiful, I can see,
a bald little hedgehog, without any sprouts or fins,
no fleas, that's true, but also no fur,
yes, really, really good,
oh, what are you doing my dear . . . ?

And what about your own daytime sonnets, daytime sonatas?
I too, I too will come, and you will show me,
I'll also smile with all my iron teeth
and cut down not just the ultimate flesh—to put it crudely,
        the foreskin—
but all the way down to the ultimate measure
and so utterly clean and beautiful, tasty and strong
will be your two lines, your two legs,
my two arms

Translated by Vitaly Chernetsky

* A reference to Anna Akhmatova's poem "The Gray-Eyed King" (translator's note).

Tomato
[*From the cycle* Erotic Fruit]

Tomato is so vulgar and so lustful
and more depraved than pomegranate or, say, grapefruit,
with their insatiable fiery insides,
and with its own brutal, greedy kiss,
when it is being turned completely inside out,
and it's unclear who is sucking whom.
It takes you over through hypnosis, like a boa,
and you cannot escape it anymore.

Translated by Vitaly Chernetsky

RAISA MOROZ

[There's a cinnamon tree that grows on the Moon]

1

There's a cinnamon tree that grows on the Moon
There's a hare who sits under that tree
And he's grinding some magic powder

2

My eyes are round and shining
My step is light and serene
My voice is ringing with beauty

Full Moon is my name
My face fair shines with a smile
When I see you, my sweet one

3

Will you come to me when you're in trouble
Will you come to me when you're in pain
I'll make all your bad times go away

Thunder is loud and yet it gets softer
Rain is pouring and yet it gets thinner
The cloud is black but it will fade away

Like a silver orchid
The full moon will be shining
By the hour when you must come to me

4

See, the shadow at the fence,
Isn't this my sweet one coming?
Oh no, it's just my lamp there, shaken
By the cunning gust of wind

Hear, the footsteps in the yard,
Isn't this my sweet one coming?
Oh no, it's just some old leaves there, swept
By the evil gust of wind

5

The night is oh so long
Tonight
The night is oh so long
Tonight
Only one speck of moonray
Glides along the windowsill

I promised you yesterday
And I'm waiting for you
I promised you all the time
And I'm waiting for you
I refused everyone,
All my lovers and friends

Oh why don't you come to me,
To your Menwol the Full Moon?

6

There's the cinnamon tree that grows on the Moon
There's the jasper hare who sits under that tree
And he's grinding the powder of the undying

7

Moonfrost is creeping into my soul
Sadness is whispering in the reeds
I'll put the snares for my moonhare

But what do I need his powder for
When my sweet one has forgotten all his roads to me?
Maple is groping for me with its leaves that are fair

I'll climb my maple bridge to the very Moon
I'll be crying in my moonpalace all by myself
I'll be looking into your windows when the Moon is full

Translated by Max Nemtsov

NEGAR

[*Forgive me that I opened your door silently*]

Forgive me that I opened your door silently,
without knocking entered your fate,
that I lit the fire but then turned cool,
that I searched but did not find.
Forgive me that I trusted, did not know shame,
that I charmed you with my boldness.
Forgive me that I became now and forever
an indelible scar on your soul.
Forgive me for laughter, forgive me for tears,
forgive me for sincerity that you didn't accept.
Forgive me, my dear, for rosy dreams,
for your never understanding me.
Forgive everything in the present,
forgive everything in the past
which by chance followed on your heels,
for my once opening your door,
well, now I'll slam it behind me.

Translated by Richard McKane

Dust

The dead ringing of distant steps
   Dust
The first breath in, the last groan out
   Dust
Cruel laughter at time
   Dust
Sin holding sway over the world
   Dust
Unbuilt granite of walls
   Dust
That light attracts
   Dust

Now the lament of yesterday's heights
   Dust
The convicted and the executioner
   Dust
The rainbow crown of its beginning
The end of which was never dreamed
   Dust

Nothing over nothing
   Dust
That is called fate

Translated by Richard McKane

OLESIA NIKOLAEVA

[*Once I used to study languages dead for millennia*]

Once I used to study languages dead for millennia,
Losing sleep over the other-worldly verbs:
My voice broke on the fall of a line-break
As it tried to keep up with night's bolting car.

Once I was a confidante of midnight, a rival of day's plain speaking,
I tried to curb my gestures and rein up sight:
But still I took a flame-red stallion to water
And I'd dive into his jet-black shade.

I shivered in fever heat as I walked onward,
Toward things that hated me—the coffin, the mausoleum,
The day of judgment. And the earth swam under my footstops
Slick as an ice floe on the deafening waters of spring.

Now my lips are set hard, and my eyes like paper:
So dry. Once a week, with my hand on an armchair's spine,
I teach university students to write their verses,
Unhobble their rhythms, and close a thought with a rhyme,

Make the voice fly up en pointe, clean out the odd passage
That jangles— the sound of Anon filling in a lost line—
Bracketing earth-bound passion not metamorphosed
Into words, in the margins, I press down my pen.

So, with a glimpse of myself reflected—a demon
In the depths of a polished gold mirror—I ask no gift:
Put me in a closed coffin and burn me to ashes,
Or fix a dragon's jaws to the top of a stake.

Translated by Catriona Kelly

[*You can go on holiday now, you can dabble in verse*]

You can go on holiday now, you can dabble in verse,
Or buy yourself a red coat with buttons in shocking pink:
You can make good money, or bad, or worse;
You can play the Lotto, you can take your friends for a drink.

You can get your house seen to, get your car fixed, or your teeth:
You can demonstrate, stop the world going down the drain;
You can say what you like about politics, or the police,
Or sit and look all morning at the falling rain.

You can rig up a darkened mirror on your own windowsill
To tell your fortune by the stars, draw down the kindly light:
You can pack up a parcel with a purple wax seal
And send it to Chile, or doodle with ash off your cigarette.

Now there aren't any rules and we've torn up the script,
You can do all that, and more. But what's the point?

Translated by Catriona Kelly

REA NIKONOVA

[*The earth is burning*]

The earth is burning
But the fiber of laughter
is indissoluble

Translated by Gerald Janecek

[*Six charred leaves drift*]

Six charred leaves drift
fools down the road
touching their damp roots
to the acrid warm earth

Sick barred leaves
drink transparent water
so that temples of fallen stems
can be raised up as a crown

Translated by Gerald Janecek

[*Along the threads of veins*]

Along the threads of veins
run mice

Along the spines of songs
crawl groans

Translated by Gerald Janecek

[*I sit over grief*]

I sit over grief
I warm myself . . .
I sit over grief
I chop into a log
I sit I say nothing over grief
while it seethes

Translated by Gerald Janecek

VERA PAVLOVA

Grass

Oh praise the lowly stalk
that will not sing alone
enfolds its single talk
in general conversation
commingles with the lawn
and, neighborlike, will share
the shade, the rain, the air
and, standing tall, will hide
the unofficial mint,
the bridegroom and the bride.

When flakes of white are blent,
and no one is beside,
then stands alone the blade
as if it never leant,
and reaches to the skies
for seeds of paradise.

Translated by Maura Dooley and Terence Dooley

Heaven and Earth

You began with the heavens
formed from the primitive darkness
as an ice-breaker breaks ice

You began with heaven and earth
when darkness was over the earth
and might have overwhelmed it

if you had not made both

And the spirit of God
moved on the face of waters
uncreated, still distant
and the rusty firmament
rose above the waters

before it was time
and disbelieved it was, in fact,
a mountain on dry land, as in the book
because the book
dissolves into the dark
original waters as before

and does not
reflect His face
and there is no Law
and the burden of eternal night
drags on, until the awful moment
when, through the universe,
explodes the light.

Translated by Maura Dooley and Terence Dooley

from Signs of Life

JUICE

My parents were virgins.
At 22 — even then it was a bit much.
Yes, Papa had a reputation as a skirt chaser around the women's dormitory
but he "went" to the women in order to eat a little,
because he lived on his stipend . . .
He starting going to Mama also in order to eat.
And when there started to be talk of a wedding at the Institute,
they slipped her a copy of
"How a Girl Becomes a Woman."
Mama threw it out unopened.
It was scary for them to make me.
It was strange for them to make me.
It was painful for them to make me.
It was funny for them to make me.
And I absorbed:
To live is scary.
To live is strange.
To live is painful.
To live is very funny.

Funniest of all was birth.
—Go—growled the nurse
and waved her
out into the hallway.
She held her stomach from below, and walked out.
Walked, walked, suddenly—a mirror,
and in the mirror—a belly
in a shirt to the navel,
on thin, shivering,
lilac legs.

She laughed for five minutes.
After another five she gave birth.

Translated by Jason Schneiderman

[*This is the way a row of official tulips*]

This is the way a row of official tulips
commands you "Do not pick the flowers,"
hoping that they'll be picked up when it gets dark.

This is the way a girl's vagina, weeping
from virile fingers, pleads for mercy,
hoping that mercy will never be granted.

This is the way I pray "Don't let me live in Russia,"
knowing well my prayers will not be answered.

Translated by Derek Walcott

[*And God saw*]

And God saw
it was good
And Adam saw
it was excellent
And Eve saw
it was passable

Translated by Steven Seymour

[*On the way to you*]

On the way to you
was writing verses about you
done with writing realized
was headed in the wrong direction

Translated by Steven Seymour

[*Armpits smell of linden blossom*]

Armpits smell of linden blossom,
lilacs give a whiff of ink.
If we could only wage love-making
all day long without end,
love so detailed and elastic
that by the fall of night
we would effect at least five exchanges
of prisoners of war between us two.

Translated by Steven Seymour

from Letter from Memory

9

We are not slaves,
we are slavettes.

12

Those who refused to meet
earned the right to make a date.
Those who wouldn't be embraced
earned the right to an embrace.
Those who said no to sex
earned the right to sex.
Beloved, come tomorrow morning
so as to be instantly deprived of these rights.

17

What's lovelier
than your shoulders?
Your forearms.
Than your forearms?
Your palms.
Than your palms?
Your fingers.
Than your fingers?
Your fingers
squeezing
my fingers,
palms,
forearms . . .

Place me there like a seal.

To come on each of your fingers.

Translated by Daniel Weissbort

ALEKSANDRA PETROVA

[*Tarantino's languor and dreaming back*]

Tarantino's languor and dreaming back.
The cooling hoop of Jerusalem
Throbs.
Dull scales light up for a cruel look:
Hashishnik, child of the East.
He recoiled,
Saturnine bubbling by in grooves of drains,
Till she pumped into him one two three four slugs.

Snake croaked but by daybreak
Reddening bands of scales.

O cinema dragon, I take in your fumes,
Shadowy bodies pour from your darkening screen,
Immediate injection into your heart.

"Recognize it?" This snake city!—your brother.
Lumière's finger twitches on the trigger.
Waiting the night army of roaches.

Translated by Dennis Silk

[*Again sick*]

Again sick.
Just now somehow paler.
Saxophone riff carrying blues along spiral
In undrawn curtain twilight—
This keen light—
X-ray or ultra-sound screen—
With its eddying silhouette
More rarefied than tedious.

Above the spool of the intestines,
Scheme of channels and sluices—
A dim angel, abandoned god,
Lit up by rotating blues.
Syncope flash
Forces your eyes open.

Pillow smile.
Attempt of it.

Translated by Dennis Silk

[*In Juda desert*]

I

In Juda desert,
in sunkness,
Marusenka washed white legs.
Green slime swam.
Three toads sat.

II

"Slime, where are you going?"
"Nowhere, I'm concentrating."
"Toads: friends. And you?"

III

The toad-singer with the pea in the throat
had a guttural sound:
By the mountain we guard
the frosty body
of time.
It swells more,
we face down more.

The time till it's decoded
is called expectation
it flies so fast
with a drawing of smiles
on the fire-pollen.

Yet the double-unity rim
displaces toward dead brother,
past people past things
jostling in the wrinkles
of its body and face.
How stuffy it is!
Hollow "was"
begins to be more than "will."

Here, at earth's sonorous origin,
we'll set out the clock.
Sandstorm will spread the grain
and life-scales be equal.
Isn't it all to be obedient?
Let's stalk on with an uplifted lantern
and in redundant space
find the day that rolled under.

IV

But Marusia, heeding the desert creatures,
hesitated.
Look for what? Here's mussel or crab—
At the dead house but alive.
We're like that—
        not living is our shield—
without it we're lonely.

V

Ach, Mariya always humble,
look at the receding ball.
D'you see the redfoam
fire from its retreat?

The times of a verb change on the move,
now they're in the past, the pillar of salt
looks at the blinded, naked, voiceless
vampire time cleaned out.

Mariya sat down, her sad
palms warmed her feet,
and the creatures, choked with the wet trill,
were silent and a long way off.

The mere legs of Mariya
rayed pallor.

Translated by Dennis Silk

Poor Ruth

seems she was called Ruth
though the carpenters wondered

the nurse
you remember
she drowned herself

hid
the bottle from her old man

he didn't find it
in the water barrel
out in the kitchen-garden

he found Ruth
she was sticking out of the barrel
of water

only it was
her legs sticking out

Ruth was small
and it was raining that evening

the barrel was running over

obviously she climbed up there that evening
to look for a bottle in the barrel

felt around
couldn't reach it

couldn't stand it
dived in

poor Ruth
the carpenters
laughed put out

you can imagine
what sort of
funeral

poor
Ruth
really

Translated by Daniel Weissbort

OLGA POSTNIKOVA

Archangel Cathedral

The coffins of Russian grand princesses stand in the basement of the Moscow Kremlin.
They were brought there in the 1930s from the destroyed Voznesensky Monastery.

There where the angels weave the sky,
where there is the triumph of the last dream,
where the cellar secrets conceal,
I asked myself: For whom

have I lived and suffered this life?
I didn't fall prostrate in prayer,
I always sang my own words
in the dark storehouse of useless tsaritsas.

Here, under the gigantic splinter-bar of walls,
there is disparagement of forgetfulness.
I stand over poisoned Glinskaya,
her pillaged tomb.

And over us now red flags,
now the alcoholic madness of the country.
Only timid bones can be seen
through the robbers' hole in the sarcophagus.

In these cracks of the royal masonry,
in this mold of terrifying corners,
there are the denouements of chronic illness,
the revelation of prophetic words.

By the high iconostasis
by the column, by the colored trunk
I will say before the pupils of the Savior's eyes
in my great shame:
"Why did I live?"

So that breathing in the celestial blue
someone remembered the forgotten,
and someone heard a peasant woman wail,
falling on the zinc coffin.

Translated by Richard McKane

IRINA RATUSHINSKAYA

[*Thus you lived your life without regret*]

Thus you lived your life without regret,
Hands warmed against a kettle caked in soot,
Gaudier than cheap-jack kiddies' sweets,
The daring trash of sages on the streets,
Dressed in tinsel and torn lace, surrounded
By the stenches of a traveling zoo,
By evening, you'd grown princes, known to few;
At night you'd ask "Why follow me?", astounded.
Tomorrow the white raven laughs, and where
The noise is loudest of kids' shouts and curses,
You'll find in a new town a well to share
And give clean water to your weary horses.
The circus leaves, the posters fade and wash,
The tearaways who raved about your thrills
Will make their different ways in life. Your bells
Will not change the world. Hush, now . . . hush.

How, my girl, could you ever dream to follow?
The rib cage of the circus tent subsides.
Our women age so quickly. Far and wide
They sorrow; there's not one who does not sorrow.
Ignore the embroidered shawls that seem so rich,
The baubles spangling on the sweaty saddles;
So often were they wronged, their smiles are raddled
Grins that harden on their lips like pitch;
Their cheeks are eaten by cheap rouge, their breasts
Are sucked to rags by babies every year.
I'm leaving you, no need to lie, I can bear
This slap in the face. Forget me, it's for the best.

If God's paradise exists, my old
Parrot surely lives there—he who told
Half of Europe's fortunes, who abused
All mundane authorities, and used

To swear in every language known to man,
Who took his final breath cupped in my hands,
Who pitied no one anymore at all,
And I was the only one he called a fool.

Translated by C. J. K. Arkell

[*Penelope, the screaming is all over*]

Penelope, the screaming is all over,
Put aside that cushion!
He's returned, your broad-browed ocean rover
To son and kingly station.
And his horses too, and his retainers,
Bed made out of olive . . .
The enchantress could not long detain him,
Nor those on Olympus.
The blade now wiped, see rage to sweetness alter,
A lion breathing . . .
And since his mighty sword-arm did not falter—
No innocents lie bleeding!
Punishment descended on the wicked
With proper lawful sentence.
Slaves will wipe the blood off the mosaic—
Then happiness commences.

Translated by Alan Myers

TATYANA RETIVOVA

Elegy to Atlantis

Your mainland split
Surges within me
With Pythian ecstasy

And antediluvian recall
Of the Oracle at Delphi.
Erupting from the wrath

Of Jehovah, you, oh
Umbilicus orbis terrarum, who
Simulated the atomic splitting,

Spasmodically vulcanizing,
As if you had continentally imbibed
A lethal dose of heptyl.

Since the first high priestesses
Of Hera from Argos, I have been doomed
To declaim in hexameter the contents

Of theogonies, catalogues of ships,
Goddesses, and inventories
Of Poseidon's antebellum.

And to remember how between
The pillars of Hercules would slide
Scythian and Phoenician vessels,

Smoothly floating from Tauria
To Peru and the Mississippi valley
Kurgans, and back along Iberia.

Cypress and tree resin.
Myrtle, cane, and cedar smoke
In burners on board the ark.

The half gods, having shared
Food and lodging
With the gods, desecrated demos,

The ten Atlantic kingdoms,
And have sunken you into the depths.
Mud hailed from the nethers

Across the heavens, overthrowing
Semiramida's gardens, Hesperides apples,
With the help of all four elements.

Your seven rivers changed their courses,
Mare tenebrosum swallowed the land,
Minting itself in metallurgical shreds.

The marbles of Patros, eddas,
Cuneiform writings of the Chaldeans,
The Aztec codex of Chimalpopoc

All testify to the crack
Of your splitting backbone
Along sea cliffs to the ridges

Of the Appalachian mountains.
In the mysteries, the golden age's defeat
Flames in the blushes of maidens

From Samiya who sacrifice
Their hair to Hera's temple,
Dreaming at night of Chronos.

They often attribute to me
A hyperborean provenance.
My predictions from time

Immemorial have been copied
By five scribes, direct descendants
Of Deukalion. Bathing

In Castalian waters, with laurel
Leaves in my mouth, I predict
The future to the past, the past

To the future over the burning
Pyres of Python, who emerged
Out of your flood slime,

Until I myself will be consumed
By the flames of my own prognosis
Of the erupting Vesuvius in 1737.

Translated by the author

TATYANA RIZDVENKO

[*Frost and sun, as needed*]

Frost and sun, as needed.
But the western sky's a bit overwrought.
At 16:00 a blood-red sun rolls
into the dark wood, like a coin into the lining.
Light for another hour,
so we can spend it zealously,
imaginatively, purposefully.
. . . We observed the four-century-old elm-tree,
summers, they say, not approachable.
The clunky black grouse we scared off
with a noise like a damp sheet flapping
it broke the ice crust, then soared,
only to fall back again beyond the woods.
Heavy skis, carved by hand,
make a vague track, powdery like fine sand.
A size twelve felt boot with straps,
deceptively got stuck in a crater, a pit.
A slender leg, ankle, calf twirled around,
searching, finding no support.
Freezing in the air, as if detached,
simply as such, chilled, shoeless.

They said: put on some socks, they said,
suggested I get some warm ones, suggested.
You'll die, you'll get ill—your own fault . . .

Translated by Daniel Weissbort

[*It was such a pearly, pink season*]

It was such a pearly, pink season
that we awoke and saw the winter.
We were roused, dipped into it our monitors,
our steamed-out motors.

The grandee stands, as if in reproach,
decks us in warm sheepskin,
pours the cold of hygiene over all,
drives blue glass into our veins.

And now it has sprawled out across the route,
blaming, reproving, rapping our knuckles.
The child's cheeks have reddened, father sniffs.
Everything's paralyzed by the beauty of the moment.

At night it howls so resplendently.
As if a tale were unfolding there,
evil crushing good, jingling, raging.
But good will triumph, since there's no other option.

Say thank you for these tales,
for the penetrating, lengthy drone.
For sitting solid, like a clerk,
Like yellow glue on a dried-out edge,
and your gaze is unearthly, bewitched.

Translated by Daniel Weissbort

OLGA SEDAKOVA

Rain

"It's raining,
and still people say there's no God!"
So Granny Varia,
an old woman from near us, would say.

Now the people who said there was no God
are lighting candles in churches,
ordering masses for the dead,
shunning those of other faiths.

Granny Varia lies in her grave,
and the rain pours on,
immense, abundant, relentless,
on and on,
aiming at no one in particular.

Translated by Catriona Kelly

Sant'Alessio, Roma

Roman swallows,
swallows of the Aventina,
you fly here and there,
eyelids tightly furled

in a scowl. For ages I've known
that all creatures with wings are blind,
and that's why birds cry, "O Lord!"
in a more human voice than ours.

You fly here and there,
who knows where from, where to,
where to, where from, who knows,
past the branches of orange and stone-pine . . .
The fugitive returns to his parents' house
like water to a deep old well.

No, not everything is lost,
not everything vanishes.
That, "what's the use of it?"
That, "oh what does it matter?"
That something even a mother, a wife
will never find out—that won't disappear.
How good to know, in the end,
how good it is, that everything
people want, people beg for,
everything they'd give their all for
turns out not to matter at all.

So no one recognized it? How could they?
After all, what does last?
Nothing but putrefying flesh and bones,
bones bleached dry, as in the valley of Jehoshaphat.

Translated by Catriona Kelly

Author's note: The "Valley of Jehoshaphat" is also known as the valley of Kidron, to
the east of the Jerusalem Heights and used as a burial ground since ancient times. It is
mentioned in Jeremiah 31:40 as the "valley of the dead bodies, and of the ashes"; in
Orthodox tradition, it is the valley where the Last Judgment will begin, as anticipated in
the Prophet Ezekiel's vision of divine doom, read during the vigil for Easter Saturday.

In Memory of a Poet

It's grandeur of design that matters, as Joseph puts it.
(From a letter by Akhmatova)

1

As the glaze takes into
its upswirling reek
goods, chattels, things unclaimed,
and all before it,
staring into the blue,
into empty features,
into the straitened, clamped
azure of blindness—

    as the sepulchral sting
    of the Pierides

absorbs the lap of the lagoon,
sight, sound, and aroma,
while trying to fathom
the muteness of the singer
on the edge of
exile, beyond the edge of the end—

2

Just so, closing his book
the dead one bears off
those last days of autumn
    whose name is "with him,"
    that tower, that arch,
    that wonderful porch,
    that square of St. Mark,
    where the three of us walked.

3

Neither friend nor companion
(nor brother? nor other?)
in the jangle of harmonies
of his own melody
holding fast,
like one
who's already resolved
that life
won't beguile
and death
will not daunt—
    as the wheel
    to the helmsman,
as rain to the rider,
    as a nook
    of earth,
    as stars are to travelers:
    all passes, all wanes:
  Sound is a strange thing: Me-
lchior. Balthazar.

Turnpikes. Uplands.
A cryptic connection,
sound's a strange grief:
it is serving the Muses.

What was it he sought,
that all-forsaking soul:
the horn that trusted Charlemagne?
Smoke, searching: higher!

4

O, yes, we were hatched
in other fields
with broken backs
and blind to the living,
   under old-style compassion
   for such as ourselves
   (not the Virgin of Shame:
   the dark lumbering mass)—
      the forgotten,
      and downtrodden.
      Those murdered for nothing,
      or driven beyond the point of madness . . .

Death is no Russian world.
How did Paul put it?
Death is a German world
But prison has a Russian accent.

5

The slave in his galley,
the ogre in chains,
the convict in infinite,
infinite steppe
    their longing consign
    to the all-burning fire:
    higher!
    things are unbearable
    without it: higher!

Or else
that cannibal shame will dine out
on our endless negations,
your knife and your pot.

6

Like an open cage
to a woodland bird,
like a heart,
ill-disposed to the pull of the earth—
like a raft unfettered
by gravity's robe.
And who'll remain fixed
when he is afloat?

7

This smoke's not from bonfires,
nor mountain assaults
nor hamlets exhaling
their souls in the gloom,
nor smoldering
cinders, nor torments by fire,
a hundred-armed Shiva.

8

It staggers at first
its feet thickly wrapped,
it puffs, and it clings and it hides
in the bushes—
    and above the destruction
    the valleys of tears
    O, thanks be to God
—for it kindles at last!
it rises and kneels
like the heart of kings,
the blessed smoke
of earthly altars.

9

. . . The sea at evening,
Sappho's delight,
star after star,
verse after verse . . .
They no longer recall there
who's living, who's not.
The hireling's exhausted
the oxen unyoked . . .
        What is purer than that
which has burned into nothing?
        This: the stars have no number
        the vault has no bottom . . .

10

Like children playing:
"It's my turn first!"
on the edge
of the universe, in a land out of sight —
        Oblivion's poppy,
        memorial honey,
        the one who goes first
        let him take these alone —
to a place where the surf
offers sisters welcome,
where there's sky and an island
and "sleep, my dear"!

Translated by Robert Reid

Author's note: As the reader will immediately notice, this piece is modeled on
Akhmatova's "Through all of Earth"; Tsvetaeva's devices are also discernible. I wanted
these two Russian muses to participate in verse dedicated to Brodsky. Brodsky
himself, in his verses on the death of T. S. Eliot, took W. H. Auden's "In Memory
of W. B. Yeats" as his model.

[*A rose*]

A rose
a
shameless
red
rose
ultra
sensitive
flesh
exploded
in
fearful
black
thorns

how
love
dies

Translated by Daniel Weissbort

Sleep soundly, dear poet

"I don't like men who leave behind a smoking trail of weeping women."
(Auden)

I shall stop weeping
shall not leave, weeping, a smoking trail
so love should not annoy Auden
so Joseph can sleep soundly
a genius's sleep and save the world with his
rigorous—almost delirious—
desperate dedication to the word

Translated by Daniel Weissbort

TATYANA SHCHERBINA

About Limits

The cicadas, the cicadas are singing, Rameses.
The hemlock, Socrates, pour me my just amount.
Let the others apply to their Central Committees.
No, my brother Reason, I'm the soul, and I can't.

The buildings, my idol! Look at the buildings!
Are we really insects, with our shriveled wings
who throw down our bodies on the bunks of the hive
and drape our rags on the chairs they provide us with?

Discover her, Columbus, discover her anew.
Your descendants have grown tired of their own shadow.
What way lies open now to the stumbling Jew?
What road will tell that tired remnant where he must go?

My friend, my mutant, pliable, unstiffened,
my crazy colleague, it will come to an end.
There's a limit to vomiting and diarrhea.
So here they are, have a good look. We've made it, my dear.

Translated by Derek Walcott

[Except for love everything]

Except for love everything
can be bought. Can be stolen,
snatched, bullied, asked for nicely.
Dear, you can even be converted to Buddhism,
changed from a man into a woman or just into drag.
A hag can turn into a ravishing beauty,
an old lady knock off half a dozen years,
a black become white, or a citizen of Siberia
black, wandering through Africa.
Babies can be made in test-tubes, in the blink of an eye,
New York be reduced to dust, men fly to Mars.
Except for love

in every act of will greater than the will of fate,
the baritone sings countertenor.
Except for love and death and, okay, talent
everything's in our control. Win the battle
or fall under the foeman's blow,
but neither give up nor take the alien outpost Il Ove.

Translated by J. Kates

[*They cut off my hot water*]

They cut off my hot water,
love's juice, the verbal flow.
I'd like to complain to the nation,
but they'll shut me up, too, long before.
Without moisture, I'll dry out,
along with the dirty dishes and the washing.
I'll get moldy, gather moss,
I may even graduate to long-forgotten!

Translated by Daniel Weissbort

[*What's it you're howling, siren-telephone*]

What's it you're howling, siren-telephone,
why don't you whisper some fairytale in my ear?
So, even eternity passes:
went berserk, re-stocked.
But I invested in it years
of designer and model expertise,
looked for new approaches,
wrote "prick" on the drapes.
I spent an eternity in the doorway,
in telephonic angst.
It was always in place,
its undoubted homespun place.
And now even this has passed
and the sacred spot is empty, hazy,

the whole of eternity marks time —
*hasta la vista.**

Translated by Daniel Weissbort

*Spanish: "Until we meet again"/"Good-bye" (translator's note).

[*Where are the future's clawlets?*]

Where are the future's clawlets?
Scratches on the street
pointing the way, like spires, arrows.
And the decoys
which captured us in parentheses?
The demon of wild entertainments
had such success with just a log in the fire,
making one want to keep changing places.
Suddenly, a pause, endspiel spire-ends, post-space,
suspended there like a low ceiling.
If the computers fall into a trance,
the claw will scribble things, like inverted commas.
The world is pressed between them, traffic-wise,
in context, in the fixed habit
of running backward.

Translated by Daniel Weissbort

[*Tell me, Comrade God, how can life, over this stretch*]

Tell me, Comrade God, how can life, over this stretch,
go from tolerable to such a pain,
when everything is not as it should be,
weather, ecology, men.
And even the barking of dogs, it's not the same dogs
that beethovenly, chopinly tickled the hearing.
The grass egged on the act of love
but that was grass, not senna leaflets.
My God, it's like you're not mine, because

finally even you went over to the khazars,
abandoned our side, for which—
and I'm speaking for the marketplace—
the deeper into the forest you go, the more the wolves howl.

Translated by Daniel Weissbort

IRINA SHOSTAKOVSKAYA

[*Sailor sailor got ashore*]

Sailor sailor got ashore
For the first time in a score
For twenty years he's lived in water
His entire short life
Sailor sailor he sang a song
O mama give me back to the blue waves!
She will not answer him
The good ship Lizbeth
Sailor sailor go back home
Look how this wild shore is bare
With its sharp-edged stones it will tear
the membrane between your fingers to shreds

Translated by Daniel Weissbort

[*The boy bears a gray shield*]

The boy bears a gray shield
Tells all and sundry this is the enemy's face
Wants to carry it in his bag or instead of his own
There's our boy for you
Overdosed on Frazer*
Or Propp.**

Translated by Daniel Weissbort

*Sir James Frazer (1854–1941) was a social anthropologist and the author of
The Golden Bough (translator's note).
**Vladimir Propp was a Russian structuralist scholar who concentrated his
scholarship on the Russian folktale (translator's note).

[*Today I'm a proper king's daughter*]

Today I'm a proper king's daughter
And there's one thing I love—won't tell!
Because today I'm taking a stroll
Onto the platform with a cigarette

On the platform are soldier boys
With stripes on their pants and they too
Are eagerly awaiting the fast train
The fast train to platform two

I shall pull on a mini-skirt
And shmooze up with a fag in my mouth
And you will never forget me
The boy screws and the girl just hangs about.

There's no plane from Ashkhabad
No boat from anywhere
And I see our poor soldier lads
Blubbing while they still can

Soon I'll be old, I'll be old
And I'll gather flowers in the wood,
I'll say my hubby's away on business
he's lying on the ocean bed.

Translated by Daniel Weissbort

ELENA SHVARTS

Memorial Candle

I so love the flame
That I kiss it,
I stretch out my hand to it
And wash my face in it.
Tender spirits live
In its flower bud,
A circle of delicate forces
Rings around it.
This is their home,
Their shell, their joy.
Anything else would make
Too crude a place for them.

I burned my hair,
Singed my eyelashes,
I thought you were there,
Trembling in the flame.
Maybe you are trying
To whisper a small word of light to me.
The low flame trembles,
But in me there is only darkness.

Translated by Stephanie Sandler

Conversation with a Cat

"I'll have a drink, you take a bite,"
I say to the cat, and she
Answers with a quick
Lash of her furry tail.
"And let those that weep be as though
They wept not—puss, was it St. Peter who said that?"
No answer. Instead she gnaws silently,
Steadily at her piece of fish.

Not a word from the dead, which is strange:
Is it so hard to dig a tunnel out from death?
She purrs and drops her head,
Not once lowering her watchful gaze.

Translated by Stephanie Sandler

A Portrait of the Blockade
through Genre Painting, Still Life, and Landscape

1 *Eyewitness Account (Genre)*

Past Andreevsky market
A man walks in the blockade.
Suddenly—an incredible vision:
The aroma of soup, a soup apparition!
Two stout babas
Pour the soup into plates,
People drink, and huddle closer,
Staring down into their reflected pupils.
Suddenly the police—
Knock plates out of hands,
Fire into the air:
People, you are eating human flesh!
Human meat!
The babas' chubby arms are bent back,
Led to the firing squad,
They walk and quietly howl,
And from their eyes wolfs' paws
Claw the air.
The passerby is too late to share in the soup.
A bird pecks it up from the ground—she is worse off.
And he leaves, stepping over the dead
Or walking around them, like puddles.

2 *Still Life*

Garbage dusks lap at the window.
A youth is hunched over impatiently,
Glancing at a casserole restlessly . . .
Inside it a cat gurgles!

You arrive, he calls it "rabbit,"
You eat, he laughs so savagely.
Soon he dies. In the air you quietly
Trace with coal a *nature* (o indeed!) *morte.*
A candle, a fragment of carpenter's glue,
A ration of bread, a handful of lentils.
Rembrandt! How one wants to live and pray.
Even if frozen, even if ossified.

3 *Mixed Landscape. Stairway, yard, church.*
   (paper, coal, raven's blood)

Neither a brother nor a father anymore—
A shade they lead,
Their guns pressed against his tailbone.
A naked bulb dangles similarly,
A draft presses in from the basement.

Behind this damp blue paint— there's yellow, behind it green,
Do not scrape to the void, there's no need,
There stand plaster and vapors of hell.
Here, eat up, a potato pink color.
You have nothing more, blockade, my bone!
What have you eaten? Tell me:
Blue frost off of rocks,
Worms, a horse's snout,
A feline tail.
On barrels of human hands and tufts of hair
You have fed. On sparrows, on stars and smoke,
On trees, like a woodpecker,
On iron, like rust.
And in the yard they cut a man's throat with no knife,
Unceremoniously simply.
A voice leaks out of the steaming wound.
It sings of a mustard seed and a crumb of bread,
Of the soul of blood.
Under the weak northern lights
The sky walks on tumors.
The blockade eats up
The soul, as a wolf eats his paw in a snare,
As a fish eats a worm,

As bottomless wisdom eats words . . .
O, return all those carried far away
In the body of the flabby truck,
Jingling, like frozen firewood.

Good Friday. Empty, hungry church.
The Deacon's voice desiccated, he is barely alive,
Echoing shadows bring in the shroud—
The Priest rocks back his head:
"O, now I have seen, I have grasped—
You awoke from sick death,
And cannot recover, it's ruin for us all."
My blood becomes icy wine,
Ouroboros bites through his tail.
Teeth are scattered in the sky
In place of cruel stars.

Translated by James McGavran

NATALYA STARODUBTSEVA

[*Roundabouts solidly turn*]

Roundabouts stolidly turn
convert into a winged launch
Dzhala nervously licks a cone
trails a finger over her paunch
she's a mum in waiting and the kid
annoys her and a coolness grows
it doesn't give shit
a no-hoper stands at the door
is driving me nuts, so break
silence's golden thread
have a snooze my dearest I guess
you've no wish to speak to me

Translated by Daniel Weissbort

[*And it is cold here and a bit strange*]

And it is cold here and a bit strange:
And only a split fear rings in my ears.
And in the dark opuntia ovata flowers
And a moor with white teeth draws a bow
Don't be scared, I'm here and shall set you free
And I'm not scared of the devil and the wings of silence—
But if the beautiful Helen should summon you,
Just refuse to go, so there should be no war.

Translated by Daniel Weissbort

MARIYA STEPANOVA

Airman

When he returned from there,
he screamed in his sleep and bombed towns
and spirits appeared to him,
he used to get up to smoke and open the window,
our ragged clothes lay together in a heap
and I gathered up a bag for them in the darkness,
but that is nothing yet.

He didn't begin to and forbade me
to dig the back garden by the big house—
food and income for the family.
He put on weight, got angry, brutalized, then got thin
and rolled his own home-grown.
But life went on.

When he returned from there,
where the vessels of the civilian fleet fly,
from the heavens beyond the clouds,
when he had really come back from there,
we were all helpless
as children sucking at mama.
But that is nothing yet.

High up there they are singing at the controls,
the flight stewardesses are giving out wine,
trundling their carts down the rows,
but my one in the sky had a different role,
he leaned on the Father's shoulders
and I will not give that up.
But life went on.

When he returned forever from there,
a released man from the prison of heaven,
mysterious as a suitcase,
we went out by the works exit into the fine night,
a son in arms and a daughter around.

And he hit me in the face.
But that is nothing yet.

Like a moist blush at the word love
his blue-eyed glance slid over his face
while he hurt me.
All our family tree sat on the lawn
and saw the glow, where the horizon was,
where they hadn't yet put out the fire.
And life went on.

He drank for a week, tear after tear,
threatened someone, "Piss off" said to someone.
He held his stomach and wheezed,
then he felt silent and said quietly
that—up there—he did not look in my eyes—
the Heavenly Daughter lives.
She's a daughter, a woman, a wife
and what she was like under her clothes—
I would have forgiven the lies
but he described painstakingly
her dispassionate as the skies
colorless eyes.
First he saw her, he said,
when the snow-white town was burning
and we had completed our mission
and in her blue skirt and white scarf
she stretched to me in an empty dive
to open the parachute above me.
He added: She is more visible at dawn.
She is always in a pioneer uniform,
a bluish ribbon in her hair.
Then he snored suddenly and the house woke,
now empty, not needing a lock,
since everything in it had been drunk away.
As for me I have nothing of my own,
but this astral bitch of his,
his commissar of the air
will answer, answer for his every turn
and remember his crashed plane
and what else was fated.

But everything changed. Life healed,
as though everything was bright, more transparent
than glass and nothing was owed it.
My man stopped, looked round
and became a controller for honest trips
on the country's transport resources.
Only once he returned home different,
as before, the same stress in his voice
and looking me close in the face
said that he was fed up with life on earth:
the Heavenly Daughter had appeared to him
on the trolleybus by the ring road.
He lay on his bed and began to die,
picking invisible fluff off the sheet
and died, while I, out of my mind,
was running, screaming to buy Corvalol
and saw: the trolleybus was going round
and at the first window was—She.
She had on a pioneer uniform,
she was blushing to the roots of her hair.
She leant a little toward the window,
and roared terrifyingly in my ear.
But I took a step toward the platform
and judgment met me.
. . . Forgive me, although there can be no forgiveness,
for the killing of a twelve-year-old girl,
innocently perishing because,
in the soulless abyss, like a fish in soup,
the Heavenly Daughter is living in sin,
but with whom, no one will ever know.
. . . And life goes on.

Translated by Richard McKane

DARYA SUKHOVEY

Spring Scales

1

we'll smoke a couple cigarettes
each third a unit of time

toss out a computer
or trade in a hard disk

buy a new mouse and two books
what for what for

2

with a new mouse and two books
in a semitransparent polyethylene
bag

with dreams like a refrain

take the trolleybus take the trolleybus
what for what for

3

hello—insert someone's name here
I won't report anything new to you
absolutely nothing
except for that I have time for nothing

therefore I won't plan to meet you
in the very near future

4

our affairs however require supplemental
agreement and discussion
th-ere wh-ere we get together

I sincerely hope
a cup of tea (martini/mug of beer)
to choose the essentials
they'll be guaranteed

5

you know material complexities
I look through the window to the sky

the mini-bus is twelve roubles, metro six
I have to buy two books a month
a computer mouse polyethylene bag
shoe repairs analgesics contraception

6

a continuation of the enumeration
quick noodles
cigarettes telephone bills rent
flowers

it's not yours to worry about

as usual our everyday things are fine
I'll tell you my news when we meet

7

a signature *sincerely/regretfully*

what for what for

send by fax send by fax
pasting in new names and more new names
discovering new names for myself
which live like me

8

instead of the mini-bus I'll buy a beer

I even have enough for klinskoe
and if there's no klinskoe
then a light bavarian, baltica

eight sixty eight sixty
spring waits won't go winds whistle

9

first spring in the city center
like an unpretentious color scale
drink back a beer drink back a beer

too late to experiment with anything else
+
too early to go back
=
something else will work out

10

I go somewhere to argue with someone
I might even go far away
with this very goal

to the other end of the city for example
or to another city
under the same sky

11

strictly speaking there's nothing more I can say

I open the first door I come across
a bar or the scientific institute it doesn't matter

they let me in because of my honest eyes
hair washed in the morning
unfamiliar face

12

I can't even explain why
this text is called spring scales

probably some old inertia
trajectory

previously established laws
of ecumenical equilibrium

13

It's already a sort of egor letov
twenty-third of march in club polygon
squeeze an order of tickets an order of tickets
press here

the author indicates the heart
and leaves the scene

Translated by Christopher Mattison

OLGA SULCHINSKAYA

The Kite

My soul is like a kite
and the string is in your hands.
It is wild as the wind and disobedient
and the string is in your hands.
Now it plays merrily with the wind,
soars effortlessly in the clouds,
now it shudders and dies
and catches the air stertorously
and he, below, stands, laughs—
he loves to watch.
The kite threshes, the wind swirls,
wanting to wear through the string.

Translated by Richard McKane

Crimea

The cow's moo and the goat's meheh carry down
from the hills and the measured murmur of the sea
like breathing in and out goes off into the distance
until the soul appropriates the experience
of the great day and also observes
how the cloud in the boiling milk
sweetly settles in patterned foam.
It now remembers with difficulty
the completed roads beyond the long day.
It's good here. Where else to go?
The twilight comes. The cricket has come to
and busies itself unlearning its prenatal sound.
The pupil swims and dilates
looking into the dark-crystal horizon.

Translated by Richard McKane

[*The wind paces on the lower branch*]

The wind paces on the lower branch.
There are napkins on our knees.
You eat olives and I shrimps
and together we are wonderful kids.
We drink wine, talk in poems
and we don't know what will happen to us.
We both have families and children
but we are alone in the world.
We'd run away without permission,
had fixed ourselves a Sunday,
without a middle or continuation,
without punishment or salvation.

Translated by Richard McKane

ELENA SUNTSOVA

[*Beyond is where the passersby end*]

Beyond is where the passersby end
and where the wood begins its melting.

Beyond, the sobered spruce trees flock and
fall upside down, fall upside down.

Broken like they were home-rolled ciggies,
no brushwood on their naked bodies,

All swaying, swaying their dark trunks, and
rustling, and tickling, looking on.

A big bear lives in them, a she-bear,
She lies above, and swallows wind gusts,

And drinks hot water, asymmetrical
and breathing smoke at home in billows,

Inside which, saved and sheltered, finally
she is invisible and sleeps.

Translated by Nika Skandiaka

[*as old salts know*]

as old salts know
confounded communities
are not coordinated
while between lie
the ground earth real estate demesne
willy-nilly

Translated by Nika Skandiaka

[*city of summer you inhabit a fluff-light city of little claws*]

city of summer you inhabit a fluff-light city of little claws
a martin and his martlet grandma ever saying and i said nothing
squinted felt for some reason like crying
a pink stripe over celery blinds
grandma thought *rocks are alive and grow and crumble when you hurt them*
fell asleep at the first commercial break of her soaps

Translated by Nika Skandiaka

[*as you and i stand long*]

as you and i stand long
and watch the falling snow
i see the whirling smoke in the window
i hear the changing slang

his cigarettes are like poison dumb
his senses feed upon the earth
the sister practices a living scar
and fingers reach and touch

if you should ever call again
about being in love with me: whether you are
throw momma an SMS from the train your son
is out of clarion reception area

Translated by Nika Skandiaka

VITALINA TKHORZHEVSKAYA

Wild Rose

Rose of the Russian nation
you are frosty and wayward
like poetry and prose
in a locomotive's furnace
    like
disaster under the big top
    rose breaking out
    rose of the Russian nation
    thorn of the heart
rose of the Russian nation
mustn't pluck you with the hands
tread you under foot
you're armed with teeth
    you're made of rose flesh
    all silence and menace
    no metempsychosis in you
    a direct route to the heavens you are
of early morning neurosis
filled with an inner luminescence—
like the wonderful and dazzling
moment—Rose

Translated by Daniel Weissbort

[*He wouldn't sign the death warrant*]

He wouldn't sign the death warrant
when he read his own name among the names of the condemned
and this question I pose: Is he a good judge?

Translated by Daniel Weissbort

Silence

[This is addressed] to you—A century later,*
When you experience despair
And the tremor of fear and anger,
You'll hear my silence.

And you will follow me
Along the flight paths of eagle and hawk,
Where
Bright colored openings
Leak endlessly.

Direct speech of grief.
The sky
Is covered in crosses.
As to my god-child
I bequeath to you Silence:

Seize it—like
A song,
Whistle
It
In your quiet moments:
We are but a reprise
Of the current of the years

Of blossoming—of twittering—
Of Silence—forever.

Translated by Daniel Weissbort

* Quotes the first line of Marina Tsvetaeva's poem: "To you a century later" (author's note).

YANA TOKAREVA

Brief reflection on the greatness of God

To Ilya

details didn't concern me,
but I'm noticing now
dust specks in a sunray,
a chow-chow . . .

So wondrous are
the Almighty's deeds
that I'm a bit blown by it:
got myself some specs, see.

To Phil

growing up's like taking an icy shower
already you've stuck your belly your back under
still one of your heels is holding its breath
must be the scared soul's in residence there

Translated by Daniel Weissbort

[*Why is she sleeping on some steps*]

Why is she sleeping on some steps
in the vicinity of the station?
In this place wouldn't I too
bury my head in my knees?
Mummy didn't let her child have a rat,
but he loves them,
he's sorry for them,
what sort of people are these, Lord?
Head in the snow.
In the middle of Moscow
in a single night

a living man
turned to wax.

Translated by Daniel Weissbort

---

from On Russian Poetry (1996–2000)

2

No, we didn't get deafer or older
(Joseph Brodsky)

In this world it is noblest
to walk around town with a poet,
when it is easier for the poet to point out
that from which poems are likely to sprout.
Will I be able, more acutely than a deaf-mute,
to catch the gesture, which precedes the word-root?

Poetry has to be a bit hard of hearing,
when, in front of an audience, it tries
to provide itself with exacting
long drawn-out translations into Sign,
will I be able . . . no, I'm afraid it's too late—
it has already missed its sell-by date.

Whenever and for whatever reason it was uttered:
"Thou who hast legs, arise, on thy feet!"—
no, we'll arise neither earlier nor later
than we did from the very start.
I can say it, but will I be able to understand
there's nothing nobler in the land . . . ?

Translated by Daniel Weissbort

ELENA VASILEVA

[*I wish I could look*]

I wish I could look
Into the eyes of the happy old man
Or out of the Scottish castle windows
Or when the tail
Sheds its lizard

I wish I could read
The guide to the mind's labyrinth
Or leaf through the book of my memory
Or find the proofs
For the torn-out page

I wish I could get
The key to the enchanted door
From my childhood to the land beyond
For the boy with silver heart
And the girl with chrysolite eyes

And stay with them forever
And find my own name
And stop
Waiting
For you

Translated by Max Nemtsov

[*I used to be your echo*]

I used to be your echo
I used to be a doe for your shoulders
A frequent reason for your eye
An approaching shore for your lake of tears
A white lotus in one hundred vases

You were given to me
As the absolute answer
To the only question
I had to ask

Translated by Max Nemtsov

[*She's calling God, she wants to ask Him*]

She's calling God, she wants to ask Him
if maybe now it's time to come back to her senses
to padlock with bars of black iron
the gate to her garden

Here, the cats and the light crescent of the moon
are sitting at night on the roofs between huge aerial loops
this is the time when little old women shed their tears
and babies sob in their sleep

Translated by Max Nemtsov

EKATERINA VLASOVA

[*A little sympathy*]

A little sympathy
for the poor birds,
whose wings have grown heavy with snow.
A little compassion
for my own inner I,
who cannot attain this luxury—
wings heavy with snow . . .

Translated by Peter France

[*On an old grand piano*]

On an old grand piano
the music was scattered.
But fingers crept out
for a little hunting:
with caresses, with blows,
with rain and with color,
enfolding in heat
or in sorrowful coldness;
they danced and they laughed,
were braided and bent,
whispered and cursed,
loved and didn't care,
joked and endeavored,
beseeched and surrendered,
for a while put on airs,
awkwardly smiled
and pretended to be God . . .
And then they flew up,
fluttered off somewhere
(to sounds leaving shadows
that resembled streams)—
to look for new hunting,

for some new tasty morsel . . .
and God tidied the music
and seemed to start weeping.

Translated by Peter France

[*I see*]

I see
your hands in my nightmares,
they bring me unbearable pain . . .
and yet they are just wiping the dust
from the pale looking-glass of my soul.

Translated by Peter France

[*Create me a world*]

Create me a world
of transparent-green fibers,
of dark-snowy skies,
and opal-smoky heights;
I will depart forever,
will slip between walls, between windows
into that narrow opening,
that house, behind which is sunrise.
I shall not at all miss
all I leave behind with a smile;
in a diadem of gold
I shall forget the axe marks;
and then, of course,
somewhere at the very end
I shall make myself briefly
come down to you and shout: "Time!"
But meanwhile I keep silent,
hiding cold hands in red spots,
sails on my back,
and a look of furious hunger . . .

Give me a day:
I shall hear underground noises . . .
whisper of words on the wall:
"The film has been seen, has been dubbed, has been shot."

Translated by Peter France

[*There is a way to sew wings on arms*]

There is a way to sew wings on arms,
the needles are blunted, though, the leather
is scuffed, the sword won't leave the scabbard,
the word has vanished into sand.

And to sew wings on arms there is a way,
but sensing danger, the birds flap to death,
and wind blows out the town like a lamp,
and the sun has set before sunrise.

Translated by Peter France

TATYANA VOLTSKAYA

[*The low clouds, the shreds of dry grass*]

The low clouds, the shreds of dry grass,
Beet leaves tufting behind the decayed fence,
The gravel path staggering blind-drunk down:
This is no English landscape, sleek as fine china,
With ancestral oaks and the family silver of a brook:
No: here the snare of a dropped fir branch
Lies across every path, trees hold charred stumps
In their midst like blackened teeth:
And in fields there's no help from the storm-crossed showers
That have it in for everyone, even God.

Translated by Catriona Kelly

[*Rhyme is a woman, trying on clothes*]

Rhyme is a woman, trying on clothes,
plaiting a rose into her hair.
She splashes in blood, like a naiad,
and surfaces, when not asked to.

Rhyme is a bell, driving away evil spirits
from the solitary guilty soul,
when the wind in the thistle thickets
weeps during the cold night.

Rhyme is a celestial trumpet—that is,
it rouses me from the grave,
when you come, beloved, with shining eyes,
and kiss me on the lips.

Rhyme is a path bordered by wild strawberries,
now here, now gone—so beats the heart.
I walk but don't know where,
I distract death with smooth talk.

Translated by Daniel Weissbort

[*God is the first snow. He is a leaf, a mosquito*]

God is the first snow. He is a leaf, a mosquito.
He is Benedict burning. He is sleeping Abelard.
He is a speckled stone at the bottom of a lake.
He is steam over milk. He hides in me.
But not in the ears, catching seduction,
not in depth of eyes that have been fed on dirtiness,
not in the dull, hard coffin of the skull,
not in the skipping fledgling in the ribcage nest,
shouting "Love, love!"
He doesn't dive
in the blood and splash "Catch!"
He is uncatchable for me, in me.
Only two are powerful enough
to cover Him, like a crane
in a magical, fine net of words guiltily left unsaid and movements.
Then He is here—not everywhere—
but in the fingertips and the tips of breasts
with which I softly touch you,
standing barefoot on tiptoes.
Inasmuch as this moment is fired and pure
like a pottery pitcher, like a narrow broom leaf
God breathes in it; He is the cold between the shoulder blades,
sparkle of the sun on the shoulder and imprint of a word unsaid on dry lips:
the track of an angel. The track of sun on stones.

Translated by Richard McKane

GALINA ZELENINA (GILA LORAN)

[With grown-up clever hands]

With grown-up clever hands
You do all the proper things
Only don't stamp your heels:
Your heels
Are too high
For our promenade
Through a garden of lilies-of-the-valley

Embrace me. For this
I'll treat you to a cigarette,
All right

You and I are like boy and girl cousins
And now you seem pleased to see me
How oddly light your words are
But it wouldn't be proper to embrace you:
My cuffs are too long
For our masquerade

Phone. What if I blurt out *I love you?*

Translated by Daniel Weissbort

Shma Yisrael (Hear, O Israel)

A Jew, seeing a Christian, thinks: It's the devil brought him!
Approaching, he says: May success attend you and may God
smile on you! Leaving, he mutters: May he disappear like ice
in the fire, like Pharaoh in the sea!
(From a medieval Hebrew chronicle)

To N. K.

The rustle of a page will haunt us
And our sabbath cup is empty
And blood of that wretch from the cross

Remained with us and with them, our children
We are hounded beyond the hellish Pale
And crimson worms blossom in the mouths
Of women in their thirty-third year
Our brother devils for all eternity sold us
The power to change light into dark
Whispering a magic spell.
Let us pour poison into the rivers
Let us bring mass death to the cattle, a plague to the people,
Gout to the king

Promise we'll not do it anymore,
We'll depart from everywhere, while the going's good
And will feed only in those dining-rooms
Where there's cranberry cordial not infant's blood
Live in the usual way. We'll ask mama to let us go
Collect the suitcase: pants, a towel
Swimming shoes
An inflatable mattress
Sunglasses
Panama pyjamas
Ask Pharaoh's envoys to stamp our visa
But it's no use watching TV in the hotel
Or clambering into the hippo's jaws
Or onto the rhino's back
And measuring the Giza pyramids
And splashing in the Nile's rapids—
Other people do that sort of thing.
Let's find the Cairo Genizah*—
Crooked little letters, wonderful,
Let's read some

Let Joseph, interpreter of dreams,
Sell us the last dream,
That boy, good at fabrications.
We're so weary of all-night vigils
Over books: the legacy of generations
Grows from year to year, like the beard,
Bluey-black, of that Jew
Who was condemned to live forever. We'll not pay
The fee for the river crossing

—The waters will part—and the people will cross
That dark beggar from the Dung Gate,**
Preserver of the old manuscript,
Mumbling the morning prayer.

Let's go, let's leave Egypt,
Let's have a smoke in the wind.

Translated by Daniel Weissbort

*Genizah: a room adjoining a synagogue for the safekeeping of old or damaged books, documents, or valuables (translator's note).

**The Dung Gate is mentioned in the book of Nehemiah as the dispatch point for Jerusalem's refuse. Evidently the refuse was removed from the city through this gate (translator's note).

Strategy

And then all of them heard the voice;   It's enough to speak about words
                                                                              speak with words
                                                          That's it
                                                          That's enough
                                                          That'll do
And then (when?) all of them (who?) (did what?)
felt a doubt about what they heard
Only   conjunctions
            interjections
            and particles have been left out of question
All others that answered the question unsatisfactorily
agreed: to go, to slip away, to take cover in the mouth of the source
                like a snail
                and to grow deaf to please (whom?)
                from the ringing in the ears from the hooter of double o
                to angle on thread for the paper auricles of the fool and the monster
                the oyster of hearing will wither weary
                by the lips of the secluded ear, by the doom of the ear-ring
                and the Accountant of doleful sounds
                will fall asleep, slip away by stealth and the rosy luster of fever
                with the scorched frill on the faces . . .
                we shall not listen   we shall not hear
                                        That's enough
                                        That'll do
                                        That's it
And then the sea was split, like the big shell
seducing by its blackness like Nescafé
and spliced the edges again. It was not painful to sink.
The siren wailed for them shabbes.
But then they went out on the shore with Blacksea-usher
and drove the wave on the shore the way one drives a puck on a field,
the way one drives a pack of sheep on a pasture in the mountains,
so they drove the coastal lambs like the Tartar-Mongolian yoke,
like the enemy, with clubs in front of them.
And then they returned to the place where they tortured the clay

and crushed the wine of the jug so that ten drops be spilled
on the open spelling-book, on its pages, to wipe off the wet hand-written lines
as a wanderer wipes off sweat.
Let the Man of letters weep for them
and the spellbound Accountant be puzzled.

> (This is the image of Bewilderment—harboring itself
> and greedily turning pink, its swirling out the curve of flesh
> and knitting ligature of the notched edges
> with the pitiful gilt)

And then to see it they glided into the depth
and feeling their way found the image of the gilded warm-colored rose
but then it seemed the rosy worm of guilt or perhaps
the golden folds closed and the sea fell and shut itself.
And then they raised the pyramid of silt above themselves;
there in the overturned hut of heaven in the Delta of the source of the Nile
there was a human hair, discovered after many thousand years,
and then all of them heard the voice:

> It's enough to speak about words
> speak with words
> That'll do
> That's it
> That's enow.

And now—are you still here?
On the shore Katiusha appears:
I do not want to lie in a shrine
I want to lie in brine.

Translated by the author and edited by Ashraf Noor

[*I'm speaking to make you silent*]
(fragment of a poem)

I'm speaking to make you silent
and to hear the silence that I've broken.
Or else how can I be convinced of its existence? The cast seal
of silence is broken easily by a single movement of lips.
"I saw their temples on the snow"—
Turning over the pages of the vast epistle
I'm repeating aloud the alien silence unsealed without curiosity.

Reproachfully:

"I'm speaking to believe it.
I'm speaking to believe it."—
I'm saying twice without thinking
to believe it.—"On the snow
I saw their temples.
They stood in the equal squares like crimson bells
covered with the leaking lacquer or sealing wax,
not hollow but solid,
and their form could remind me of Cambodian constructions
if their form and content were not in fact an entity—
the crimson lacquer in and outside
or the sealing-wax, as was said earlier, the crimson sealing-wax.
They were bound by the chains perhaps of cast-iron,
                                        I don't know for sure,
but undoubtedly black and heavy."
They?—About whom was this said? About temples or about Khmers
whose temples she's seen?
"Though I didn't step over the chains
I found myself in the middle of the square."—
What does it mean? Perhaps she was hooked
by a gaff, up from the bottom of the silence,
and placed in the closed garden,
or she passed by the tongueless bells
as a trembling of fire passes, hot
and licking the leaks of the sealing-wax.

Translated by the author and edited by Ashraf Noor

Lamentation of the Border-Guard

I do not want to be a border-guard, said the border-guard.
I don't want to be a body-guard.
I don't want to be a guardian-angel.
I don't want to be a guide.
I want not to be a grinder.
I don't want to be a garnet.
I don't want to be a guerdon.
I don't want to be a gaud.

But my own unwillingness is grinding and grounding me
and I'm standing on guard, my own octagonal garden.

I don't want to be a watchman, answered the watchman.
I don't want to be a guardsman.
I don't want to be a watchguard.
But my own unwillingness is watching over me and hobbling me,
I'm standing alone, wavering in the wind.

I'm the door-keeper, observed the porter.
But nobody asked me
about my will.

Translated by the author and edited by Ashraf Noor

OLGA ZONDBERG

[*The variety of animals, said Khlebnikov*]

The variety of animals, said Khlebnikov,
derives from their ability
to see God in different ways.

If the universe, said Hawkins,
were different, we'd simply
not notice it.

From *Chanel* to *Escape* (a gorgeous
glossy journal alluded to them)
each year death has another smell.

There are people, writers,
who have written everything down,
noughts-and-crosses
instead of digital facsimiles

Translated by Daniel Weissbort

[*cockle-antarctica*]

cockle-antarctica
has been cast up onto the shore
from it fell an icy fragment
instead of the first snow

three calendar kittens
november december january

february. march.

achilles took
the tortoise for a walk
working hours on the leash
of the short day

to see how our little winter,
long as a tongue
freezing to the iron cold
will not give in to the enemy
our proud varangian*
both our hard sign and our soft**

Translated by Daniel Weissbort

*Reference to a song from the beginning of the twentieth century, in which "Our proud *Varangian*," the name of a ship, refuses to surrender to the enemy. The Varangians invaded Russia from the North, a land of ice and snow (author's note). **The hard sign and soft sign are Russian letters; their functions are indicated by their names (author's note).

[*they all but cry out*]

they all but cry out
young and not too
bald with a sky cap
with a parcel with a briefcase
white and white
because it's snow

—suvorov and his skeleton

windspeed 17 meters per sec
distance time speed

first-rate audibility but a short memory
almost said two fools

audibility. almost

didn't say

Translated by Daniel Weissbort

[*there were lots of them*]

there were lots of them
but their fear was greater

some got flowers (I wouldn't accept any
even if they themselves were overgrown with blooms
then I would) they raised children
hating the process
even more than the children
and so forth

I gave myself flowers, she says
because there's nobody else

nobody could give her or anybody
in that she didn't have anyone

well why are all my questions so hard

"You have to give yourself presents,"
croons Accident.*
"Time for yourself"—
Harlequin's slogan,
deluging the town with cheap reading matter
love in soft covers
stupid as several donkeys

Translated by Daniel Weissbort

*Name of a rock band (author's note).

[*To die. And be born as an inspector of playgrounds for tiny tots*]

To die. And be born as an inspector of playgrounds for tiny tots.
At night to write, as you hit the high spots.
Cradle songs for a play featuring a sleeping baby.
Or, more likely, being born as a timorous mushroom maybe.
Lonely tree stumps welcome the one-legged visitor.
Transformation into a tree or a mushroom is rare,
Mushroom and tree hang out together. At this sign kids
With baskets get ready to descend on the woods,
Where amid dark trunks a cobweb shimmers . . . Their eyes can't take it in—
Pity, the basket is small. This pity's the only kind known.
As for you, slender-legged mushroom, mercy is on the skids,
And no one will be born as an inspector of playgrounds for kids

Translated by Daniel Weissbort

POSTFACE

A POET'S VIEW

ELENA FANAILOVA

Art is a dialogue with Time. Of course, this may take different forms, so that to compare by contrasting one kind of art with another is not an entirely useless operation. It is in this sense that I should like to speak of the artistic world of women, of women's poetry and its place in contemporary Russia.

In 2001 and 2002, the Tretyakov Gallery mounted several major retrospective exhibitions of Russian women's painting. One of these was called "Amazons of the Avant-garde" and was dedicated to Olga Rozanova and Natalya Goncharova; there were also individual retrospectives. Among others, I remember an exhibition entitled "Art of the Female Kind," but the curators insisted that the title alluded not to gender, but rather to women as a *tribe*, a kind of separate nationality, existing side by side with the tribe of men and producing its own art. The exhibition was comprehensive and was organized chronologically. It began with artistic productions of the royal needle-workers of the sixteenth century and ended in the huge hall where twentieth-century Russian women artists, of the 70s and 80s, were represented: Irina Nakhova, Rimma Gerlovina, and others who had burst upon the Russian art-scene of the 90s, such as Olga Chernyshova, Tatyana Liberman, and Ira Waldron.

What the history of art reveals, what—from a local point of view—is becoming obvious, even in the cursory overview afforded by such an exhibition, is the total inscription of women in the male world, their auxiliary or decorative role in the world of Russian art. At least that is how it appeared prior to the Russian avant-garde. Women lacked a distinct graphic language of their own. They adhered to the canons and the stylistic norms of the epoch: Karl Briulov's manner or the academic style, Russian impressionism or Russian modernism, followed by the Stalinist art-deco of the 30s and the Soviet romanticism of the 70s.

If we were to depict these developments, say, in animated-cartoon form, this is how it would look. Women are not permitted to paint religious or secular pictures, so all that is left for them to do is to embroider. Only at the end of the eighteenth century did ladies of the nobility, amateur artists, start producing paintings. In the nineteenth century, female talent was found exclusively among aristocrats. Thus Mariya Bashkirtseva appeared on the scene as unexpectedly as a pearl on the ocean floor. The flood of names—and the first serious attempts by women to develop their own artistic language—occurs at the beginning of the twentieth century. The invincible Natalya Goncharova may be the first Russian woman artist ready to compete with men, with her own utterly authentic, powerful, and convincing language. Marina Tsvetaeva's interest in Goncharova is that of one great artist in another, following the same path of innovation. The present explosion, resulting from the evolution of these individual languages, dates from the end of the 80s. There is scarcely a single notable woman artist imitating somebody else or making use of the aesthetic means employed by men. Women and men at the end of the twentieth century spoke quite different languages, and there are many of these.

Inevitably certain parallels with what is happening today suggest themselves. The work of the first Russian women poets of the nineteenth century, such as Karolina Pavlova and Evdokiya Rostopchina, does not transgress the boundaries of the contemporary poetic style. "I am a woman! My thinking and my inspiration should be governed by meekness and modesty." This self-definition by Rostopchina makes it quite clear what the woman artist's place in the world must be. It is curious that Mariya Bashkirtseva, whose diary—she was reproached in her own time for egocentrism and concentration on her inner feelings—became one of the first manifestos of Russian feminism, thought of herself primarily as an artist, not a writer. The first real efflorescence of Russian women's poetry is associated with the "Silver Age," and later with the Revolution and its aftermath. The principal poets, competing with men on equal terms, are still, symbolically, Anna Akhmatova and Marina Tsvetaeva.

Not a single other poet on a par with Akhmatova or Tsvetaeva has yet emerged, perhaps because the culture and the spirit of the times which created these preeminent figures have become irretrievable. By the 30s the creativity of the Russian (Soviet) people was forced to serve ideologically correct (purely celebratory) ends. Female emancipation, coinciding with the Russian Revolution, ended in the "equality of the sexes." The social lie forced on it is totally alien to the language of women, which is natural and spontaneous. A woman forced to remain within the officially decreed boundaries will produce vacuities or withdraw into a private world. But in poetry a socially significant voice, however paradoxically, is achieved through personal application; and women in the country named the USSR, following the lead of the men, allowed themselves to be deprived of the right of sincere self-expression. In Russia, World War II produced a totally male atmosphere and masculine literature. To women was allotted the passive role of mourners or nurses, Olga Berggolts being one exception. Eccentric, natural talent, such as that of Kseniya Nekrasova, was not taken seriously by the Union of Soviet Writers.

The end of the 50s and early 60s, the period after Joseph Stalin's death or the era of what we call "Khrushchev's Thaw" (with space travel, the virgin lands project, and so forth), is in fact a pale copy of the revolutionary years, similarly optimistic, in a romantic spirit, about the reconstruction of the world. Russians learned to hope and also acquired three musketeers: Robert Rozhdestvensky, Andrey Voznesensky, and Evgeny Evtushenko, plus a woman, Bella Akhmadulina. To her credit, Akhmadulina has continued to write brilliantly up to the present. The isolated but resolute voices of Natalya Gorbanevskaya, Irina Ratushinskaya, Inna Lisnianskaya, Yunna Morits, Novella Matveeva, and younger writers Tatyana Bek, Olesia Nikolaeva, and Marina Kudimova have maintained and continue to maintain the high standard of Russian women's literature. Until the end of the 80s, Elena Shvarts, Olga Sedakova, and Svetlana Kekova, poets virtually unknown to a wider public and with powerful metaphysical gifts, had a major influence.

Fortunately, poets, including women, who wrote for the "desk drawer" are now able to publish freely. But the "professional ban," even in the relatively liberal 70s and 80s, did enormous damage to Russian culture in general and women's poetry in particular. And this is especially true of the provinces. Only during the 90s did it become evident that major writers of the "feminine gender" were at work in these distant outposts of the former Soviet empire.

At the end of the 80s, political changes and the information explosion that accompanied these made poetry of "metametaphorism" accessible and led to the publication of conceptualist writers and the poets of the so-called Leningrad school. Nina Iskrenko became the star of the Moscow club "Poetry," and Rea Nikonova began appearing at poetry festivals. On the threshold of the 90s effulgent personalities like Tatyana Shcherbina, Larisa Berezovchuk, Tatyana Voltskaya, and Inna Kabysh began to emerge. The atmosphere of the inevitably changing times, the open archives and publications, and acquaintance with the legacy of uncensored Russian literature nurtured a new generation of women poets who continued in the tradition of Akhmatova and Tsvetaeva. Among these are the neo-classicist Polina Barskova, the postconceptualist Mariya Stepanova, Vera Pavlova, and Aleksandra Petrova. Each is drawn to a particular tradition. Stepanova employs the entire palette of Nikolay Zabolotsky and rehabilitates the classical ballad, including its Soviet form; Vera Pavlova, heir to the conceptualists, is more a Dmitry Aleksandrovich Prigov in skirts than an apologist for the "eternal feminine," as superficial critics believe. "Feminine" themes and erotic motifs are for Pavlova just the coating for occasionally more bitter pills. Aleksandra Petrova's poetics largely derives from the OBERIU (Association for Real Art) poets, from Leonid Dobychin, and from conceptualist verse. The intertextuality of these poets is extensive, as if they had emerged with computers in their brains, permitting them to mount poems like video-clips—that is, to work with the texture of temporality in a nonlinear fashion.

Several significant female names have appeared in the Russian diaspora in Israel and America, for instance, and this concerns not only immigrants of the 70s and 80s but quite young women. New cosmopolitan poets like Linor Goralik, Elena Kostyleva, or the above-mentioned Polina Barskova and Aleksandra Petrova are not émigrés but rather individuals who have experienced life in diverse countries and who write about the reality familiar to them as Russians encountering the world. These are poems by writers who keep changing countries of domicile and therefore linguistic milieus. Their texts are contributing something new and unexpected, from a tonal and acoustic point of view, not just to women's poetry but to Russian poetry as such. And there is a completely new generation of women poets—"the generation of twenty-year-olds"—which works in the mass media, on Internet publications, or in advertising. These poets embody media reality in their writing.

The division of poets according to gender is, of course, a theoretical notion. The actual contribution of any author is defined by the quality of his or her writing, not by gender. But physically and psychologically men and women are different, and this inevitably leads to differences on a linguistic level. It is well known that in ancient cultures there were distinct "female" languages, that is, those used by women, conversing among themselves. A woman expresses herself in all respects differently from men. The map of the post-Soviet female world is only now beginning to acquire specific features, and the world of women—not just of Russian women—is now in urgent need of self-definition.

Translated by Daniel Weissbort

APPENDIX

THE VAVILON PROJECT AND WOMEN'S VOICES
AMONG THE YOUNG LITERARY GENERATION

DMITRY KUZMIN

It is already fifteen years since the first issue of the samizdat journal *Vavilon* appeared, in February 1989, as a platform for young Russian writers. The Vavilon project never intended to draw a line of division between male and female writing. Indeed, from the very start, the project was supposed to unite, not to divide. The very name "Vavilon" comes from a song by famous Russian rock musician Boris Grebenshchikov, who was hugely influential in the youth world of the 1980s:

> Vavilon is a city like any other,
> one shouldn't complain about this.
> If you go, we'll go one way—
> there simply is no other.

The guiding notion was universal coexistence and fruitful interaction between various artistic discourses and views on life and literature. In those years, so critical for Russian society and especially for Russian literature, beginning authors seemed uniquely placed. Every day new data about Russian and world history, culture, and domestic and foreign literature of the present and the recent past flooded in. In the first place, readers now had access to the forbidden works of the Silver Age as well as to the products of over three decades of the samizdat literature of the second half of the twentieth century. The world in general and culture in particular seemed to these young authors unstable, continually changing, each new publication demanding a reappraisal of set ideas. Therefore, it cannot be said of the majority of significant young writers who entered literature from the late 80s to the early 90s that they inherited any particular tradition, based on earlier Russian poetry. From the very onset of their literary careers, they found themselves at an intersection of many paths, with the option of freely combining different ones, that is, of combining incompatibles.

There were five originators of the project, all of them male (aged between sixteen and twenty in 1989), among them such contemporary young stars as Stanislav Lvovsky and Vadim Kalinin. Our samizdat journal was produced on an ordinary typewriter and was not intended for wide circulation: we simply wanted to record the emergence of a young literary generation, because other publishers, who had published Nabokov and Brodsky for the first time, were not interested in young writers. It was quite understandable, therefore, that our energies went into discovering new writers. And very soon the two first women appeared in Vavilon: the Petersburg prose-writer Marina Sazonova and the Moscow poet Olga Zondberg. These key figures of the early Vavilon represented two very different concepts of women's writing. The prose of Sazonova was experimental, multivoiced, disruptive of gender stereotypes (her story "Triptikh" [Triptych] of the early 90s remains to this day the most distinctive example of Russian lesbian prose). Zondberg's poetry, on the contrary, startled with its systematic rejection of any kind of artificiality or affectation, a clearly focused intimacy, a tendency to preserve all the elements of traditional Russian verse, investing it, however, with a uniquely individual emotionality. With time this archetype of woman as conserver of traditions became too restrictive for Zondberg. She migrated from poetry to prose, bidding the former farewell with the graceful cycle "Seven Hours One Minute," which exhibited a brilliant mastery of modernist literary devices and a modernist view of the world. Zondberg's poetry of the early 90s became for the young literary generation one of the most significant experiments in the interpretation of their relationship to the poetic tradition.

Gradually acquiring new creative energy, the Vavilon circle, about 1991, felt confident enough to launch an All-Union competition for young poets. An extensive advertising campaign and a jury consisting of such prominent writers as Yury Levitansky, Aleksandr Kushner, Viktor Krivulin, and Ivan Zhdanov encouraged a whole range of young poets to compete. At the poetry festival which concluded the competition, the focus of attention was the youngest participant, the fifteen-year-old Petersburg poet Polina Barskova, whose sensual, somber verse recalled the French "poètes maudits." The late Soviet period knew many female infant prodigies who did not fulfill their early promise. Strength of character, professional training in philology, and intensive creative and personal links with other prominent young writers protected Barskova from such a fate. The Barskova of today is an acknowledged poet, her juvenile misanthropy having settled into a mature stoicism, the occasional decorativeness having transformed itself into a mercilessly precise description of reality on both sides of the ocean—in St. Petersburg and in California, the two localities where Barskova leads her life. Barskova's two most recent books appeared in one of the most prestigious Russian poetry series, published by the Pushkin Fund publishing house—but it was Vavilon that initiated all this, in 1993, with a booklet by Barskova (together with a collection by another celebrated Vavilon author, Nikolay Zviagintsev).

Not finding anyone in Russia ready to help the young poetry with money, I turned to the well-known scholar Valentina Polukhina, whom I had met a few years previously at the first Petersburg Conference on Brodsky. The $30 that she sent was at that time sufficient to enable us to bring out the first two books of our publishing house (ARGO-RISK). Ten years later, we have published over 150 collections, mainly of poetry (along with the young writers, under the ARGO-RISK imprint have appeared acknowledged masters of Russian verse, including Dmitry A. Prigov, Genrikh Sapgir, Viktor Krivulin, Nina Iskrenko, and Svetlana Kekova).

In the mid 90s, Russian literary life gradually became less agitated, and traditional publishers began to pay attention to young writers—often, unfortunately, to those who were more familiar, somewhat resembling their older colleagues. Sometimes, however, they were surprised: poetics, seemingly quite innocent, turned out to be explosive and apt to take unexpected turns. So it was with Mariya Stepanova, who appeared in Vavilon after being published in *Yunost* and *Znamia*. Stepanova's début was distinguished by brilliant poetic technique and a purity of style, behind all of which stood the shade of Akhmatova, to whose early portraits Stepanova bore a resemblance. Progress along this route would virtually have assured Stepanova of success with the reading public and with the critics, but she chose another and far riskier strategy. Each publication produced something unexpected. At times she engaged in a dialogue with the Russian tradition, with the archaic language and poetry of the eighteenth century; at others she introduced casual contemporary diction, close to slang, into a classical stanza reminiscent of Catullus. At one time, in a lyric miniature, she reached the heights of estrangement, observing the sufferings of the spirit and the body from some point of passionless elevation; at another, a sonnet cycle looked like total parody, aimed partially at Brodsky's famous sequence of twenty sonnets but mainly at his many imitators, also attempting this difficult form. Her text was suddenly invested with genuine, penetrating lyricism. In some texts Stepanova hovers on the edge of misogyny; thus, she is true to her conviction that the artist must be many-sided, Protean.

The end of the 90s was a time in which new literary organizations came into being. Poetry turned from the problematical customary path, "from journal to book," to the oral presentation of texts in literary clubs and via mass accessibility on the Internet. In both cases the youngest generation could hardly fail to have a head start: the literary club Avtornik was established in late 1996, under the aegis of Vavilon. Since then, young authors not only appear each week but invite literary individuals of all generations. So a picture of contemporary literature from the standpoint of the young generation has emerged. Similarly significant is the Internet anthology of contemporary Russian literature *www.vavilon.ru*, which was inaugurated in autumn 1997 and today includes a vast array of contemporary writing. At the same time the Internet led to an influx of many talented new authors into Vavilon—and here a particularly characteristic and significant figure is Linor Goralik, who made her début on the Internet initially with her early poems and later with strikingly audacious social and political commentary (including material on sexual problems, unparalleled for its frankness and in-depth treatment). Later on the Vavilon website she contributed texts which were on the border between verse and prose, broaching almost all the painful and taboo cultural topics, especially those relating to female sexuality and interaction between the Russian and Jewish peoples.

The start of the new millennium was marked for Vavilon by the initiation of a fruitful rivalry with the young writers prize "Debiut," the first such award to have been established in Russia. The first winner, in 2000, was the present manager of the Vavilon project, poet and prose-writer Danila Davydov. Young Russian writers cannot now complain of a lack of interest in their work. This coincides with the appearance on the literary scene of a whole pleiad of talented poets born after 1978, most of them female. The latter have something in common which encourages one to call them "angry young women." The forerunner of this poetics, the worldview proclaimed by these writers, is the scarcely older Anna Górenko—a rising star of Russian poetry in Israel, who died of drug abuse at the age of twenty-seven and whose work has only now become accessible to Russian readers. Independently of Gorenko, in Russia, Moscow authors Elena Kostyleva, Irina Shostakovskaya, and Kseniya Marennikova as well as representatives of the new wave of Ural Poetry—Elena Suntsova, Natalya Starodubtseva, and others—also subscribed to this poetics. The leitmotiv of their work is a tendency to convey the fragmented consciousness of the youthful writer of today, swamped by all kinds of information, hardly able to achieve or retain self-awareness. Against the background of such perceptions, love is experienced as extremely painful, traumatic, the high price demanded of the individual wishing to acquire wholeness and purposefulness. This poetry does not make easy reading: the disintegration of syntactic connections, unpredictable associational moves, abundant intertextuality—not so much quotations from classical poetry as fragments of information that make up the background to contemporary life (advertising slogans, pop lyrics, items of news footage). At its best, however, this writing does possess a striking authenticity.

In its fifteen years of existence the Vavilon project has essentially fulfilled its task: today the young literary generation (from very young, twenty-year-old authors) forms an inalienable part of the literary landscape. Critics and publishers have to reckon with it, and so, above all, does the reading public. Each year, women's voices ring out more clearly in its midst.

Translated by Daniel Weissbort

BIBLIOGRAPHY

VALENTINA POLUKHINA AND DMITRY KUZMIN

Our bibliography does not aim to present a comprehensive list of writings and publications by women poets. It is more specialized and, we feel, more useful than that, because it includes the most significant poets of the old generation and the most outstanding young writers, likely, in general critical estimation, to be central figures in the future.

We have included only publications in Russian and English. To facilitate use, anthologies and periodical publications are listed alphabetically and include the date and place of publication. The publication date of specific poems is not always provided, because some journals are numbered continuously and can be identified not by the date of publication but by the issue number. In most cases the poet's date of birth is given, but in a few instances we were unable to provide this information, because poets declined to furnish it. Where two places are given after the name of the poet, the first is the place of birth, and the second is the place of current residence. Where three places are given, the second is the place of residence before the current one.

ACKNOWLEDGMENTS

Additional names and information about some authors were proposed by Ivan Akhmetev, Tatyana Milova, Darya Sukhovey, and Yury Tsaplin.

ANTHOLOGIES

100 let poezii Primorya. Vladivostok, 1998.

Against Forgetting: Twentieth-Century Poetry of Witness. Ed. Carolyn Forche. New York/London, 1995.

An Anthology of Russian Women's Writing, 1977–1992. Ed. Catriona Kelly. Oxford, 1994.

Antologiya "Dvoetochiya." Ed. Nega Grezina. Jerusalem, 2000.

Antologiya poezii russkogo zarubezhya, 1920–1990. Ed. Evgeny Vitkovsky. Moscow, 1997.

Antologiya russkogo verlibra. Ed. Karen Dzhangirov. Moscow, 1991.

Antologiya: Sovremennaya uralskaya poeziya (1997–2003). Ed. Vitaly Kalpidi. Cheliabinsk, 2003.

Antologiya sovremennoi russkoi poezii tretei volny emigratsii. Ed. Aleksandr Glezer and Sergey Petrunis. Paris/New York, 1986.

Antologiya sovremennoi russkoi poezii Ukrainy. Ed. Mikhail Krasikov. Kharkov, 1998.

The Blue Lagoon Anthology. Ed. Konstantin Kuzminsky and Grigory Kovalev. 9 vols. Newtonville, Mass., 1980–1986.

Child of Europe: A New Anthology of East European Poetry. Ed. Michael March. London, 1990.

Contemporary Russian Poetry. Ed. and tr. Gerald S. Smith. Bloomington and Indianapolis, 1993.

Crossing Centuries: The New Generation in Russian Poetry. Ed. John High et al. Jersey City, N.J., 2000.

Deviat izmerenii: Antologiya noveishei russkoi poezii. Ed. Ilya Kukulin. Moscow, 2004.

Dictionary of Russian Women Writers. Ed. Marina Ledkovsky, Charlotte Rosenthal, and Mary Zirin. London, 1994.

Dikoe pole: Stikhi russkikh poetov Ukrainy kontsa XX veka. Vol. 1. Ed. Andrey Dmitriev, Irina Evsa, and Stanislav Minakov. Kharkov, 2000.

A Double Rainbow/Dvoinaya raduga. Ed. Marat Akchurin. Moscow, 1988.

Gorod-Tekst v stikhakh peterburgskikh poetov. Ed. Olga Beshenkovskaya. Munich, 2002.

Grazhdane nochi: Neizvestnaya Rossiya. Ed. Olga Chugay. 2 vols. Moscow, 1991.

In the Grip of Strange Thoughts: Russian Poetry in a New Era. Ed. J. Kates. Brookline, USA/Newcastle upon Tyne, UK, 1999.

I vsiakie: Antologiya noveishei poezii. Holyoke, Mass., 1993.

Krug. Ed. Boris Ivanov and Yury Novikov. Leningrad, 1985.

Legko byt' iskrennim: Po sledam IX festivalia verlibra. Ed. Dmitry Kuzmin. Moscow, 2002.

Molodaya poeziya 89. Ed. Arkady Tiurin. Moscow, 1989.

Nestolichnaya literatura: Poeziya i proza regionov Rossii. Ed. Dmitry Kuzmin. Moscow, 2001.

Nezamechennaya zemlia. Ed. Valery Shubinsky and Igor Vishnevetsky. Moscow/St. Petersburg, 1991.

Orientatsiya na mestnosti. Ed. Margarita Shklovskaya. Jerusalem, 2002.

Poet for Poet. Ed. Richard McKane. London, 1998.

The Poetry of Perestroika. Ed. Peter Mortimer and S. J. Litherland. Newcastle, 1991.

Poeziya bezmolviya. Ed. Anatoly Kudriavitsky. Moscow, 1999.

Poeziya vtoroi poloviny XX veka. Ed. Ivan Akhmetev and Mikhail Sheinker. Moscow, 2002.

Poryv: Sbornik stikhov—Novye imena. Moscow, 1989.

Pozdnie peterburzhtsy. Ed. Vladimir Toporov. St. Petersburg, 1995.

Reference Guide to Russian Literature. Ed. Neil Cornwell. London/Chicago, 1998.

Russian Poetry: The Modern Period. Ed. John Glad and Daniel Weissbort. Iowa City, 1978.

Russian Women Poets. Ed. Daniel Weissbort and Valentina Polukhina. *Modern Poetry in Translation* 20. London, 2002.

Russian Women Writers. Vol. 2. Ed. Christine D. Tomei. New York/London, 1999.

Russkaya poeziya: XX vek. Ed. Vladimir Kostrov and Gennady Krasnikov. Moscow, 1999.

Samizdat veka. Ed. Genrikh Sapgir (poetry section). Moscow/Minsk, 1997.

Samoe vygodnoe zaniatie: Po sledam X festivalia verlibra. Ed. Dmitry Kuzmin. Moscow, 2003.

Skopus-2. Ed. Margarita Shklovskaya. Jerusalem, 1990.

Sovremennaya uralskaya poeziya. Ed. Vitaly Kalpidi. Cheliabinsk, 1996.

Sovremennye russkie poety: Spravochnik-antologiya. Ed. V. V. Agenosov and K. N. Ankudinov. Moscow, 1998.

Strofy veka. Ed. Evgeny Evtushenko. Moscow, 1995.

Ten Russian Poets: Surviving the Twentieth Century. Ed. Richard McKane. London, 2003.

Third Wave: The New Russian Poetry. Ed. Kent Johnson and S. M. Ashby. Ann Arbor, 1992.

Three Russian Poets. Tr. Elaine Feinstein. Manchester, 1979.

To vremia—eti golosa: Leningrad: Poety "Ottepeli." Ed. Maya Borisova. Leningrad, 1990.

Twentieth-Century Russian Poetry. Ed. John Glad and Daniel Weissbort. Iowa City, 1992.

20th-Century Russian Poetry: Silver and Steel. Selected, with an introduction, by Yevgeny Yevtushenko. Ed. Albert Todd and Max Hayward. New York, 1993.

Vremia Ch: Stikhi o Chechne i ne tolko. Ed. Nikolay Vinnik. Moscow, 2001.

A Will and a Way. Ed. Natasha Petrova and Arch Tait. Glas, no. 13. Moscow and Birmingham, UK, 1996.

PERIODICALS

22 (Tel Aviv); *Absinthe* (Detroit); *Arion* (Moscow); *Ars-Interpres* (New York / Moscow/Stockholm); *Avrora* (St. Petersburg); *Avtornik* (Moscow); *Chelovek i priroda* (Moscow); *Chernovik* (Fair Lawn, USA / Moscow); *Collegium* (Kiev); *Den i noch* (Krasnoyarsk); *Den poezii* (Leningrad); *Den poezii* (Moscow); *Dirizhabl* (Nizhnii Novgorod); *Druzhba narodov* (Moscow); *Dvoetochie* (Jerusalem); *Ekho* (Paris); *Grani* (Frankfurt / Moscow); *Ierusalimskii zhurnal* (Jerusalem); *Istoki* (Moscow); *Kolokol* (London); *Kommentarii* (Moscow/St. Petersburg); *Kontinent* (Paris / Moscow); *Kreshchatik* (Heringhausen, Germany); *Literaturnoe obozrenie* (Moscow); *Macguffin* (Livonia, Mich.); *Mitin zhurnal* (St. Petersburg / Tver); *Mnogotochie* (Donetsk); *Narod i zemlia* (Jerusalem); *Nash sovremennik* (Moscow); *Nemiga* (Minsk); *Nesovremennye zapiski* (Cheliabinsk); *Neva* (St. Petersburg); *Novaya yunost* (Moscow); *Novoe literaturnoe obozrenie* (Moscow); *Novyi mir* (Moscow); *Novyi zhurnal* (New York); *Obitaemyi ostrov* (Jerusalem); *Odessa* (Odessa); *Okrestnosti* (Moscow); *Oktiabr* (Moscow); *Petropol* (St. Petersburg); *Poberezhye* (Philadelphia); *Poetry* (London); *Poeziya* (Moscow); *Polden* (St. Petersburg); *Poslednii ekzempliar* (Saratov); *Postscriptum* (St. Petersburg); *Potomac Review* (Port Tobacco, Md.); *Predlog* (Moscow); *Raduga* (Kiev); *RISK* (Moscow); *Rodnik* (Riga); *Rubezh* (Vladivostok); *Seraya loshad* (Vladivostok / Moscow); *Slovo/ Word* (New York / Moscow); *Soglasie* (Moscow); *Solnechnoe spletenie* (Jerusalem); *Solo* (Moscow); *Soty* (Kiev); *©oyuz pisatelei* (Kharkov); *Stetoskop* (Paris); *Strelets* (New York / Paris / London); *Sumerki* (St. Petersburg); *Tallinn* (Tallinn); *Targum* (Moscow); *Teplyi stan* (Moscow); *Triton* (Moscow); *Ulov* (Moscow); *Ural* (Ekaterinburg); *Uralskaya nov'* (Cheliabinsk); *Urbi* (Nizhnii Novgorod/St. Petersburg); *Vavilon* (Moscow); *Vestnik Evropy* (Moscow); *Vestnik molodoi literatury* (Moscow); *Vestnik novoi literatury* (St. Petersburg); *Vestnik: Russian-American Magazine* (Baltimore, USA); *Volga* (Saratov); *Vremia i my* (New York); *Vsemirnye odesskie novosti* (Odessa); *Vyshgorod* (Tallinn); *Zerkalo* (Tel Aviv); *Zerkalo zagadok* (Berlin); *Zhurnal stikhov* (St. Petersburg); *Znamia* (Moscow); *Zvezda* (St. Petersburg); *Zvezda Vostoka* (Tashkent).

ALMANACS

XXI poet (Moscow, 2003); *24 poeta i 2 komissara* (St. Petersburg, 1994); *Almanakh-99 Kluba russkikh pisatelei* (New York, 1999); *Anatomiya angela* (Moscow, 2002); *Chernym po belomu* (Moscow, 2002); *Cross Current* (New York); *Deribasovskaya-Reshilevskaya* (Odessa); *Dom s khimerami* (Kiev, 2000); *Elka dlia menia* (Moscow, 1992); *Enter 2000* (Donetsk, 2001); *Ierusalimskii poeticheskii almanakh* (Jerusalem, 1993); *Indeks-2* (Moscow, 1993); *Iz arkhiva "Novoi literaturnoi gazety"* (Moscow, 1997); *Kamera khraneniya* (St. Petersburg/Frankfurt); *Kliuch* (St. Petersburg, 1995); *Laterna Magica* (Moscow, 1990); *Molodaya poeziya* (Moscow); *Molodoi Leningrad 89* (Leningrad, 1989); *Molodye poety Rossii* (Moscow, 2003); *Oboinyi gvozdik v grob moskovskogo romanticheskogo kontseptualizma* (Moscow, 1998); *Plotnost ozhidanii* (Moscow, 2001); *Poluostrov* (Moscow, 1997); *Remissionery* (St. Petersburg, 2002); *Russkoe pole eksperimentov* (Moscow, 1994); *Salt* (Cambridge); *Skladchina* (Omsk, 1996); *Slovo/Word* (New York); *Vstrechi* (Philadelphia).

NEWSPAPERS

AKT (St. Petersburg); *Gumanitarnyi fond* (*GF*) (Moscow); *Literaturnaya gazeta* (Moscow); *Novaya literaturnaya gazeta* (Moscow); *Russkaya mysl* (Paris).

WEBSITES

Biblioteka Moshkova, http://lib.ru/
Lavka yazykov, http://www.vladivostok.com/Speaking_In_Tongues/
Literaturnyi ariergard, http://poetry.liter.net/
Liter.Net, http://www.liter.net/
Mitin zhurnal, http://www.mitin.com/
Molodaya russkaya literatura, http://vernitski.narod.ru/
Neofitsialnaya poeziya, http://www.rvb.ru/np/
Novaya Kamera Khraneniya, http://www.newkamera.de/
Opushka, http://www.opushka.spb.ru/
Ostrakon, http://members.tripod.com/~barashw/
Poberezhye, http://www.thecoastmagazine.org/
Poeziya Moskovskogo Universiteta, http://www.poesis.ru/poeti-poezia/
Russkaya poeziya 60-kh, http://www.ruthenia.ru/60s/
Seraya loshad, http://www.gif.ru/greyhorse/
Setevaya slovesnost, http://www.litera.ru/slova/
Solnechnoe spletenie, http://www.plexus.org.il/
Sovremennaya russkaya literatura s V. Kuritsynym, http://www.guelman.ru/slava/
Soyuz pisatelei, http://sp-issues.narod.ru/
Stikhiya, http://www.litera.ru/stixiya/authors/
Stranitsa Alexandra Levina, http://www.levin.rinet.ru/FRIENDS/
VAVILON: Sovremennaya russkaya literatura, http://www.vavilon.ru/
Zhurnalnyi zal, http://magazines.russ.ru/

An asterisk before a name indicates the poet's inclusion in this anthology.
A: = Anthologies; B: = Books; P: = Periodicals and almanacs; E: = In English;
I: = Internet (the validity of all sites has been checked as of November 2004)

Abelskaya, Natalya (1957, St. Petersburg)

A: *Pozdnie peterburzhtsy*; B: *Avtorskii list* (1995); P: *Kliuch*; *Molodoi Leningrad 89*

Ainova, Tatyana (Kiev)

A: *Antologiya sovremennoi russkoi poezii Ukrainy*; B: *Vmesto menia* (2000);
P: *Kreshchatik 4*; I: http://www.litera.ru/slova/ainova/; http://www.poezia.ru/
user.php?uname=ainova

*Akhmadulina, Bella (1937, Moscow)

A: *Russkaya poeziya: XX vek*; *Strofy veka*; *Poeziya vtoroi poloviny XX veka*; B: *Skazka
o dozhde* (1962, 1975); *Stikhi* (1962); *Struna* (1962); *Moya rodoslovnaya* (1964);
Prikliuchenie v antikvarnom magazine (1967); *Oznob* (1968); *Uroki muzyki* (1969);
Stikhi (1975); *Metel* (1977); *Sny o Gruzii* (1977); *Svecha* (1977); *Taina* (1983); *Sad*
(1987); *Izbrannoe* (1988); *Stikhotvoreniya* (1988); *Poberezhye* (1991); *Larets i
kliuch* (1994); *Griada kamnei* (1995); *Shum tishiny* (1995); *Stikhotvoreniya* (1995);
Zvukukazuyushchii (1995); *Odnazhdy v dekabre* (1996); *Izbrannye proizvedeniya*, 3
vols. (1997); *Sozertsanie stekliannogo sharika* (1997); *Druzei moikh prekrasnye cherty*
(1999); *Vozle elki: Kniga novykh stikhotvorenii* (1999); *Stikhotvoreniya: Esse* (2000);
Vlechet menia starinnyi slog (2000); P: *Vremia i my 96*; *Oktiabr* (1988) 3; *Znamia*
(1993) 10, (1999) 7, (2001) 1, (2002) 10, (2003) 1, (2004) 1; *Arion* (1995) 2, (1996) 1;
Kontinent 97; *Druzhba narodov* (2000) 10; E: *Fever and Other New Poems* (1969);
A Double Rainbow; *The Garden: New & Selected Poems* (1990); *Twentieth-Century
Russian Poetry*; *Contemporary Russian Poetry*; *An Anthology of Russian Women's
Writing*; *Reference Guide to Russian Literature*; *Russian Women Writers*; *The Poetic
Craft of Bella Akhmadulina* by Sonia Ketchian (1993), *In the Grip of Strange
Thoughts*; *Russian Women Poets*; I: http://www.litera.ru/stixiya/authors/
axmadulina.html; http://lib.ru/POEZIQ/ahmadulina.txt; http://magazines
.russ.ru/authors/a/ahmadulina/

Akselrod, Elena (1932, Minsk/Israel)

B: *Okno na sever* (1976); *Lodka na snegu* (1986); *Stikhi* (1992); *V drugom okne* (1994);
Lirika (1997); P: *Ierusalimskii zhurnal 3*, 10; *Kontinent 111*, 114; I: http://magazines
.russ.ru/authors/a/akselrod/

Akulenko, Natalya (1957, Kiev)

A: *Vremia Ch*; *Samoe vygodnoe zaniatie*; B: *Labirint i drugie stikhotvoreniya* (1995)

Alaverdova, Liana (Baku/New York)

B: *Rifmy* (1997); E: *Russian Women Poets*; I: http://liana.synnegoria.com/

Alchuk (Mikhalchuk), Anna (1955, Moscow)

A: *Samizdat veka*; *Poeziya bezmolviya*; *Vremia Ch*; B: *Dvenadtsat ritmicheskikh
pauz* (1994); *Sov sem* (1994); *Ovols* (1998); *Dvizhenie* (1999); *Slovarevo*
(2000); P: *Chernovik 4*; I: http://www.rvb.ru/np/publication/01text/44/
02alchuk.htm

Alferova, Tatyana (1958, St. Petersburg)

   B: *Stantsiya Gorelovo* (1993); *Ogovorki* (1996); *Perevodnye kartinki* (1999); *P: Neva*
   (1998) 9, (2000) 7, (2001) 11, (2003) 3; *I:* http://litera.ru/slova/alferova/

Andreeva, Galina (1933, Moscow)

   A: Samizdat veka; *P: Novyi mir* (1994) 4; *I:* http://poetry.liter.net/andreeva.html;
   http://rvb.ru/np/publication/02comm/04/01andreeva.htm

Andreeva, Viktoriya (1942–2002, Moscow/USA)

   A: Samizdat veka; *B: Son tverdi* (1986); *Son tverdi* (2002); *I:* http://www.rvb.ru/
   np/publication/01text/32/02andreeva.htm

Andriuts, Valentina (1954, Vladivostok)

   A: Russkaya poeziya: XX vek; *B: Bukhta Svetlaya* (1982); *Toska po lotosu* (1991);
   P: Seraya loshad 3, 4; *I:* http://www.gif.ru/greyhorse/gh4/andriuts4.html

Andrukovich, Polina (1968, Moscow)

   A: Deviat izmerenii; *Legko byt' iskrennim*; *Samoe vygodnoe zaniatie*; *B: Menshe
   na odin golos* (2004); *P: Avtornik* 6, 7, 9, 10, 11; *Vavilon* 7, 8, 9, 10; *Triton* 4;
   I: http://www.vavilon.ru/texts/andrukovicho.html

Anistratova, Irina (Moscow)

   P: GF (1992) 29; *Iz arkhiva "Novoi literaturnoi gazety"*; *I:* http://www.vavilon.ru/
   metatext/nlg-arch/anistratova.html

Anserova, Vera (1958, Donetsk district)

   A: Antologiya russkogo verlibra; *E: Russian Women Poets*

Arefeva, Olga (Moscow)

   B: Kovcheg (1996); *P: Znamia* (1998) 8; *I:* http://www.ark.ru/ins/poems/
   index.html

Argutina, Irina (1963, Cheliabinsk)

   A: Antologiya: Sovremennaya uralskaya poeziya (1997–2003); *B: Svobodnye skitaltsy*
   (1999); *Vremia poit' peski* (2001); *P: Uralskaya nov'* 15; *I:* http://magazines.russ.ru/
   authors/a/argutina/

Arishina, Natalya (Moscow)

   A: Antologiya russkogo verlibra; *Novaya volna* (1991); *B: Ternovnik* (2003);
   P: Novyi mir (1993) 5, (1999) 9; *Soglasie* (1993) 5; *I:* http://magazines.russ.ru/
   authors/a/arishina/

Astafeva, Natalya (1922, Moscow)

   A: Antologiya russkogo verlibra; *Novaya volna* (1991); *B: Devchata* (1959); *Gordost*
   (1961); *V ritme prirody* (1977); *Liubov* (1982); *Zavety* (1989); *Iznutri i vopreki* (1994);
   I: http://magazines.russ.ru/authors/a/astafeva/

Astina, Marina (1972, Moscow/Israel)

   P: Druzhba narodov (1990) 7; *Znamia* (1993) 9; *Okrestnosti* 4

Avvakumova, Mariya (1943, Arkhangelsk/Moscow)

   A: Dvoinaya raduga; *Novaya volna* (1991); *Strofy veka*; *Russkaya poeziya: XX vek*;
   B: Severnye reki (1982); *Zimuyushchie ptitsy* (1984); *Neosedlannye koni* (1986); *Iz
   glubin* (1990); *Nochnye gody* (2000); *P: Ural* (1985) 8; *Novyi mir* (1987) 7, (1989) 2,
   (1991) 10; *Volga* (1988) 6; *Znamia* (1988) 5, (1990) 4; *Nash sovremennik* (1994)
   4 and 10, (1995) 8, (1997) 1, (1998) 7, (2000) 3; *Moskva* (2003) 7 and 8; *E: A Double
   Rainbow*; *20th-Century Russian Poetry*; *Russian Women Poets*

Balalaikina, Yuliya (Saratov)

> A: *Nestolichnaya literatura*; I: http://dk.ufanet.ru/bibl/konkurs/balalaykina01 .htm

Barakhtina, Larisa (1960, Novgorod)

> P: *Kommentarii* 6; I: http://www.opushka.spb.ru/name/barahtina_name .shtml

*Barskova, Polina (1976, St. Petersburg/Berkeley, USA)

> A: *Deviat izmerenii*; B: *Rozhdestvo* (1991); *Rasa brezglivykh* (1994); *Memory* (1996); *Evridei i Orfika* (2000); *Arii* (2001); P: *Plotnost ozhidanii*; *Ulov* 1; *Urbi* 8; *Vavilon* 2, 4, 7, 8, 9, 10; *Zvezda* (2001) 3; *Poberezhye* 11; E: *Crossing Centuries*; *Russian Women Poets*; I: http://www.vavilon.ru/texts/prim/barskovao.html; http://www .sguez.com/za-granizza/polibars.html

Batkhen, Veronika (1974, St. Petersburg/Moscow)

> B: *Shosse Ekkleziastov* (2001); I: http://www.litera.ru/slova/bathen/; http:// www.nikab.narod.ru/

*Bek, Tatyana (1949–2005, Moscow)

> A: *Russkaya poeziya: XX vek*; B: *Skvoreshniki* (1974); *Snegir* (1980); *Smeshannyi les* (1987); *Zamysel* (1987); *Oblaka skvoz derevya* (1997); *Uzor iz treshchin* (2002); P: *Novyi mir* (1992) 2 and 3, (1995) 9, (1997) 1, (1999) 12; *Arion* (1996) 1, (1998) 4 and 9, (1999) 1, (2001) 3; *Zvezda* (1997) 3; *Kontinent* (1999) 101; *Znamia* (2000) 4, (2001) 11, (2003) 5; E: *Dictionary of Russian Women Writers*; *In the Grip of Strange Thoughts*; *Russian Women Poets*; I: http://magazines.russ.ru/authors/b/bek/; http://lib.ru/POEZIQ/BEK_T/

*Belchenko, Natalya (1973, Kiev)

> A: *Antologiya: Sovremennoi russkoi poezii Ukrainy*; *Dikoe pole*; B: *Smotritel sna* (1997); *Tranzit* (1998); *Karman imen* (2002); P: *Mitin zhurnal* 35; *Chernovik* 11; *Chernym po belomu*; *Collegium* (1997) 1; *Soty* 3, 5; *Vavilon* 4, 8, 9, 10; I: http://www.litera.ru/ slova/belchenko/

*Berezovchuk, Larisa (1948, Kiev/St. Petersburg)

> B: *Tsvetenie reliktov* (1997); *Obrechennye na falstart* (1999); P: *Kreshchatik* 14; *Soty* 5; *Mitin zhurnal* 35; E: *Russian Women Poets*; I: http://www.vavilon.ru/texts/prim/ berezovchuko.html

Beshenkovskaya, Olga (1947, St. Petersburg/Germany)

> A: *Krug*; *The Blue Lagoon Anthology*, 5B; *Pozdnie peterburzhtsy*; *Strofy veka*; B: *Peremenchivyi svet* (1987); *Podzemnye tsvety* (1996); *Pesni pyanogo angela* (1999); *Peterburgskii albom* (2003); P: *Den poezii* (Leningrad, 1989); *Molodoi Leningrad* 89; *Kontinent* 65; *Mitin zhurnal* 17; *Literaturnaya gazeta*, 25 March 1992; *Teplyi stan* (1992); *Zvezda* (1992) 3, (2003) 8; *Oktiabr* (1996) 9, (1997) 4, (2001) 6, (2003) 8; *Den poezii* (Moscow, 2000); *Neva* (2001) 5, (2003) 1; *AKT*; E: *20th-Century Russian Poetry*; I: http://magazines.russ.ru/authors/b/beshenkovskaya/

Besprozvannaya, Polina (1951, St. Petersburg)

> A: *Pozdnie peterburzhtsy*; B: *Teni na snegu* (1980); *Smalta* (1984); *Suglinok* (1990); P: *Kliuch*; *AKT*

Bessarabova, Irina (Moscow)

> B: *Neuznannaya zhizn* (1999)

Bialosinskaya, Nina (1923, Moscow)

    B: Moi dorogoi chelovek (1959); *Poslednii sneg* (1978); *P: Kontinent* 64

Bliznetsova, Ina (1958, Orenburg/Leningrad/USA)

    A: Antologiya sovremennoi russkoi poezii tretei volny; *The Blue Lagoon Anthology*, 3A; *B: Dolina tenet* (1988); *Vid na nebo* (1991); *Zhizn ognia* (1995)

Bode, Veronika (1961, Moscow)

    A: Samizdat veka; *B: Dlia sveta i snega* (1995); *Muzyka i bumaga* (1996); *I:* http://www.liter.net/=/Bode/poems.html

Bodrunova, Svetlana (1981, St. Petersburg)

    B: Pesni Peterburga (2000); *Veter v komnatakh* (2001); *P: Vavilon* 10; *I:* http://www.litera.ru/slova/bodrunova/

Bogdanova, Svetlana (1970, Moscow)

    B: Rodstvo s predmetami (2000); *P: Chernovik* 13; *I:* http://www.guelman.ru/slava/writers/bogd9.htm

Bondarenko, Mariya (1973, Vladivostok/Moscow)

    P: Vavilon 8, 9, 10; *Chernym po belomu*; *Seraya loshad* 4; *Avtornik* 2; *Znamia* (2001) 9; *I:* http://magazines.russ.ru/authors/b/bondarenko/; http://www.gif.ru/greyhorse/bondarenko.html

Borinevich, Tatyana (1963, Moscow)

    B: Neletalnost (2001); *Obraz zhizni* (2003); *P: Remissionery*; *I:* http://www.litera.ru/slova/borinevich/

*Boroditskaya, Marina (1954, Moscow)

    A: Molodaya poeziya; *Strofy veka*; *Russkaya poeziya: XX vek*; *B: Ya razdevayu soldata* (1994); *Odinochnoe katanie* (2000); *God loshadi* (2002); *P: Novyi mir* (1994) 11, (1998) 1, (2001) 8, (2003) 11; *Arion* (1998) 4, (2002) 3; *Ierusalimskii zhurnal* (2002) 13; *Novaya yunost* (2003) 5; *Voprosy literatury* (2003) 3; *E: Russian Women Poets*; *Poetry London* (2003) 46; *I:* http://magazines.russ.ru/authors/b/boroditskaya/

*Boyarskikh, Ekaterina (1976, Irkutsk)

    A: Nestolichnaya literatura; *P: Vavilon* 8, 9; *Plotnost ozhidanii*; *E: Russian Women Poets*; *I:* http://www.vavilon.ru/texts/boyarskikh0.html; http://vernitski.narod.ru/boyarskikh.htm

Bukovskaya, Tamara (1947, St. Petersburg)

    A: Samizdat veka; *Pozdnie peterburzhtsy*; *B: Otchayanie i nadezhda* (1991); *Svidetelstvo ochevidtsa* (1999); *Neveshchestvennoe dokazatelstvo* (2002); *P: Zvezda* (2001) 4; *AKT*; *Kolokol* (2002) 4

Bushueva, Katia (1973, Ekaterinburg)

    A: Sovremennaya uralskaya poeziya

*Bykova, Zinaida (Ukraine, Chernovtsy)

    A: Legko byt' iskrennim; *B: Nezrimye ptitsy* (2000); *P: Druzhba narodov* (1997) 6, (1998) 7, (1999) 12, (2003) 3; *Arion* (1998) 4, (2003) 1; *Znamia* (1998), 4; *I:* http://magazines.russ.ru/authors/b/bykova/

Bystrova, Mariya (Pskov)

    A: Nestolichnaya literatura; *B: Neproverennye dannye* (1999)

Chastikova, Elvira (Obninsk, Kaluga district)

    A: Antologiya russkogo verlibra; *B: Dva gorizonta* (1990); *Triada* (2003)

Chebrova, Tatyana (Kiev)

B: Vverkh po techeniyu (1994); *I:* http://poetry.liter.net/mar01chb.html

Cheredeeva, Lidiya (1971, Vladivostok/St. Petersburg)

P: Vavilon 9, 10; *Seraya loshad* 4; *I:* http://www.cheredeeva.rbcmail.ru/

Chernavina, Rimma (1949, Moscow)

A: Antologiya russkogo verlibra; B: V pustynnom vremeni (1992); *Barer otdelnosti*
(1994); *P: Arion* (1998) 1, (2000) 2, (2002) 2; *Novaya yunost* (2001) 3; *I:* http://
magazines.russ.ru/authors/c/chernavina/

Chernykh, Natalya (1970, Moscow)

A: Deviat izmerenii; B: Priyut (1996); *Vidy na zhitelstvo* (1997); *Roditelskaya subbota*
(1999); *Tretii golos* (2000); *Tikhii prazdnik* (2002); *P: Avtornik* 11; *Vavilon* 2, 5, 7, 8;
E: Crossing Centuries; I: http://www.vavilon.ru/texts/chernykho.html

Chinakhova, Elena (1971, Donetsk/Australia)

B: Tysiachi otkrovenii (2002); *P: Uralskaya nov'* 13; *I:* http://e4book.spb.ru/

Chizhevskaya, Vera (1946, Obninsk, Kaluga district)

A: Antologiya russkogo verlibra; B: Chekanka (1990); *Makov tsvet* (1996); *Plius ko*
vsemu (1996); *Piatoe vremia goda* (2000); *Koltso gorizonta* (2001); *P: Kreshchatik*
20; *E: Russian Women Poets*

Chizhova, Elena (1957, St. Petersburg)

B: Tragediya Marii Stiuart (1991), *Peterburgskie dushi* (1993); *P: Novyi zhurnal* 179;
E: Dictionary of Russian Women Writers; Anthology of Russian Women's Writing

Chugay, Olga (1944, Moscow)

B: Sudba gliny (1982); *Svetlye storony tmy* (1995)

Chulkova, Svetlana (1958, Moscow)

A: Molodaya poeziya 89; Antologiya russkogo verlibra; Russkaya poeziya: XX vek;
B: Lesgorod (1993); *E: Russian Women Poets*

Chuprina, Evgeniya (1972, Kiev)

B: Sochineniya (1997); *Vid snizu* (2002); *P: Kreshchatik* 1, 2; *Neva* (2001) 6;
I: http://www.litera.ru/slova/chuprina/

Delaland, Nadia (1978, Rostov-na-Donu)

A: Nestolichnaya literatura; B: Eto Vam, Doktor (2000); *Kiziak mestnykh yakov*
(2002); *P: XXI poet; I:* http://ndelaland.narod.ru/

Delfinova, Dina (Perm)

P: Vavilon 8, 9; *Ural* (2001) 2

*Dengina, Svetlana (1968, Samara)

A: Antologiya russkogo verlibra; B: Osennee ravnodenstvie (1992); *E: Russian Women*
Poets

Denisova, Olga (1944, Kiev/Germany)

A: The Blue Lagoon Anthology, 3B; *P: Arion* (1995) 2; *Dom s khimerami; Chernovik* 1

*Derieva, Regina (1949, Kazakhstan/Israel/Sweden)

A: Antologiya russkogo verlibra; B: Pocherk (1978); *Uzel zhizni* (1980); *Po pervoputku*
(1985); *Poseshchenie* (1992); *Otsutstvie* (1993); *Molitva dnia* (1994); *Zimnie lektsii*
dlia terroristov (1997); *De Profundis* (1998); *Begloe prostranstvo* (2001); *Poslednii*
ostrov (2002); *P: Kreshchatik* 19; *Zvezda* (2001) 4, (2003) 9; *Poberezhye* 11; *Den i*
noch (2002) 5/6; *Novyi zhurnal* (2002) 229; *Oktiabr* (2003) 8; *Stetoskop* (2003) 35;

Vstrechi (2003) 27; *E: The Inland Sea and Other Poems* (1998), *In Commemoration of Monument* (1999); *Instructions for Silence* (1999); *Cross Current* (2002) 52; *Salt* (2002) 15; *Russian Women Poets*; *Ars-Interpres* (2003) 1; *I:* http://www.geocities .com/pilgrim_star_1999/Absence.html; http://medlem.spray.se/hylaea/ authors.ru.r.d.html

Diagileva, Yanka (1966–1991, Novosibirsk)
    P: Russkoe pole eksperimentov; *E: Crossing Centuries*; *I:* http://www.farpost.com/ music/yanka/; http://www.grob-records.go.ru/texts/janka/

Dizhur, Bella (1904, Sverdlovsk/USA)
    P: Znamia (1992) 2; *E: Shadow of the Soul* (1990); *In the Grip of Strange Thoughts*

Dobrushina, Irina (1928, Moscow)
    A: Samizdat veka; *B: Koliuchii kust* (1996); *P: Arion* (1994) 3; *I:* http://www.poesis .ru/poeti-poezia/dobrushina/biograph.htm

Dobrynina, Viktoriya (1950, Kharkov)
    A: Antologiya sovremennoi russkoi poezii Ukrainy; *Dikoe pole*; *B: Svetlym-svetlo* (1993); *Vas liubiashchei naveki ostayus* (1993); *Vechernie temy* (2002)

*Dolia, Marina (1951, Kiev)
    B: Sirotskie pesni (1998); *Mezhzerkalye* (1999); *Znaki na stene: Concerto Grosso: Pamiati I. Brodskogo* (2000); *U vorot* (2001); *P: Kreshchatik* 3; *E: Russian Women Poets*; *I:* http://www.vladivostok.com/Speaking_In_Tongues/marina.html

Dolina, Veronika (1956, Moscow)
    A: Strofy veka; *Russkaya poeziya: XX vek*; *B: Ili kot ili ptitsa* (1988); *Moya radost* (1988); *Vozdukhoplavatel* (1989); *Nevingrad* (1993); *Nevingrad: 10 let spustia* (2003)

Dubovskaya, Sofya (1933, St. Petersburg)
    A: Antologiya russkogo verlibra; *B: Sezon chesti* (1997); *Miniatiury* (1998); *Vse bylo krome nas* (2000); *P: Molodoi Leningrad* 89

Dunaevskaya, Elena (1950, St. Petersburg)
    B: Pismo v pustotu (1994); *P: Molodoi Leningrad* 89; *Kontinent* 59; *Zvezda* (1999) 3, (2002) 12; *I:* http://www.opushka.spb.ru/name/dunayevskaya_name.shtml

Dyachenko, Evgeniya (1966, Ekaterinburg)
    A: Nestolichnaya literatura

Efendieva, Di (Estonia)
    B: Stikhotvoreniya (1995); *Stikhotvoreniya* (1997); *Dzhaz dekabria* (2000); *I:* http:// www.litera.ru/slova/efendieva/

Elagina, Elena (1947, St. Petersburg)
    B: Mezhdu Piterom i Leningradom (1995); *Narushenie simmetrii* (1999); *Geliofobiya* (2004); *P: Kontinent* 97; *Neva* (1990) 12, (2003) 7; *Novyi mir* (1996) 7, (1998) 4; *Zvezda* (1996) 1, (2002) 12, (2004) 1; *Arion* (1999) 4; *AKT*; *I:* http://magazines .russ.ru/authors/e/elagina/

Eltang, Elena (St. Petersburg/France/Lithuania)
    B: Stikhi (2003); *P: Znamia* (2002) 11; *I:* http://www.litera.ru/slova/eltang/

*Ermakova, Irina (1951, Kerch/Moscow)
    A: Russkaya poeziya: XX vek; *B: Provintsiya* (1991); *Vinogradnik* (1994); *Stekliannyi sharik* (1998); *Kolybelnaya dlia Odisseya* (2002); *P: Arion* (1996) 3, (1999) 2, (2001)

1, (2002) 2, (2003) 4; *Oktiabr* (1997) 12, (1998) 8, (2003) 3; *Druzhba narodov* (2001)
7; *Novyi mir* (2003) 3; *Ulov* 1; *Voprosy literatury* (2003) 4; *E: Russian Women Poets*;
I: http://www.vavilon.ru/texts/prim/ermakovao.html; http://magazines
.russ.ru/authors/e/ermakova/

Ermolaeva, Olga (1947, Novokuznetsk/Moscow)

    A: Russkaya poeziya: XX vek; *B: Podmasterye* (1966); *Nastasya* (1978); *Tovarniak*
(1984); *Yuryev den* (1988); *Aniutiny glazki* (1999); *P: Novyi mir* (1988) 11, (1991) 7,
(1996) 10, (1997) 11, (1999) 3; (2003) 7; *Soglasie* (1993) 5; *E: A Double Rainbow*;
I: http://magazines.russ.ru/authors/e/ermolaeva/

*Ermoshina, Galina (1962, Samara)

    A: Antologiya russkogo verlibra; *Nestolichnaya literatura*; *B: Okno dozhdia* (1990),
Oklik (1993), *Vremia gorod* (1994); *P: Chernovik* 13; *E: Crossing Centuries*; *Russian
Women Poets*; *I:* http://magazines.russ.ru/authors/e/ermoshina/

Evsa, Irina (1956, Kharkov)

    A: Dikoe pole; *Antologiya sovremennoi russkoi poezii Ukrainy*; *B: Otzvuk* (1976);
Dykhanie (1978); *Avgust* (1985); *Den sedmoi* (1985); *Sad* (1986); *Den sedmoi* (1992);
Izgnanie iz raya (1995); *Navernoe, snilos . . .* (1999); *Lodka na fayanse* (2000); *Opis
imushchestva* (2003); *P: Raduga* (2001) 11, 12, (2003) 5; *Kreshchatik* (2003) 5;
©*oyuz pisatelei* (2003) 5; *I:* http://kharkov.vbelous.net/iambus/evsa.htm;
http://sp-issues.narod.ru/5/evsa.htm

*Ezrokhi, Zoya (1946, St. Petersburg)

    A: Pozdnie peterburzhtsy; *B: Koshachya perepiska* (1993); *Shestoi etazh* (1995); *Na
vsiakii sluchai* (2002); *P: Molodoi Leningrad 89*; *Kontinent* 53; *Den poezii* (Leningrad,
1989); *Kreshchatik* 12; *E: Dictionary of Russian Women Writers*; *Russian Women
Poets*; *I:* http://ok.zhitinsky.spb.ru/ezrohi/O_SEBE.HTM

*Fanailova, Elena (1962, Voronezh/Moscow)

    A: Vremia Ch; *B: Puteshestvie* (1994); *Teatralnyi roman* (1999); *S osobym tsinizmom*
(2000); *Transilvaniya bespokoit* (2002); *P: Rodnik* (1990, 1991, 1992); *Mitin zhurnal*
42, 49; *Novoe literaturnoe obozrenie* 62; *Znamia* (1995, 1996) 1, (1997, 1998, 1999) 3,
(2000) 1, (2002) 1, (2004) 1 and 6; *Arion* (1996) 3; *Zerkalo*; *Chernym po belomu*;
E: Russian Women Poets; *I:* http://www.vavilon.ru/texts/fanailovao.html

FC, Olga (Ivanovo)

    A: Nestolichnaya literatura; *Samoe vygodnoe zaniatie*; *P: Triton* 2

*Gabrielian, Nina (1953, Moscow)

    A: Molodye golosa (1981); *Antologiya russkogo verlibra*; *Russkaya poeziya: XX vek*;
B: Trostnikovaya dudka (1987); *Zerno granata* (1992); *Khoziain travy* (2002);
P: Arion (1995) 2; *E: Dictionary of Russian Women Writers*; *Russian Women Poets*;
The Master of Grass (2004)

*Galina, Mariya (1958, Odessa/Moscow)

    B: Vizhu svet (1993), *Signalnyi ogon* (1994); *P: Yunost* (1990) 9; *Teplyi stan* (1991);
Arion (1998) 1, (2000) 1 and 4, (2003) 1; *Soty* 5; *Kreshchatik* 11, 20; *Avtornik* 5, 6, 7, 9,
10, 11; *Postscriptum* 5, 7; *Ulov* 2; *Polden* (2003) 3; *E: Russian Women Poets*; *I:* http://
www.vavilon.ru/texts/galinao.html; http://magazines.russ.ru/authors/g/
galina/

Galkina, Natalya (1943, St. Petersburg)

A: Strofy veka; *B: Gorozhanka* (1974); *Zal ozhidaniya* (1984); *Golos iz khora* (1989); *Okkervil* (1990); *Milyi i dorogaya* (1993); *Pogoda na vchera* (1999); *P: Den poezii* (Leningrad, 1989)

Galushko, Tatyana (1937–1988, St. Petersburg)

A: To vremia—eti golosa; *B: Monolog* (1966); *Ravnodenstvie* (1971); *Obraz* (1981); *Drevo vremeni* (1988); *Zhizn: Poeziya: Pushkin* (2003)

Gamper, Galina (1938, St. Petersburg)

A: Strofy veka; *B: Kryshi* (1965); *Tochka kasaniya* (1970); *Krylo* (1977); *Zaklinanie* (1983); *Na iskhode leta* (1987); *Dukh sam sebe otchizna* (1996); *I v Novom svete dozhd i v Starom svete . . .* (1998); *Chto iz togo, chto lestnitsa kruta . . .* (2002); *P: Novyi mir* (1993) 11; *Arion* (2001) 1; *Zvezda* (2002) 6; *E: The Glass Zoo* (1998); *I:* http://magazines.russ.ru/authors/g/gamper/

Garrido, Alex (1963, Kaliningrad)

A: Nestolichnaya literatura; *B: Soprano* (2003); *I:* http://zhurnal.lib.ru/g/garrido_a/versos-1.shtml; http://poetry.liter.net/augoogar.html; http://www.enet.ru/~writers/garrido/stixi.html

*Gatina, Dina (1981, Engels, Saratov district)

A: Deviat izmerenii; *Legko byt' iskrennim*; *Samoe vygodnoe zaniatie*; *P: Vavilon* 9, 10; *Avtornik* 7, 9, 10; *Chernym po belomu*; *Anatomiya angela*; *I:* http://www.vavilon.ru/texts/gatinao.html

Gatovskaya, Irina (1956, Kharkov/Germany)

A: Dikoe pole; *B: Okonchanie spektaklia* (1995)

Geide, Marianna (1980, Moscow/Pereslavl-Zalesskii)

A: Deviat izmerenii; *P: Novoe literaturnoe obozrenie* 62; *Arion* (2003) 3; *Ulov* 5; *I:* http://vernitski.narod.ru/heide.htm

Genina, Natalya (Moscow/Germany)

B: Piatyi ugol (1996)

Georgadze, Marina (Moscow/Georgia/New York)

B: Marshrut (1998); *Chernym po belomu* (2002); *P: Poeziya* 56; *Teplyi stan* (1990); *Novyi zhurnal* 183, 184–185, 188, 190–191, 194; *Postscriptum* 6; *Kontekst-9* 5; *Slovo/Word* 31–32; *I:* http://www.niworld.ru/poezia/georgadze/georg.htm

*Glazova, Anna (1973, Moscow/Chicago)

A: Deviat izmerenii; *B: Pust' i voda* (2003); *P: Vavilon* 6, 7; *Chernovik* 14; *Stetoskop* 32; *Kommentarii* 21; *E: Russian Women Poets*; *I:* http://www.vladivostok.com/Speaking_In_Tongues/anna.htm

Goldenberg, Marina (1978, Cheliabinsk district/Moscow)

A: Antologiya: Sovremennaya uralskaya poeziya (1997–2003); *I:* http://magazines.russ.ru/authors/g/goldenberg/

Golosova, Evgeniya (1974, St. Petersburg)

B: Na trogatelnoi ploshchadi Vosstaniya (1999); *Iz lichnoi pochty* (2001); *I:* http://www.litera.ru/slova/golosova/

*Goralik, Linor (1975, Ukraine/Israel/Moscow)

A: Deviat izmerenii; *B: Tsitatnik* (1999); *Ne mestnye* (prose poetry, 2003); *P: Avtornik* 9, 10, 11; *Vavilon* 10; *I:* http://www.vavilon.ru/texts/goraliko.html

*Gorbanevskaya, Natalya (1936, Moscow/Paris)

   *A: Antologiya sovremennoi russkoi poezii tretei volny emigratsii; Nezamechennaya
   zemlia; Sovremennye russkie poety; Poeziya vtoroi poloviny XX veka; B: Stikhi* (1969);
   Poberezhye: Stikhi (1973); *Tri tetradi stikhotvorenii* (1975); *Pereletaya snezhnuyu
   granitsu* (1979); *Angel dereviannyi* (1982); *Chuzhie kamni: Stikhi 1979–1982* (1983);
   Gde i kogda: Stikhi 1983–1985 (1985); *Peremennaya oblachnost* (1985); *Tsvet
   vereska* (1993); *Nabor* (1996); *Ne spi na zakate: Izbrannaya lirika* (1996); *Kto o
   chem poet* (1998); *13 vosmistishii . . .* (2000); *Poslednie stikhi togo veka* (2001);
   *Russko-russkii razgovor: Izbrannye stikhotvoreniya: Poema bez poemy: Novaya
   kniga stikhov* (2003); *P: Znamia* (1966) 6, (1990) 8; *Oktiabr* (1990) 7, (1992) 11,
   (1994) 41/42, (1995) 2; *Novyi mir* (1992) 11; *Kontinent* 69, 114; *Zvezda* (1994) 7,
   (2003) 6; *Arion* (1997) 3; *Neva* (2001) 5; *Kamera khraneniya* 2, 3, 4; *Ulov* 3;
   Russkaya mysl (2002) 4411; *Novyi zhurnal* 196; *Slovo/Word* (2003) 38/39;
   Ierusalimskii zhurnal (2004) 17; *E: Selected Poems* (1972); *The Other Voices* (1976);
   Russian Poetry: The Modern Period; Post-War Russian Poetry (1993); *Against
   Forgetting; Twentieth-Century Russian Poetry; Contemporary Russian Poetry;
   Reference Guide to Russian Literature; Russian Women Writers; 20th-Century
   Russian Poetry; Russian Women Poets; I:* http://www.vavilon.ru/texts/
   gorbanevsk/

Gorbovskaya, Ekaterina (1964, Moscow/London)

   A: Molodaya poeziya 89; Russkaya poeziya: XX vek; B: Pervyi bal (1980); *Sredi kukol i
   sobak* (1990)

*Gorenko (Karpa), Anna (1972–1999, Moldova/Israel)

   A: Deviat izmerenii; B: Maloe sobranie (2000); *Stikhi* (2000); *Prazdnik nespelogo
   khleba* (2003); *P: Solnechnoe spletenie* 2, 4/5, 6, 9; *I:* http://www.nlo.magazine.ru/
   bookseller/gotov/gorenko.html

*Gorlanova, Nina (1947, Perm)

   P: Znamia (1994) 3, (2001) 2; *Volga* (1995) 2/3; *Arion* (1999) 4, (2003) 4; *Novyi mir*
   (1999) 11; *E: Russian Women Poets*

Grebennikova, Olga (Uzbekistan/New York)

   A: Deviat izmerenii; P: Vavilon 7; *24 poeta i 2 komissara; Zvezda Vostoka,* (1993) 3;
   Mitin zhurnal 57; *I:* http://library.ferghana.ru/almanac/pers/olga.htm

Grechko, Olga (1947–1998, Penza/Moscow)

   A: Antologiya russkogo verlibra; Russkaya poeziya: XX vek; B: Ya shagayu po zemle
   (1983); *Zemli i neba krug* (1986); *Predosterezhenie* (1989); *Izbrannye stikhi* (1995);
   Lazurnyi sad (1997); *P: Novyi mir* (1989) 3, (1993) 10, (1995) 11, (1997) 12; *Oktiabr*
   (1993) 12; *Druzhba narodov* (1996) 2; *I:* http://magazines.russ.ru/authors/g/
   grechko/

Grigoreva, Lidiya (1945, Ukraine/Moscow/London)

   A: Strofy veka; B: Svidanie (1978); *Maiskii sad* (1981); *Svet vinogradnyi* (1984);
   Krug obshcheniya (1988); *Liubovnyi golod* (1993); *Sumasshedshii sadovnik* (1999);
   Vospitanie sada (2001); *Ne bednye liudi* (2002); *P: Arion* (1999) 1; *Druzhba narodov*
   (2001) 12, (2002) 4; *E: A Double Rainbow; Selected Poems* (1995); *MPT* (2001) 17;
   Russian Women Poets; I: http://magazines.russ.ru/authors/g/grigoreva/; http://
   www.erfolg.ru/hall/sad.htm

*Grimberg, Faina (1951, Moscow)

    A: Vremia Ch; Legko byt' iskrennim; Samoe vygodnoe zaniatie; B: Zelenaya tkachikha
    (1993), *Andreeva liubovnaya khrestomatiya* (2002); *P: Chernym po belomu; Ulov* 1;
    Avtornik 1, 2, 3, 5, 6, 7, 11; *RISK* 3; *Okrestnosti* 4; *Arion* (1994) 3; *Kontinent* 103;
    E: Crossing Centuries; Russian Women Poets; I: http://www.vavilon.ru/texts/prim/
    grimberg0.html

Idlis, Yuliya (1981, Moscow)

    B: Skazki dlia (2003); *P: XXI poet; Vavilon* 9, 10; *I:* http://www.litera.ru/slova/idlis/

*Ignatova, Elena (1947, St. Petersburg/Israel)

    A: Krug; The Blue Lagoon Anthology, 5B; *Strofy veka; Gorod-Tekst; B: Stikhi o*
    prichastnosti (1976); *Zdes, gde zhivu* (1983); *Stikhotvoreniya* (1985); *Teplaya zemlia*
    (1989); *Nebesnoe zarevo* (1992); *P: Molodoi Leningrad 89; Indeks-2; Kontinent* 51 and
    70; *Ogonek* (1993) 9–10; *Novyi mir* (1994) 10; *Znamia* (1999) 9; *Kreshchatik* 9;
    Ierusalimskii poeticheskii almanakh; E: Dictionary of Russian Women Writers; In
    the Grip of Strange Thoughts; Russian Women Poets; I: http://members.tripod
    .com/~barashw/ipa/ignatova.htm; http://www.antho.net/library/ignatova/
    index.php

Isachenko, Olga (1953, Sverdlovsk district)

    A: Antologiya: Sovremennaya uralskaya poeziya (1997–2003); I: http://magazines
    .russ.ru/authors/i/isachenko/

Isaeva, Elena (1956, Moscow)

    A: Russkaya poeziya: XX vek; B: Mezh mirom i soboi (1992); *Molodye i krasivye*
    (1993); *Sluchainaya vstrecha* (1995); *Lishnie slezy* (1997); *Nicheinaya muza* (2000);
    P: Vremia i my 152; *Druzhba narodov* (2002) 9; *I:* http://isaeva.1977.ru/

*Iskrenko, Nina (1951, Saratov–1995, Moscow)

    A: Molodaya poeziia 89; Antologiya russkogo verlibra; Strofy veka; Russkaya poeziya:
    XX vek; B: Ili (1991); *Neskolko slov* (1991); *Referendum* (1991); *Interpretatsiya*
    momenta (1996); *Neposredstvenno zhizn* (1997); *O glavnom* (1998); *Stikhi o rodine*
    (2000); *Gosti* (2001); *Izbrannoe* (2001); *Znaki vnimaniya* (2002); *U nas i u nikh*
    (2003); *P: 22* 67; *Chernovik* 5; *Arion* (1995) 2; *Novyi mir* (1996) 11; *Znamia* (2001) 7;
    Chernovik 3; *E: The Right to Err* (1995); *Third Wave: The New Russian Poetry;*
    Dictionary of Russian Women Writers; 20th-Century Russian Poetry; In the Grip of
    Strange Thoughts; Crossing Centuries; Russian Women Poets; I: http://www.vavilon
    .ru/texts/iskrenoo.html

*Ivanova, Olga (1965, Moscow), also as *Polina Ivanova*

    A: Russkaya poeziya: XX vek; B: Kogda nikogo (1997); *Ofeliya Gamletu* (1999);
    P.S. (1999); *Oda ulitse* (2000); *P: Novyi mir* (1988) 3, (1998) 11, (2002) 11, (2003) 12;
    Kontinent (1992) 71; *Arion* (1998) 2, (1999) 3, (2000) 3, (2003) 2; *Avtornik* 1, 2, 3;
    Druzhba narodov (2001) 2; *E: The Poetry of Perestroika; Russian Women Poets;*
    I: http://poetry.liter.net/ivanova.html; http://magazines.russ.ru/authors/i/
    oivanova/

*Ivanova, Svetlana (1965, St. Petersburg/Moscow)

    A: Antologiya russkogo verlibra; Nezamechennaya zemlia; B: Ten na kamne (1990);
    Poyavlenie babochki (1995); *Nebesnaya fontanka* (2001); *P: Den poezii* (Moscow,
    1989); *Molodoi Leningrad 89; Zvezda* (1994) 11, (1996) 3, (1997) 9, (1999) 2, (2000)

3, (2001) 6; *Arion* (1998) 3, (2000) 4; *Petropol* (2000) 9; *Kamera khraneniya* 2;
E: Crossing Centuries; *Russian Women Poets*; *I:* http://www.vavilon.ru/texts/
ivanova_so.html

Izmailova, Viktoriya (Chita)

B: Zhavoronkovy sny (1995); *Talisman* (1999); *P: Kolokol* (2003) 3/4; *Novyi mir*
(2003) 3; *I:* http://www.litera.ru/slova/Izmajlova/

Izvarina, Evgeniya (1967, Ekaterinburg)

A: Vremia Ch; *B: Sny o Velikom plavanii* (1996); *Po zemnomu krugu* (1998); *Strany
nochi* (1999); *P: Ulov* 5; *Znamia* (2000) 10, (2002) 1, (2003) 4; *Uralskaya nov'*
(2000) 2; *Ural* (2001) 8, (2002) 8, (2003) 9; *I:* http://magazines.russ.ru/authors/
i/izvarina/

*Kabysh, Inna (1963, Moscow)

A: Strofy veka; *Dvoinaya raduga*; *Russkaya poeziya: XX vek*; *B: Lichnye trudnosti*
(1994); *Detskii mir* (1996); *Detstvo-Otrochestvo-Detstvo* (2003); *P: Molodaya poeziya
89*; *Druzhba narodov* (1989) 3, (1997) 6, (1998) 3, (2000) 4, (2001) 1 and 8, (2002)
2, (2003) 3; *Znamia* (1989) 3, (1993) 1; *Novyi mir* (1994) 12, (1995) 9, (1996) 1; *Istoki*
(1999) 6; *Kolokol* (2002) 3; *E: A Double Rainbow*; *Russian Women Poets*; *I:* http://
magazines.russ.ru/authors/k/kabysh/; http://www.erfolg.ru/hall/inna_
kabysh.htm

Kachalova, Irina (Riga)

P: GF (1993) 3; *Iz arkhiva "Novoi literaturnoi gazety"*; *I:* http://vernitski.narod.ru/
kachalova.htm

Kadikova, Irina (1973, Cheliabinsk/USA)

A: Antologiya: Sovremennaya uralskaya poeziya (1997–2003); *B: 21 stikhotvorenie*
(1996); *Ursulika* (1998); *I:* http://magazines.russ.ru/urnov/2003/16/kadik.html

Kamenkovich, Mariya (1962, St. Petersburg/Germany)

B: Reka Smorodina (1996); *Mikhailovskii zamok* (1999); *P: Kreshchatik* 1, 2, 9

*Kapovich, Katia (1960, Kishinev/Boston)

A: Russkie poety v Amerike (1999); *B: Den angela i noch* (1992); *Sufler: Roman v
stikhakh* (1998); *Proshchanie s shestikrylymi* (2001); *Perekur* (2002); *Veselyi
distsiplinarii* (2004); *P: Novyi mir* (1997) 12; *Znamia* (1997) 7; *Zvezda* (1999) 10;
Arion (2000) 2; *Neva* (2000) 12; *Ulov* 3; *Ierusalimskii poeticheskii almanakh*; *E: Poet
for Poet*; *Russian Women Poets*; *Ten Russian Poets*; *Stanzas to the Stairwell* (2003);
Gogol in Rome (2004); *I:* http://www.vavilon.ru/texts/kapovicho.html; http://
magazines.russ.ru/novyi_mi/portf/kapov/; http://members.tripod.com/
~barashw/ipa/kapovich.htm

Kapustina, Veronika (1962, St. Petersburg)

B: Zal ozhidaniya (1993); *Blagodaria Lune* (1999); *P: Neva* (1992, 2001) 6, (2003) 7;
Kreshchatik, 8, 22; *Novyi mir* (2002) 9; *I:* http://magazines.russ.ru/authors/k/
kapustina/

Kassirova, Elena (Moscow)

B: Kofe na Golgofe (2001); *P: Avtornik* 7, 10, 11

Katsiuba, Elena (1946, Rostov/Moscow)

A: Strofy veka; *Samizdat veka*; *B: Krasivye vsegda pravy* (1999); *Pervyi
palindromicheskii slovar . . .* (1999); *eR-eL* (2002); *Igr rai* (2003); *P: Indeks-2*;

Petropol (1990); *Strelets* 73; *E: Crossing Centuries*; *I:* http://www.rvb.ru/np/
publication/01text/40/02katsyuba.htm; http://slovart.narod.ru/; http://
flashpoetry.narod.ru/

*Kekova, Svetlana (1951, Sakhalin/Saratov)

B: Pesochnye chasy (1995); *Stikhi o prostranstve i vremeni* (1995); *Po obe storony imeni*
(1996); *Korotkie pisma* (2000); *Vostochnyi kaleidoskop* (2001); *P: Kontinent* 65; *Mitin
zhurnal* 9/10, 20, 22/23; *Postscriptum* 1, 10; *Volga* (1990) 10, (1996) 4; *Znamia*
(1990) 10, (1992) 5 and 11, (1994) 1, (1995) 3, (1997) 4, (1998) 7, (2000) 1 and 8,
(2001) 4 and 11, (2002) 5, (2003) 7; *Novyi mir* (2001) 3, (2002) 4, (2003) 7; *Zvezda*
(2002) 1, (2003) 1 and 7; *Chernym po belomu*; *Ulov* 1, 5; *E: In the Grip of Strange
Thoughts*; *Russian Women Poets*; *I:* http://www.vavilon.ru/texts/kekovao.html;
http://magazines.russ.ru/authors/k/kekova/

*Khagen, Marina (1974, Cheliabinsk)

A: Nestolichnaya literatura; *Antologiya: Sovremennaya uralskaya poeziya
(1997–2003)*; *Samoe vygodnoe zaniatie*; *B: Teni otrazhenii* (2001); *Dnevnik bez
nabliudenii* (2002); *P: Chernym po belomu*; *Triton* 1, 2, 3, 4; *Uralskaya nov'* (1999) 5,
(2003) 16; *Vavilon* 10; *Arion* (2002) 2; *Ural* (2002) 9; *I:* http://www.litera.ru/
slova/golda/; http://magazines.russ.ru/urnov/2003/16/hagen.html

Khatkina, Natalya (1956, Donetsk)

A: Antologiya russkogo verlibra; *Strofy veka*; *B: Ot serdtsa k serdtsu* (1988); *Poemy*
(1998); *Lekarstvo ot liubvi* (1999); *Ptichka dozhila* (2000); *P: Enter 2000*; *Arion*
(2001) 2; *Kreshchatik* 17 and 22; *I:* http://magazines.russ.ru/authors/h/hatkina/

Khodynskaya, Liudmila (Moscow/Netherlands)

A: Samizdat veka; *P: Indeks-2*; *GF*

*Khvostova, Olga (1965, Tadzhikistan/Krasnodar district)

P: Pamir; *Znamia* (1994) 11, (2000) 5, (2002) 2, (2003) 2; *Arion* (2000) 3, (2002) 4,
(2003) 3; *Chernym po belomu*; *E: Russian Women Poets*; *I:* http://magazines.russ
.ru/authors/h/hvostova/

*Kildibekova, Mariya (1976, Moscow)

P: Arion (2001) 1; *Vavilon* 7; *Chernym po belomu*; *Molodye poety Rossii*; *E: Russian
Women Poets*

Kiseleva, Vera (1940, Cheliabinsk)

A: Antologiya: Sovremennaya uralskaya poeziya (1997–2003); *B: Polotno* (2002);
I: http://magazines.russ.ru/urnov/2003/16/kisel.html

Kisina, Yuliya (1966, Kiev/Moscow/Germany)

P: Mitin zhurnal 19, 27, 30, 35; *Zvezda Vostoka* (1992) 6

Kliuchareva, Natalya (1981, Yaroslavl)

A: Deviat izmerenii; *Samoe vygodnoe zaniatie*; *P: XXI poet*; *Vavilon* 9, 10; *I:* http://
www.vavilon.ru/texts/klyucharevao.html

Kondakova, Nadezhda (1949, Orenburg/Moscow)

A: Strofy veka; *B: Den chudesnyi* (1975); *Dom v chistom pole* (1981); *Strela* (1983);
Ptitsa nepereletnaya (1985); *Inkognito* (2001); *P: Novyi mir* (1990) 9, (1994) 10;
Literaturnaya gazeta, 9 June 1993; *E: Third Wave*; *Crossing Centuries*; *I:* http://
magazines.russ.ru/authors/k/kondakova/

Koroleva, Nina (1933, Moscow/St. Petersburg)

A: Strofy veka; B: Medlennoe chtenie (1993); *P: Literaturnaya gazeta*, 13 February 1991; *Zvezda* (1997) 10, (2001) 8; *Neva* (2001) 2, (2003) 1; *Novyi zhurnal* 232

*Kossman, Nina (1959, Moscow/New York)

B: Pereboi (1990); *Po pravuiu ruku sna* (1996); *P: Novoe russkoe slovo* (1980, 1994, 1996, 1998, 2000); *Novyi zhurnal* (1985) 159, (1991) 184/185, (1993) 192/193; *E: Dictionary of Russian Women Writers; Russian Women Poets*

*Kostyleva (Popova), Elena (1977, Moscow)

A: Deviat izmerenii; B: Legko dostalos (2001); *P: Vavilon* 6, 7, 8; *Mitin zhurnal* 60; *Plotnost ozhidanii; I:* http://www.mitin.com/books/kostyleva/easy.shtml

Kotliar, Elmira (1925, Kazan/Moscow)

A: Antologiya russkogo verlibra; B: Vetka (1958); *Svet-gorod; Akvareli; V ruki tvoi; P: Kontinent* 104; *Novyi mir* (1992) 12, (1995) 1, (1996) 4, (1997) 4 and 10, (1998) 5, (1999) 7, (2001) 10; *I:* http://magazines.russ.ru/authors/k/kotlyar/

*Kovaleva, Irina (1964, Moscow)

B: Kukolnyi yashchik (2002); *V proshedshem vremeni* (2002); *Yubileinyi gimn* (2003); *P: Vavilon; Novyi zhurnal* 181; *Slovo/Word* (2001) 29/39, (2003) 40; *Florida: Russkie stranitsy* (2003) 1; *E: Russian Women Poets; I:* http://www.niworld.ru/poezia/irina/irin_1.htm; http://www.poesis.ru/poery-poezia/kovaleva/biograph.htm

Krasnova, Nina (1950, Riazan/Moscow)

A: Antologiya russkogo verlibra; Russkaya poeziya: XX vek; B: Razbeg (1979); *Takie krasnye tsvety* (1984); *Poteriannoe koltso* (1986); *Plach po rekam* (1989); *Intim* (1995); *Semeinaya neidilliya* (1995); *Zaletochka* (1997); *P: Vremia i my* 143 and 148; *Novyi mir* (1990) 2; *Istoki* (1999) 6; *Den poezii* (Moscow, 2000)

Kriukova, Elena (1956, Nizhnii Novgorod)

A: Poryv: Sbornik stikhov—Novye imena; Strofy veka; B: Kolokol (1986); *Kupol* (1990); *Sotvorenie mira* (1997); *P: Neva* (1988) 1; *Novyi mir* (1989) 3, (1993) 1; *Volga* (1989) 2, (1990) 6; *Literaturnaya gazeta*, 11 December 1991; *Znamia* (1993) 2, (1998) 12; *Druzhba narodov* (1996) 9, (1997) 8, (1999) 11; *I:* http://magazines.russ.ru/authors/k/kryukova/

Krutilina, Vera (Kiev)

B: Mimicheskie skobki (1997); *P: Oktiabr* (1996) 12; *Zvezda* (1997) 3

*Krylova, Ella (1967, Moscow/St.Petersburg)

A: Strofy veka; B: Proshchanie s Peterburgom (1993); *Apokrif* (1998); *Sozertsatel* (1999); *Spasi i sokhrani* (2000); *Pchela na levkoe: Izbrannoe* (2001); *Sineva* (2001); *Chaiki nad Letoi* (2003); *P: Znamia* (1991) 8, (1995) 10, (1997) 2, (1999) 1; *Druzhba narodov* (1992) 3, (1996) 4, (1997) 9, (1999) 2, (2000) 11; *Zvezda* (1996) 8, (1999) 9, (2001) 9, (2003) 3; *Arion* (1997) 1, (1998) 4; *Kreshchatik* 9; *E: Russian Women Poets; I:* http://poetry.liter.net/krylova.html; http://magazines.russ.ru/authors/k/krylova/

Kuchkina, Olga (1936, Moscow)

B: Soobshchayushchii sosud (1991); *Italyanskaya babochka* (1999); *Visokosnyi god* (2002); *P: Arion* (1995) 2 and 3, (1997) 2, (1999) 3, (2003) 2; *Novyi mir* (1995) 12, (1998) 12, (2004) 2; *Druzhba narodov* (1996) 11; *Neva* (1996) 12; *Zvezda* (1996) 12;

Oktiabr (1997) 11, (1999) 3, (2003) 7; *Znamia* (1998) 11, (1999) 10, (2000) 9;
Kontinent 113; *I:* http://magazines.russ.ru/authors/k/kuchkina/

*Kudimova, Marina (1953, Tambov/Moscow)

    A: Russkaya poeziya: XX vek; B: Perechen prichin (1982); *Chut chto* (1987); *Arys-pole*
(1989); *Oblast* (1990); *P: Molodaya poeziya 89; Znamia* (1989) 8, (1999) 2; *Volga*
(1990) 7; *Kontinent* 73, 88, 113; *Novyi mir* (1994) 9, (1996) 6, (1998) 7, (1999) 10;
Druzhba narodov (1995) 8, (1998) 12; *E: A Double Rainbow; 20th-Century Russian*
Poetry; Russian Women Poets; I: http://magazines.russ.ru/authors/k/kudimova/

Kulakova, Marina (1962, Nizhnii Novgorod)

    A: Antologiya russkogo verlibra; B: Kogda by ne yunost (1986); *Fantazii na temy*
realnosti (1991); *Stikhi Aleksandriny* (1995); *Gosudarstvennyi zapovednik* (1999);
P: Moskva (1984) 3; *Neva* (1984) 2; *Novyi mir* (1987) 1, (1988) 3; *Novaya*
literaturnaya gazeta 8

Kulieva, Elizaveta (1973, Moscow)

    A: Den poezii (Moscow, 2000); *P: Kreshchatik* 15; *Arion* (2002) 3; *I:* http://
magazines.russ.ru/authors/k/kulieva/

*Kulishova, Inna (1969, Tbilisi/Israel)

    B: Na okraine slova (2000); *P: Vstrechi* (2001) 25, (2003) 27; *Poberezhye* (2002) 11,
(2003) 12; *E: Russian Women Poets; I:* http://www.litera.ru/slova/kulishova/;
http://poetry.liter.net/decookul.html; http://vernitskii.liter.net/kulishova
.htm

*Kunina, Yuliya (1966, Moscow/USA)

    A: Strofy veka; B: Kairos (1991); *Stikhi* (1992); *Diurer pered zerkalom* (1996);
P: Poberezhye; Kontinent 70; *Arion* (1996) 4; *E: Crossing Centuries; Russian Women*
Poets

Kunovskaya, Marina (Minsk)

    B: Second Hand (1998); *P: Nemiga* (1999) 3

Kupriashina, Sofya (1968, Moscow)

    P: Oboinyi gvozdik; Vavilon 5; *I:* http://www.vavilon.ru/texts/kupryashinao.html

Kurchatova, Natalya (1977, St. Petersburg)

    P: Vavilon 9

Kursanova, Marina (1963, Lvov)

    B: Lodka naskvoz (1995); *P: Arion* (2003) 2; *Znamia* (2004) 2; *I:* http://magazines
.russ.ru/authors/k/kursanova/

Kutsubova, Tatyana (1959, Kaluga/Tarusa)

    I: http://www.litera.ru/slova/kutsubova/

Kuzmina, Natalya (Moscow)

    B: Izdaleka i vblizi (1999); *P: Arion* (1994) 4 and 6, (1998) 4; *Kreshchatik* 17;
Novaya literaturnaya gazeta 6; *Triton* 2, 4; *I:* http://www.vladivostok.com/
Speaking_In_Tongues/kuzmina2.html

*Kuznetsova, Inga (1974, Moscow)

    A: Deviat izmerenii; B: Sny-sinitsy (2002); *P: Arion* (1998) 3, (2001) 4; *Druzhba*
narodov (2000) 9; *Novyi mir* (2000) 6, (2003) 9; *Novaya yunost* (2002) 1; *Oktiabr*
(2003) 9; *Chernym po belomu; Vavilon* 5; *Molodye poety Rossii; I:* http://magazines
.russ.ru/authors/k/ikuznetsova/

Kuznetsova, Olga (1975, Riga/Moscow)

   P: Daugava (1994) 3; *Arion* (1995) 2; *Novyi mir* (1995) 7; *Znamia* (1995) 4; *I:* http://
   magazines.russ.ru/authors/k/okuznetsova/

*Lavut, Evgeniya (1972, Moscow)

   A: Deviat izmerenii; *B: Stikhi pro Gleba, Dobrogo Barina, tsaria Davida* . . . (1994);
   Amur i dr. (2001); *P: Vavilon* 9, 10; *Chernym po belomu*; *Ulov* 1; *Okrestnosti* 4;
   E: Russian Women Poets; *I:* http://www.vavilon.ru/texts/lavuto.html

*Lazutkina, Elena (1975, Krasnodar/Moscow)

   P: Arion (1995) 1, (1997) 4; *Znamia* (1999) 3, (2001) 4; *E: Russian Women Poets*;
   I: http://magazines.russ.ru/authors/l/lazutkina/

Legkaya (Vandellos-Pushkareva), Iraida (1932, Latvia/USA)

   A: Antologiya poezii russkogo zarubezhya; *B: Poputnyi veter* (1968); *Podzemnaya reka*
   (1999)

Leskina, Yuziya (1976, Saratov)

   A: Nestolichnaya literatura; *P: Vavilon* 6, 7; *I:* http://amber2002.narod.ru/leskina
   .htm

Liaskovskaya, Natalya (1958, Ukraine/Moscow)

   A: Molodaya poeziya 89; *Russkaya poeziya: XX vek*; *B: Okno v vishnevyi sad* (1986);
   Svetaet (1991); *Dusha Natashi* (2001); *P: Nash sovremennik* (2000) 8, (2002) 3;
   I: http://www.vcu.ru/vcu/poets/n_lyask.htm

Limanova, Natalya (Togliatti)

   A: Nestolichnaya literatura; *P: GF* (1992) 1; *Novaya literaturnaya gazeta* 8; *Arion*
   (1995) 3

Linkova (Pukhanova), Liudmila (Moscow)

   A: Molodaya poeziya 89; *P: Okrestnosti* 4

Linkova, Vera (1954, Kazakhstan/Moscow)

   B: Videniya v gorode nishchikh (1991); *Babochka v chasakh* (1993); *I:* http://www
   .poesis.ru/poeti-poezia/linkova/biograph.htm

Lipanovich (Ioffe), Berta (1959, Ivanovo/Israel)

   B: Iskliuchenie pchel (1996)

*Lisnianskaya, Inna (1928, Baku/Moscow)

   A: Russkaya poeziya: XX vek; *Poeziya vtoroi poloviny XX veka*; *B: Eto bylo so mnoiu*
   (1957); *Vernost* (1958); *Ne prosto—liubov* (1963); *Iz pervykh ruk* (1966); *Vinogradnyi
   svet* (1978); *Dozhdi i zerkala* (1983); *Na opushke sna* (1984); *Stupeni: Nakhodka
   otdykhayushchego* (1990); *Vozdushnyi plast* (1990); *Stikhotvoreniya* (1991); *Posle
   vsego* (1994); *Odinokii dar* (1995); *Veter pokoya* (1998); *Muzyka i bereg* (2000);
   V prigorode Sodoma (2002); *Odinokii dar* (2003); *P: Metropol* (1979); *Kontinent* 38,
   47, 64, 117; *Znamia* (1987) 9, (1988) 3, (1989) 9, (1990) 12, (1992) 11, (1994) 7,
   (1997) 6, (1998) 2, (2000) 6, (2001) 9, (2002) 4 and 9, (2003) 9; *Novyi mir* (1988)
   6, (1990) 6, (1992) 10, (1993) 12, (1995) 5, (1997) 7, (1998) 2, (1999) 2 and 10,
   (2000) 3, (2001) 1, (2002) 1, (2003) 1 and 10; *Oktiabr* (1988) 11, (1990) 9; *Druzhba
   narodov* (1989) 2, (1996) 3, (1997) 3, (1998) 2, (1999) 3, (2000) 8, (2001) 4, (2002)
   5, (2003) 12; *Volga* (1990) 1; *Arion* (1995) 4, (1998) 1, (1999) 2, (2000) 1, (2001) 1,
   (2002) 1, (2003) 3; *Zvezda* (2001) 3; *Vestnik Evropy* (2002) 5; *E: 20th-Century
   Russian Poetry*; *In the Grip of Strange Thoughts*; *Russian Women Writers*; *Russian

Women Poets; *I:* http://www.vavilon.ru/texts/prim/lisno.html; http://
magazines.russ.ru/authors/l/lisnyanskaya/

*Litvak, Sveta (1959, Moscow)

    A: Samizdat veka; *Antologiya russkogo palindroma* (2002); *B: Raznotsvetnye prokazniki*
    (1992); *Pesni uchenika* (1994); *Eto liubov* (2002); *P: Kontinent* 47; *Znamia* (1987) 9,
    (1990) 12, (1995) 12, (1997) 5, (1998) 10, (1999) 10, (2001) 10, (2002) 7, (2003) 11;
    Arion (1996) 2, (1998) 1 and 4, (2000) 2, (2001) 3, (2003) 2; *Volga* (1996) 8/9;
    E: Crossing Centuries; *Russian Women Poets*; *I:* http://www.rvb.ru/np/publication/
    01text/46/08litvak.htm; http://magazines.russ.ru/authors/l/litvak/; http://
    litvak.rema.ru/

Litvinova, Elena (Obninsk, Kaluga district)

    A: Nestolichnaya literatura; *B: Stikhi kak priem* (2001); *I:* http://www.litera.ru/
    slova/litvinova/

Lovina-Lovich, Ekaterina (1961, Syktyvkar)

    A: Nestolichnaya literatura; *P: Arion* (1998) 3; *I:* http://www.vavilon.ru/textonly/
    issue4/lov_lov.htm

Maksimova, Mariya (1960, Moscow)

    A: Samizdat veka; *B: Uroki ritoriki* (1995); *Kanuny* (2002); *P: GF* (1992) 1; *Novaya*
    literaturnaya gazeta 1; *Poluostrov*; *Kreshchatik* 15; *Volga* (1996) 4; *Mitin zhurnal* 53;
    Okrestnosti 4; *Chernovik* 12; *E: Crossing Centuries*; *I:* http://www.liter.net/=/
    POLUOSTROV/book1/Maksimova.html

Maksimova, Svetlana (1958, Kharkov/Moscow)

    A: Grazhdane nochi; *Molodaya poeziya 89*; *Russkaya poeziya: XX vek*; *B: Nevedomye*
    travy (1988); *Volnomu volia* (1988); *Rozhdennye sfinksami* (1994); *P: Oktiabr* (1996)
    7, (1997) 3, (1998) 3, (2000) 6, (2003) 4; *Kreshchatik* 13; *I:* http://magazines.russ
    .ru/authors/m/maksimova/

*Malanova, Mara (1970, Leningrad/Ulan-Ude/Moscow)

    A: Deviat izmerenii; *B: Ekspress* (2002); *P: Vavilon* 8, 9, 10; *E: Absinthe: New European*
    Writing (2003) 1; *I:* http://www.vavilon.ru/texts/malanovao.html

Malshina, Olga (1981, Samara)

    P: XXI poet; *Vavilon* 9, 10; *I:* http://www.vavilon.ru/texts/malshinao.html

Maltseva, Nadezhda (1945, Moscow)

    A: Strofy veka; *Russkaya poeziya: XX vek*; *P: Druzhba narodov* (1989) 9; *Poberezhye*
    11; *Novyi zhurnal* 231; *I:* http://www.thecoastmagazine.org/Poetry/
    NadezhdaMaltseva.htm

*Marennikova, Kseniya (1981, Kaliningrad/Moscow)

    A: Deviat izmerenii; *P: XXI poet*; *Avtornik* 11; *Vavilon* 9, 10; *I:* http://maren.pisem
    .net/

*Martynova, Olga (1962, Krasnoyarsk/Leningrad/Frankfurt)

    A: Nezamechennaya zemlia; *B: Postup yanvarskikh sadov* (1989); *Sumasshedshii*
    kuznechik (1993); *Chetyre vremeni nochi* (1998); *P: Kamera khraneniya* 2–6; *Avrora*
    (1990) 3; *Kontinent* 65; *Sumerki* (1991) 11; 22 (1997) 104; *Volga* (1997) 3–4; *Zerkalo*
    zagadok (2000) 9; *Ural* (2001) 1; *Novyi mir* (2003) 2; *Zhurnal stikhov* (2003) 1;
    Zvezda (2003) 10; *Russkaya mysl*; *E: Crossing Centuries*; *Russian Women Poets*;

I: http://www.newkamera.de/omartynova1.html; http://magazines.russ.ru/authors/m/omartynova/

*Mashinskaya, Irina (1958, Moscow/New Jersey)

    A: Strofy veka; *Vremia Ch*; *B: Potomu chto my zdes* (1995); *Posle epigrafa* (1996); *Prostye vremena* (2000); *Stikhotvoreniya* (2001); *Putniku snitsia* (2004); *P: Arion* (1997) 3, (2000) 3; *Zvezda* (1997) 1, (1998) 11; *Novaya yunost* (1999) 6, (2002) 5; *Novyi mir* (2001) 2, (2003) 10; *Vremia i my* (2002) 116; *Znamia* (2002) 2, (2003) 11; *Poberezhye* (2003) 12; *Russkaya mysl* (2003) 4465; *Petropol* 8, 9; *Slovo/Word* 15, 21, 23, 28, 36, 38/39; *Kreshchatik* 13, 22; *Chernovik* 8; *Ulov* 5; *Ierusalimskii zhurnal* 11; *Vstrechi* (2003) 27; *Zerkalo* 2; *E: Because We Are Here* (1995); *Ars-Interpress* (2003) 1; *I:* http://www.vavilon.ru/texts/prim/mashinskayao.html; http://stetoscop .narod.ru; http://lib.ru/NEWPROZA/MASHINSKAYA/stihotworeniya.txt

Matveeva, Novella (1934, Leningrad/Moscow)

    A: Russkaya poeziya: XX vek; *Poeziya vtoroi poloviny XX veka*; *B: Lirika* (1961); *Korablik* (1963); *Dusha veshchei* (1966); *Lastochkina shkola* (1973); *Shpaly* (1973); *Reka* (1978); *Strana priboya* (1983); *Zakon pesen* (1983); *Krolichya derevnia* (1984); *Izbrannoe* (1986); *Khvala rabote* (1987); *Proza v stikhakh* (1989); *Bormatukha: Stikhi i poemy* (1991); *Nerastorzhimyi krug* (1991); *Menuet* (1994); *Kasseta snov* (1998); *Melodiya dlia gitary* (1998); *Pastusheskii dnevnik* (1998); *Sonety* (1998); *Karavan* (2000); *P: Znamia* (1986) 3, (1992) 3/4, (1995) 1, (1996) 1, (1997) 4, (1998) 1, (1999) 3, (2000) 1 and 7, (2001) 6, (2002) 5; *Arion* (1995) 4, (2001) 1; *Druzhba narodov* (1997) 4, (1999) 4; *E: Dictionary of Russian Women Writers*; *Twentieth-Century Russian Poetry*; *20th-Century Russian Poetry*; *I:* http://www.ruthenia.ru/60s/matveeva/; http:// magazines.russ.ru/authors/m/nmatveeva/; http://www.litera.ru/stixiya/ authors/matveeva/all.html

Medvedeva, Natalya (1958–2003, Leningrad/USA/France/St. Petersburg)

    A: The Blue Lagoon Anthology, 2B; *B: Ya reyu znamenem . . .* (1995); *P: Chelovek i priroda* (1992) 1; *Arion* (1999) 2; *Chernovik* 1

Mikhailichenko, Elizaveta (Stavropol/Israel)

    B: Na styke sekund (1987); *Kazhdyi okhotnik zhelaet znat* (1990): *Tsvety vinovnosti* (1999); *I:* http://www.litera.ru/slova/mihaylichenko/

Mikhailovskaya, Tatyana (1943, Moscow)

    B: Solnechnoe spletenie: Kniga odnostishii (1995); *To est* (1998); *P: AKT*; *Kreshchatik* 15; *Chernovik* 9, 11, 14

*Miller, Larisa (1940, Moscow)

    A: Strofy veka; *Russkaya poeziya: XX vek*; *B: Bezymiannyi den* (1977); *Zemlia i dom* (1986); *V ozhidanii Edipa* (1993); *Motiv: K sebe, ot sebia* (2002); *"Gde khorosho? Povsiudu i nigde . . ."* (2004) *P: Novyi mir* (1993) 6 and 7, (1999) 3, (2000) 2, (2002) 3, (2003) 4; *Arion* (1996) 4, (2002) 1 and 3, (2003) 4; *Druzhba narodov* (2000) 5; *Vremia i my* (2000) 146; *Kontinent* 103 and 115; *Vestnik* (2002) 21 (306); *Predlog* 8; *Voprosy literatury* (2003) 6; *E: A Will and a Way*; *Poet for Poet*; *Between the Cloud and the Pit* (2001); *Russian Women Poets*; *I:* http://magazines.russ.ru/novyi_ mi/redkol/miller/miller.html; http://poetry.liter.net/miller.html; http:// magazines.russ.ru/authors/m/miller/

*Milova, Tatyana (1965, Moscow)

A: *Russkaya poeziya: XX vek*; *Vremia Ch*; B: *Nachalniku khora* (1998); P: *Petropol*; *Yunost*; *GF* (1993) 21; *Arion* (1996) 4, (1997) 4, (1999) 2, (2002) 2; *Druzhba narodov* (1998) 10; *Novaya yunost* (1999) 2; *Novyi mir* (2001) 9, (2003) 9; *Kreshchatik* 10; *Avtornik* 1, 2; *Ulov* 4; *Okrestnosti* 3; E: *Russian Women Poets*; I: http://www.vavilon .ru/texts/prim/milovao.html; http://magazines.russ.ru/authors/m/milova/

Minakova, Anna (1985, Kharkov)

A: *Anatomiya angela*; B: *Zolotaya zola* (2000); *Dorogoe moe* (2002); P: *Soty* (2001); *Literaturnaya gazeta* (2003) 7; *Novaya yunost* (2003) 2; I: http://www.pereplet.ru/ kot/104.html; http://www.stihi.ru/autor.html?annam; http://kharkov.vbelous .net/minakova.htm

Mirkina, Zinaida (1926, Moscow)

A: *Sovremennye russkie poety*; B: *Poteria poteri* (1991); *Zerno pokoya* (1994); *Moi zatishya* (1999); *Odin na odin* (2002); I: http://www.poesis.ru/poeti-poezia/ mirkina/biograph.htm

Mnatsakanova, Elizaveta (1922, Baku/Moscow/Vienna)

A: *The Blue Lagoon Anthology*, 2A; *Samizdat veka*; B: *Shagi i vzdokhi: Chetyre knigi stikhov* (1982); *Beim tode zu gast/U smerti v gostiakh* (1986); *Das Buch Sabeth: Kniga v piati chastiakh* (1988); *Vita Breve* (1994); P: *Apollon* 77; *Vremia i my* (1978) 27; *Sintaksis* (1983) 11; *Rodnik* (1990) 9; *Mitin zhurnal* (1992) 45/46; *Kommentarii* 6; *Segodnia*, 31 May 1996; *Chernovik* 12, 13; *Novoe literaturnoe obozrenie* (2003) 62; E: *Russian Women Poets*

Mogilever, Yuliya (1948, Leningrad/Israel)

I: http://www.litera.ru/slova/mohilever/

Morits, Yunna (1937, Kiev/Moscow)

A: *Dvoinaya raduga*; *Strofy veka*; *Russkaya poeziya: XX vek*; *Poeziya vtoroi poloviny XX veka*; B: *Razgovor o schastye* (1957); *Mys zhelaniya* (1961); *Schastlivyi zhuk* (1969); *Loza: Kniga stikhov, 1962–1969* (1970); *Surovoi nityu* (1974); *Malinovaya koshka* (1976); *Pri svete zhizni* (1977); *Poprygat—poigrat* (1978); *Tretii glaz* (1980); *Izbrannoe* (1982); *Zakhodite v gosti* (1982); *Sinii ogon* (1985); *Domik s truboi* (1986); *Na etom berege vysokom* (1987); *Muskul vody* (1990); *V logove golosa* (1990); *Litso* (2000); *Rasskazy o chudesnom* (2002); P: *Oktiabr* (1997) 7, (1998) 10, (1999) 5; E: *Russian Poetry: The Modern Period*; *Three Russian Poets*; *The Poetry of Perestroika*; *A Double Rainbow*; *Dictionary of Russian Women Writers*; *Contemporary Russian Poetry*; *Twentieth-Century Russian Poetry*; *20th-Century Russian Poetry*; *Russian Women Writers*; *In the Grip of Strange Thoughts*; *Russian Women Poets*; I: http://owl.ru/ morits/; http://magazines.russ.ru/authors/m/morits/; http://lib.ru/ POEZIQ/MORIC/stihi.txt

*Morotskaya, Stella (1962, Gorkii/Moscow)

A: *Antologiya russkogo verlibra*; *Samizdat veka*; B: *Metodika svobodnogo poleta* (1993); *Vse 33 i drugie* (2001); P: *Oktiabr* (1991) 12; *Arion* (1995) 2, (1999) 2; *Druzhba narodov* (1995) 4; *Chernovik* 12; I: http://www.levin.rinet.ru/FRIENDS/Stella/index.html

*Moroz, Raisa (1949, Primorye/South Korea)

A: *100 let Primorya*; B: *Otchii dom* (1982); *Nochnye tsykady* (1985); *Pesni poberezhya* (1986); *5 po 50* (1999)

Moseeva, Tatyana (1983, Moscow)

P: *Vavilon* 10; *XXI poet*; *I:* http://www.terless.front.ru/

Nal, Anna (1942, Moscow)

B: *Imia* (1990); *Vesy* (1995); P: *Novyi mir* (1993) 11; *Kontinent* 84, 96; *Znamia* (1995) 5

Nechay, Svetlana (1963, Ukraine/Riazan)

A: *Nestolichnaya literatura*; P: *GF* (1992) 1; *Novaya literaturnaya gazeta* 8

*Negar, Hazan-Zadeh (1975, Baku/London)

B: *Pod chuzhimi oblakami* (2004); E: *On Wings over the Horizon: Selected Poems* (2002); *Russian Women Poets*

Nemirovskaya, Yuliya (1962, Moscow/USA)

B: *Moya knizhechka* (1998); *I:* http://www.poesis.guru.ru/poeti-poezia/nemirov/ biograph.htm; http://periferia.kulichki.net/r11.htm

Neshumova, Tatyana (Moscow)

B: *Neptitsa* (1999); P: *GF* (1993) 2; *Iz arkhiva "Novoi literaturnoi gazety"*

*Nikolaeva, Olesia (1955, Moscow)

A: *Dvoinaya raduga*; *Strofy veka*; *Russkaya poeziya: XX vek*; B: *Sad chudes* (1980); *Na korable zimy* (1986); *Smokovnitsa* (1990); *Zdes* (1990); *Amor fati* (1997); *Ispanskie pisma* (2000, 2004); P: *Novy mir* (1988) 8, (1990) 1, (1994) 7, (1996) 2, (1998) 9, (1999) 11, (2001) 5, (2003) 3; *Znamia* (1989) 3, (1994) 2, (1996) 11, (2000) 3; *Arion* (1994) 2, (1996) 3, (1998) 2, (2000) 4; E: *The Poetry of Perestroika*; *A Double Rainbow*; *20th-Century Russian Poetry*; *Dictionary of Russian Women Writers*; *In the Grip of Strange Thoughts*; *Russian Women Poets*; *I:* http://magazines.russ.ru/authors/n/ onikolaeva/

Nikolaeva-Baturova, Olga (1945, Leningrad/Riga)

A: *Russkaya poeziya: XX vek*; B: *Nemerknushchii sad* (1976); *Zhivye iskry* (1980); *Vysokaya gornitsa* (1986)

*Nikonova, Rea (Anna Tarshis) (1942, Sverdlovsk/Eisk/Germany)

A: *Samizdat veka*; P: *Urbi* 8; *Arion* (1996) 2, (1998) 1; *Chernovik* 1, 3, 4, 5, 6, 7; E: *Crossing Centuries*; *Dictionary of Russian Women Writers*; *Russian Women Poets*; *I:* http://www.rvb.ru/np/publication/01text/27/01nikonova.htm

Nikulina, Maya (1937, Ekaterinburg)

A: *Strofy veka*; *Antologiya: Sovremennaya uralskaya poeziya (1997–2003)*; B: *Moi dom i sad* (1969); *Imena* (1977); *Dusha prava* (1983); *Koleya* (1983); *Babya trava* (1987); *Stikhi* (2002); *I:* http://magazines.russ.ru/urnov/2003/16/nikul.html

Novitskaya, Ira (1946, Moscow)

A: *Antologiya russkogo verlibra*; *Legko byt' iskrennim*; *Samoe vygodnoe zaniatie*; B: *Dorogi temnyi konus* (1993); P: *Arion* (1995) 4, (2000) 3, (2003) 2; *Triton* 1, 2, 3, 4

Orlova, Marina (1960, Donetsk/Moscow)

A: *Antologiya russkogo verlibra*; B: *Ustnoe plavanie* (1992); P: *Kreshchatik* 17; *Dom s khimerami*; *Kontinent* 96

Osipova, Natalya (1958, Moscow)

A: *Vremia Ch*; *Legko byt' iskrennim*; *Samoe vygodnoe zaniatie*; B: *Neskolko rasskazov i stikhotvorenii* (2001); P: *Avtornik* 1, 5; *I:* http://www.vavilon.ru/textonly/issue2/ osipova.htm

Pakhomova, Valentina (1954, Moscow)

A: *Antologiya russkogo verlibra*; B: *Dykhanie derevev* (1997); P: *Novyi mir* (1993) 9; *Arion* (1997) 2; *Iz arkhiva "Novoi literaturnoi gazety"*; I: http://magazines.russ.ru/authors/p/pahomova/

Pavlova, Muza (1916, Perm/Moscow)

A: *Antologiya russkogo verlibra*; P: *Grani* 58; I: http://www.rvb.ru/np/publication/05supp/syntaxis/1/pavlova.htm

*Pavlova, Vera (1963, Moscow)

B: *Nebesnoe zhivotnoe* (1997); *Vtoroi yazyk* (1998); *Chetvertyi son* (2000); *Liniya otryva* (2000); *Intimnyi dnevnik otlichnitsy* (2001); *Sovershennoletie* (2002); *Vezdes* (2002); P: *Yunost* (1990); *Arion* (1995) 3, (1998) 4, (2002) 2, (2003) 2; *Volga* (1995) 4; *Ulov* 1; *Novyi mir* (1996) 3, (1999) 4, (2004) 5; *Solnechnoe spletenie* 20/21; E: *Russian Women Poets*; I: http://www.vavilon.ru/texts/prim/pavlovao.html; http://magazines.russ.ru/authors/p/pavlova/; http://magazines.russ.ru/novyi_mi/redkol/pavl.html

*Petrova, Aleksandra (1964, St. Petersburg/Rome)

A: *Nezamechennaya zemlia*; *Samizdat veka*; B: *Liniya otryva* (1994); *Vid na zhitelstvo* (2000); P: *Kontinent* 69; *Mitin zhurnal* 51 and 53; *Zvezda* (1995) 11; *Znamia* (2001) 2; *Zerkalo* 1–2, 13–14; *Ulov* 2; *Kriticheskaya massa* (2003) 2; E: *Crossing Centuries*; *Russian Women Poets*; I: http://www.vavilon.ru/texts/prim/petrovao.html

Petrova, Elina (1968, Donetsk)

B: *Belaya ploshchad* (1998); P: *Novaya yunost* (1999) 4; *Arion* (2001) 2

Petrova, Olga (Moscow)

B: *Storonnii nabliudatel* (1994)

*Petrushevskaya, Liudmila (1939, Moscow)

B: *Karamzin: Derevenskii dnevnik* (2000); P: *Oktiabr* (2002) 5; E: *Dictionary of Russian Women Writers*; *Russian Women Poets*

Pivovarova, Irina (1939–1986, Moscow)

A: *Strofy veka*

Pivovarova, Yuliya (1964, Novosibirsk)

B: *Okhotnik* (1993); P: *Kreshchatik* 12; I: http://www.nsk.su/~sibogni/Pivovar.html

Pogreb, Sara (Israel)

B: *Ya domolchalas do stikhov* (1990); *Ariel* (2003); P: *Druzhba narodov* (1985) 3; *Yunost* (1987) 8; *Poeziya* (1988) 55

Pokrovskaya, Svetlana (Saratov)

P: *Poslednii ekzempliar* (1993) 1

Poletaeva, Tatyana (1953, Moscow)

A: *Samizdat veka*; B: *Nauka liubvi* (1995); P: *Kontinent* 28; *Znamia* (1992) 3, (1993) 7, (1994) 3, (1996) 6; *Novyi mir* (2002) 5; I: http://magazines.russ.ru/authors/p/poletaeva/

Poliachenko, Tatyana (1960, Moscow)

A: *Molodaya poeziya 89*; P: *Kontinent* 67

Poliushkina, Elena (1973–1993, Moscow)

B: *Vozmozhnost* (1995); I: http://vernitski.narod.ru/poliushk.htm

Popova, Sofya (1968, Cheliabinsk/Moscow)

A: *Sovremennaya uralskaya poeziya*; *Nestolichnaya literatura*; B: *Lesnoi pozhar* (1997)

Poriadina, Mariya (1973, Moscow)

B: *Liniya otchuzhdeniya* (2003); P: *Vavilon* 4

*Postnikova, Olga (1943, Voronezh/Moscow)

A: *Grazhdane nochi*; *Poryv* (1993); *Strofy veka*; B: *Visokosnyi god* (1984); *Pontiiskaia sol* (1992); *Krylatyi lev* (1993); *Babyi pesni* (1995); *Ferrum* (1998); P: *Novyi mir* (1988) 3, (1994) 1, (1995) 6, (1997) 3, (1998) 3, (2002) 3, (2003) 3; *Znamia* (1989) 6, (1993) 12, (1994) 12, (1997) 11; *Soglasie* (1991) 7; *Teplyi stan* (1991); *Poberezhye* 11; E: *Dictionary of Russian Women Writers*; *Russian Women Poets*; I: http://magazines .russ.ru/authors/p/postnikova/

Potapova, Polina (1978, Cheliabinsk)

A: *Antologiya: Sovremennaya uralskaya poeziya (1997–2003)*; I: http://magazines .russ.ru/urnov/2003/16/potapova.html

Pudovkina, Elena (1950, St. Petersburg)

P: *Indeks-2*; *Den poezii* (Leningrad, 1989); *Molodoi Leningrad 89*; *Znamia* (1997) 1; *Novyi mir* (2002) 4; *AKT*; I: http://magazines.russ.ru/authors/p/pudovkina/

Rakhlina, Marlena (1925, Kharkov)

A: *Dikoe pole*; B: *Dom dlia liudei* (1965); *Mayatnik* (1968); *Nadezhda silnee menia* (1990); *Drugu v pokolenye* (1994); *Poteriavshiesia stikhi* (1996); *Oktiabr, na iyul pokhozhii* (2000); P: *Russkaya mysl*, 5 June 1987; *Kontinent* 60

Rakitskaya, Evelina (1960, Moscow)

B: *Dozhit do 30* (1993); P: *Oktiabr* (1997) 12, (2000) 10; *Den poezii* (Moscow, 2000); I: http://magazines.russ.ru/authors/r/rakitskaya/

Rashkovskaya (Slepaya), Irina (1963, Kaluga/Germany)

A: *Antologiya russkogo verlibra*; *Samizdat veka*; B: *Prevrashcheniya* (1990); P: *Novaya literaturnaya gazeta* 5; *Yunost* (1989) 1

*Ratushinskaya, Irina (1954, Odessa/Kiev/London/Moscow)

A: *Russkaya poeziya: XX vek*; *Dikoe pole*; B: *Stikhi, Poems, Poèmes* (1984); *Vne limita* (1986); *Ya dozhivu* (1986); *Stikhi* (1988); *Stikhi* (1993); P: *Grani* (1985) 137, (1987) 143; *Kontinent* (1985) 43; *Novyi mir* (2001) 1, (2003) 4; E: *Against Forgetting*; *In the Grip of Strange Thoughts*; *No, I Am Not Afraid* (1986); *Beyond Limit* (1987); *Pencil Letter* (1988); *Dance with a Shadow* (1992); *20th-Century Russian Poetry*; *Reference Guide to Russian Literature*; *Wind of the Journey* (2000); *Russian Women Poets*

*Retivova, Tatyana (1954, New York/Kiev)

E: *Potomac Review* (Fall 1997); *Russian Women Poets*; *Macguffin* (2003) 1/2; I: http:// www.vladivostok.com/Speaking_In_Tongues/tatiana.html

Rits, Evgeniya (1977, Nizhnii Novgorod)

P: *Oktiabr* (2002) 12; *Vavilon* 10; I: http://stihi.ru/author.html?riz

*Rizdvenko, Tatyana (1969, Moscow)

A: *Russkaya poeziya: XX vek*; B: *Lichnyi vozdukh* (1999); *Dlia Rozhdestva, dlia bukvaria* (2002); P: *Oktiabr* (1997) 10, (2002) 2; *Druzhba narodov* (1998) 4, (1999) 3; *Arion* (1999) 3; *Ulov* 5; *Znamia* (2002) 12; *Yunost* (2003) 11; I: http://www.levin.rinet.ru/ FRIENDS/RIZDVENKO/; http://magazines.russ.ru/authors/r/rizdvenko/

Rodionova, Olga (1959, Omsk/Leningrad/USA)

　　B: *Moi ptitsy—na vetkakh* (1999); *Za krysolovom* (2001); *Ne letai* (2003); P: *Skladchina* (1996); *Istoki* (2000) 7; *Poberezhye* 11; I: http://www.litera.ru/slova/verochka/

Romanova, Anastasiya (1979, Moscow)

　　B: *Rasputye: Samshity: Osoka* (2001); P: *Vavilon* 9, 10; *Anatomiya angela*; *XXI poet*; I: http://www.kastopravda.ru/verse/romanova/nastia.htm; http://www.litera.ru/slova/romanova/

Romanova, Natalya (St. Petersburg)

　　B: *Mashina navazhdeniya* (1994); *Publichnye pesni* (1999); *Raspisnaya stena* (1999); *Pesnia angela na igle* (2001); I: http://litpromzona.narod.ru/romanova/; http://www.opushka.spb.ru/name/romanova_name.shtml

Rozenblium, Madlen (Tbilisi/USA)

　　B: *Nevostrebovannyi chas* (1998); *Venok sonetov* (2001); P: *Almanakh-99 Kluba russkikh pisatelei*; I: http://www.vechny.com/ludislov/ls100800_2.htm

Rozhanskaya, Olga (Moscow)

　　B: *Stikhi po-russki* (1993); P: *Kontinent* 62; *Chernovik* 1

Rychkova, Olga (1970, Tomsk)

　　A: *Nestolichnaya literatura*; B: *Kazhdyi okhotnik* (1997); P: *Yunost* (1997) 2; *Arion* (1999) 1; *Literaturnaya gazeta*, 6–12 March 2002

Sannikova, Natalya (1969, Ekaterinburg)

　　A: *Antologiya: Sovremennaya uralskaya poeziya (1997–2003)*; B: *Intermezzo* (2003); P: *Ural* (2001) 7; I: http://magazines.russ.ru/urnov/2003/16/sannnat.html

Sarancha, Nina (Omsk)

　　A: *Nestolichnaya literatura*; P: *Novaya literaturnaya gazeta* 4

Savushkina, Nina (1964, St. Petersburg)

　　B: *Stikhi* (1996); *Pansionat* (1999); P: *Postscriptum* 10; *Neva* (2002) 8; I: http://www.piiter.ru/view.php?cid=10&gid=39

*Sedakova, Olga (1949, Moscow)

　　A: *Nezamechennaya zemlia*; *Samizdat veka*; B: *Vrata, okna, arki* (1986); *Kitaiskoe puteshestvie: Stely i nadpisi: Starye pesni* (1990); *Stikhi* (1994); *Puteshestvie volkhvov: Izbrannoe* (2001); *Stikhi* (2001); *Starye pesni* (2003); P: *Grani* 130; *Laterna Magica*; *Mitin zhurnal* 9/10; *Druzhba narodov* (1988) 10, (1992) 9, (1993) 11, (1998) 5; *Vestnik novoi literatury* 2; *Novyi mir* (1990) 5; *Volga* (1991) 10 and 12, (1992) 7; *Znamia* (1991) 6, (1992) 8, (1996) 2; *Arion* (1994) 2; *Kontinent* 95, 116; E: *The Poetry of Perestroika*; *Third Wave*; *Dictionary of Russian Women Writers*; *Contemporary Russian Poetry*; *An Anthology of Russian Women's Writing*; *Crossing Centuries*; *Russian Women Writers*; *In the Grip of Strange Thoughts*; *The Silk of Time* (1994); *The Wild Rose* (1997); *Poet for Poet*; *Reference Guide to Russian Literature*; *Russian Women Poets*; *Poems and Elegies* (2003); I: http://www.poesis.ru/poeti-poezia/sedakova/biograph.htm

Shadrina, Yuliya (1976, Vladivostok)

　　A: *Nestolichnaya literatura*; P: *Seraya loshad* 1, 2, 3, 4; I: http://www.gif.ru/greyhorse/shadrina.html

Sharapova, Alla (1949, Moscow)

　　A: *Strofy veka*; B: *Sredi vetvei* (1996); P: *Arion* (1994) 1; *Novyi mir* (1995) 1

*Shats, Evelina (Odessa/Milan)

B: *Variazioni sul nero* (1992); *Poezia per Armanda* (1997); *Hotel Londonskaya* (1999, 2001); *Ieroglif beskonechnosti* (1999); *Pivnoi larek* (2001); *Mytinskii zamok* (2002); *Semeinaya khronika goroda Mykina* (2002); P: *Vsemirnye odesskie novosti* (1992) 5, (2000) 40, (2002) 48; *Odessa* (1996) 2; *Deribasovskaya-Reshilevskaya* (2002) 8, (2003) 13 and 15; E: *Russian Women Poets*

Shchapova, Elena (1950)

A: *Samizdat veka*; *Strofy veka*; B: *Stikhi* (1985); P: *Vremia i my* 38; *Kontinent* 25; *Ekho* (1979) 2–3, (1980) 1; *GF* (1992) 8; *Istoki* (1999) 5; I: http://lib.ru/POEZIQ/ RUSSAMERICA/SHAPOWA/kriminalist.txt

*Shcherbina, Tatyana (1954, Moscow)

A: *Poryv*; *Strofy veka*; *Samizdat veka*; *Molodaya poeziya 89*; B: *Nol Nol* (1991); *Zhizn bez* (1997); *Dialogi s angelom* (1999); *Kniga o khvostatom vremeni. . .* (2001); *Prozrachnyi mir* (2002); P: *Mitin zhurnal* 14, 20, 22/23, 31, 38, 50, 52, 54, 55, 57; *Rodnik* (1988) 10, (1989) 12; *Chernovik* 5; *Yunost* (1992) 6–8; *Oktiabr* (2001) 8, (2003) 11; E: *Third Wave*; *Dictionary of Russian Women Writers*; *In the Grip of Strange Thoughts*; *Crossing Centuries*; *Russian Women Poets*; *The Score of the Game* (2003); *Life Without* (2004); I: http://www.mitin.com/people/sherbina/

Shcherbino, Kseniya (1980, Moscow)

B: *Evgenika* (2002); P: *Vavilon* 9, 10; *XXI poet*; I: http://www.litera.ru/slova/ sherbino/; http://www.piiter.ru/view.php?cid=10&gid=8

Shevchenko, Ekaterina (1956, Moscow)

B: *Stikhi* (1995); P: *Okrestnosti* 3; *Novyi mir* (1995) 7, (1997) 1; *Arion* (1997) 2; I: http:// magazines.russ.ru/authors/s/eshevchenko/

Shneiderman, Asia (1968, St. Petersburg)

A: *Poeziya bezmolviya*; B: *Oboznachit molchanie slovom* (1998); P: *Arion* (1996) 2; *Vavilon* 3

*Shostakovskaya, Irina (1978, Moscow)

A: *Deviat izmerenii*; B: *Irina Shostakovskaya* (1999); *Tsvetochki* (2004); P: *Vavilon* 5, 6, 7, 8, 9, 10; *Chernovik* 13; *Chernym po belomu*; *Avtornik* 1, 5, 10; *Remissionery*; *Okrestnosti* 3; *XXI poet*; *Arion* (2001) 1; I: http://www.vavilon.ru/texts/ shostakovskayao.html

*Shvarts, Elena (1948, St. Petersburg)

A: *Krug*; *Nezamechennaya zemlia*; *Strofy veka*; *Samizdat veka*; B: *Tantsuyushchii David* (1985); *Stikhi* (1987); *Trudy i dni Lavinii iz ordena obrezaniya serdtsa* (1987); *Storony sveta* (1989); *Stikhi* (1990); *Lotsiya nochi* (1993); *Paradise* (1993); *Pesnia ptitsy na dne morskom* (1995); *Mundus imaginalis* (1996); *Opredelenie vetra v durnuyu pogodu* (1997); *Zapadno-vostochnyi veter* (1997); *Solo na raskalennoi trube* (1998); *Stikhotvoreniya i poemy* (1999); *Dikopis poslednego vremeni* (2000); *Sochineniya* (2002); P: *22* 5; *Ekho* (1978) 1, (1979) 2, (1980) 1 and 4; *Strelets* 3; *Kovcheg* 5, 6; *Gnozis*; *Glagol*; *Grani*; *Neva* (1988) 9; *Rodnik* (1988) 5; *Den poezii* (Leningrad, 1989); *Molodoi Leningrad 89*; *Urbi* 1; *Yunost* (1991) 10; *Volga* (1992) 7–8; *Znamia* (1992) 12, (2001) 8, (2003) 6; *Zvezda* (1992) 5–6, (1997) 6, (2001) 1, (2002) 6, (2003) 12; *Vestnik novoi literatury* 2, 5, 8; *Kamera khraneniya* 2, 3, 4; *Novyi mir* (1993) 3, (2000)

7, (2003) 5; *Arion* (1995) 1; *Novoe literaturnoe obozrenie* (1999) 1; *Oktiabr* (2003) 11;
E: Child of Europe; *The Poetry of Perestroika*; *Paradise* (1993); *Contemporary Russian Poetry*; *Third Wave*; *Twentieth-Century Russian Poetry*; *20th-Century Russian Poetry*; *An Anthology of Russian Women's Writing*; *Reference Guide to Russian Literature*; *Russian Women Writers*; *In the Grip of Strange Thoughts*; *Crossing Centuries*; *Russian Women Poets*; *I:* http://www.vavilon.ru/texts/shvartso.html; http://www.newkamera.de/escwarz_01.html; http://magazines.russ.ru/authors/s/shvarts/

Simonova, Ekaterina (1977, Nizhnii Tagil)

A: Antologiya: Sovremennaya uralskaya poeziya (1997–2003); *P: Uralskaya nov'* 12; *Ural* (2000) 9, (2002) 9 and 11; *Vavilon* 10; *I:* http://magazines.russ.ru/authors/s/esimonova/

Sineva, Albina (1968, Voronezh)

B: Zabytoe iskusstvo byt' liubimym (1993); *Devochka-rech* (1997); *P: Vavilon* 2, 10; *Russkaya mysl*; *I:* http://www.stihi.ru/author.html?albina; http://www.zapovednik.litera.ru/N50/index.html

Sinkevich, Valentina (1926, Kiev/USA)

A: Antologiya poezii russkogo zarubezhya; *Russkaya poeziya: XX vek*; *B: Ogni* (1973); *Nastuplenie dnia* (1978); *Tsvetenie trav* (1985); *Zdes ia zhivu* (1988); *P: Kontinent* 102

Sizova, Zhanna (1969, Moscow/Irkutsk/St. Petersburg)

B: Izhitsy (1998); *P: Vavilon* 8; *Arion* (1999) 4; *Chernovik* 5; *I:* http://www.vavilon.ru/textonly/issue5/sizova.htm

Skandiaka, Nika (1978, Moscow/USA/Britain)

A: Deviat izmerenii; *P: Vavilon* 7, 8, 9, 10; *E: Absinthe: New European Writing* (2003) 1; *I:* http://www.vavilon.ru/texts/skandiakao.html

Skorodumova, Yuliya (1964, Moscow)

A: Russkaya poeziya: XX vek; *B: Chtivo dlia paltsev* (1993); *Otkuda prikhodit mysh* (1993); *Sochiniaya sebe litso* (1997); *P: Arion* (1994) 4; *Avtornik* 2, 11; *E: Crossing Centuries*; *I:* http://www.vavilon.ru/texts/skoroo.html

Slepakova, Nonna (1936–1998, St. Petersburg)

A: Samizdat veka; *To vremia—eti golosa*; *Strofy veka*; *B: Lampa* (1992); *Polosa otchuzhdeniya* (1998); *P: Novyi mir* (1991) 6; *I:* http://www.ruthenia.ru/60s/leningrad/slepakova/; http://www.rvb.ru/np/publication/02comm/13/04slepakova.htm

Slutskina, Polina (1947, Moscow)

B: Puteshestvie po vremeni (2002); *P: Chernovik* 14; *Arion* (1998) 4; *I:* http://poetry.liter.net/jano2slu.html

Smolovskaya (Kolesnikova), Elena (Moscow/Australia)

B: Povorotnyi krug (1992); *P: Arion* (1998) 2

Sobenina, Lelia (1981, Ekaterinburg)

P: Ural (2002) 9; *Vavilon* 9; *I:* http://vernitski.narod.ru/sobenina.htm

Son, Anna (1962, Odessa)

B: Zemlia-Zemlia-Vozdukh (1998); *P: Soty*; *Collegium* (1997) 1

Spirina, Elena (1964, Nizhnii Novgorod)

P: Dirizhabl (2001) 9

*Starodubtseva, Natalya (1979, Nizhnii Tagil)

  A: *Antologiya: Sovremennaya uralskaya poeziya (1997–2003)*; B: *Kitaiskaya skripka* (2000); *Opuntsiya ovata* (2002); P: *Uralskaya nov'* 12; *Vavilon* 9, 10; *Anatomiya angela*; *RISK* 4; I: http://www.vavilon.ru/texts/starodubtsevao.html

Stegny, Natalya (1965, Moscow)

  B: *Kniga stikhotvorenii* (1999)

*Stepanova, Mariya (1972, Moscow)

  A: *Deviat izmerenii*; B: *O bliznetsakh* (2001); *Pesni severnykh yuzhan* (2001); *Tut-svet* (2002); *Schastye* (2003); P: *Elka dlia menia*; *Yunost* (1988) 3; *Znamia* (1993) 3, (1997) 3, (1998) 6, (2000) 6; *Istoki* (1999) 6; *Zerkalo* 17–18; *Vavilon* 4, 7, 8, 9, 10; *Chernym po belomu*; *Ulov* 1; *Okrestnosti* 4; *Kriticheskaya massa* (2003) 1; E: *Russian Women Poets*; I: http://www.vavilon.ru/texts/stepanovao.html

Suchkova, Nata (1976, Vologda)

  A: *Vremia Ch*; *Nestolichnaya literatura*; *Deviat izmerenii*; B: *Lanilovyi bliuz* (1997); *Nezhneishaya pytka* (1997); *Piat poem* (1999); P: *Vavilon* 9, 10; *Novaya yunost* (1999) 4; I: http://www.stihi.ru/author.html?ctrekoza

Sudina, Yuliya (1979, Nizhnii Tagil)

  A: *Antologiya: Sovremennaya uralskaya poeziya (1997–2003)*; I: http://magazines .russ.ru/urnov/2003/16/sud.html

Suglobova, Irina (1958, Tambov/Moscow)

  A: *Russkaya poeziya: XX vek*; B: *I grekh moi predo mnoi est' vynu* (1997); *Stikhi kontsa aprelia* (1997); I: http://lib.ru/ZHURNAL/suglobowa.txt

*Sukhovey, Darya (1977, St. Petersburg)

  A: *Vremia Ch*; *Legko byt' iskrennim*; *Deviat izmerenii*; B: *AVTOM* (1997); *Katalog sluchainykh zapisei* (2001); P: *AKT*; *Vavilon* 6, 7, 8, 9, 10; *Chernym po belomu*; *Ulov* 3, 5; *Anatomiya angela*; *Okrestnosti* 3; E: *Russian Women Poets*; I: http://www.levin .rinet.ru/FRIENDS/SUHOVEI/index.html; http://www.vavilon.ru/texts/ suhoveio.html

*Sulchinskaya, Olga (1966, Moscow)

  B: *Stikhotvoreniya* (2000); P: *Arion* (1997) 2, (1999) 1, (2002) 1; *Znamia* (1998) 12, (2001) 3; *Novyi mir* (1999) 6, (2000) 11; *Oktiabr* (2000) 9; *Kreshchatik* 22; E: *Russian Women Poets*; I: http://magazines.russ.ru/authors/s/sulchinskaya/

*Suntsova, Elena (1976, Nizhnii Tagil)

  A: *Antologiya: Sovremennaya uralskaya poeziya (1997–2003)*; B: *Kniga stikhotvorenii* (2000); *Plokhoi idealnyi mayatnik* (2003); P: *Vavilon* 8, 9, 10; *Uralskaya nov'* (2001) 12; *Chernovik* (2003) 18; *Ural* (2003) 1, (2004) 3; I: http://www.vavilon.ru/texts/ suntsovao.html

Svitneva, Evgeniya (Moscow)

  P: *Arion* (1997) 3

Tarasova, Marina (Moscow)

  B: *Vozdushnyi most* (1993); P: *Arion* (1999) 2; *Druzhba narodov* (2000) 4; *Novyi mir* (2000) 11, (2001) 12; *Kontinent* 105; I: http://magazines.russ.ru/authors/t/ tarasova/

Tatarinova, Olga (1939, Moscow)

  B: *Stikhi* (1995); P: *Kreshchatik* 15; *Den poezii* (Moscow, 2000)

Temkina, Marina (1948, New York)

    A: The Blue Lagoon Anthology, 2B; *Antologiya sovremennoi russkoi poezii tretei volny emigratsii*; *Strofy veka*; *B: Chasti chast* (1985); *V obratnom napravlenii* (1989); *Kalancha* (1995); *P: Kontinent* 51 and 56; *Novyi zhurnal* 196; *E: Dictionary of Russian Women Writers*; *I:* http://www.thecoastmagazine.org/Poetry/MarinaTemkina .htm

Tinovskaya, Elena (1964, Ekaterinburg)

    A: Nestolichnaya literatura; *Antologiya: Sovremennaya uralskaya poeziya (1997–2003)*; *B: Krasavitsa i ptitsa* (2002); *P: Ural* (2000) 2; *Znamia* (2000) 10, (2001) 9, (2002) 5 and 8, (2003) 8; *Chernym po belomu*; *I:* http://magazines.russ.ru/authors/t/ tinovskaya/

Titova, Tatyana (1962, Nizhnii Tagil)

    A: Sovremennaya uralskaya poeziya (1997–2003); *B: Derevya* (2003); *P: Nesovremennye zapiski*

*Tkhorzhevskaya, Vitalina (1971, Ekaterinburg); also as *Vita Te*

    A: Samizdat veka; *Sovremennaya uralskaya poeziya*; *Antologiya russkogo verlibra*; *Antologiya: Sovremennaya uralskaya poeziya (1997–2003)*; *B: Ptichya pamiat* (1991); *Puteshestvie v obratnuyu storonu* (1994); *Tretye puteshestvie* (1996); *Smirennyi gnev* (1997); *P: Chernovik* 14; *Nesovremennye zapiski* 2; *Oktiabr* (1996) 12; *Ural* (1999) 8, (2001) 10; *E: Crossing Centuries*; *Russian Women Poets*; *I:* http://sp-issues.narod .ru/4/tkhorzh.htm; http://magazines.russ.ru/urnov/2003/16/thor.html

*Tokareva, Yana (1976, Moscow)

    A: Legko byt' iskrennim; *Deviat izmerenii*; *B: Teplye veshchi* (2004); *P: Okrestnosti* 3, 4; *Vavilon* 7, 8, 10; *Chernym po belomu*; *Anatomiya angela*; *Kreshchatik* 15; *Avtornik* 5, 10; *I:* http://www.vavilon.ru/texts/tokarevao.html

Trubacheva, Anastasiya (Moscow)

    A: Deviat izmerenii; *P: Vavilon* 7, 10; *I:* http://vernitski.narod.ru/trubatch.htm

Tyshkovskaya, Lesia (1969, Kiev)

    A: Antologiya russkogo verlibra; *Vremia Ch*; *B: Sny na beregu zhizni* (1992); *Ostavshimsia zdes* (1994); *Vremia polutonov* (2000); *P: GF* (1991) 15; *Kreshchatik* 2, 8; *Chernovik* 14; *Vavilon* 4; *Soty* 3; *I:* http://www.litera.ru/slova/tyshkovskaya/

Ukhanova, Marina (Nizhnii Novgorod)

    A: Nestolichnaya literatura; *P: Vavilon* 4; *E: Crossing Centuries*

Unksova, Kari (1941–1983, St. Petersburg)

    A: Antologiya russkogo verlibra; *Samizdat veka*; *B: Izbrannoe* (1985); *P: Arion* (1994) 1

Ushakova, Elena (Nevzgliadova,1945, St. Petersburg)

    A: Strofy veka; *B: Nochnoe solntse* (1991); *Metel* (2000); *P: Novyi mir* (1992) 1, (1993) 6, (1995) 10, (1997) 4, (1999) 3, (2000) 6, (2001) 11, (2003) 11; *Neva* (1993) 2; *Znamia* (1993) 11; *Zvezda* (1993) 3, (1997) 5, (2002) 4, (2003) 4; *Arion* (1996) 1, (1999) 4; *E: Dictionary of Russian Women Writers*; *Russian Women Poets*; *I:* http://magazines .russ.ru/authors/u/ushakova/

Vagurina, Liudmila (Moscow)

    B: O mnogom i ob odnom (1994); *P: Novoe literaturnoe obozrenie* 35

Vankhanen, Natalya (1951, Moscow)

A: *Vremia Ch*; B: *Dnevnoi mesiats* (1991); *Dalekie lastochki* (1995); *Zima imperii* (1998); P: *Arion* (1996) 2; *Strelets* (1997) 1; *Neva* (2001) 1; *Postscriptum* 7, 8; *Novyi mir* (2003) 8; I: http://www.erfolg.ru/hall/n_vankhanen.htm

*Vasileva, Elena (1964, Vladivostok)

A: *100 let poezii Primorya*; B: *Zona molchaniya* (1995); P: *Seraya loshad* 1, 2, 3, 4; *Rubezh* 4; I: http://spintongues.vladivostok.com/lena.htm; http://www.gif.ru/greyhorse/vasiljeva.htmlm

Vasileva, Elizaveta (1984, Ivanovo)

A: *Samoe vygodnoe zaniatie*; B: *Moi Amsterdam Anna* (2003); P: *XXI poet*; I: http://vernitski.narod.ru/vasilieva.htm

Vasilkova, Irina (1949, Moscow)

A: *Molodye poety Moskvy*; *Tverskoi bulvar* (1987) 25; *Den poezii* (Moscow, 1989); *Russkaya poeziya: XX vek*; B: *Poverkh lesov i vod* (2001); P: *Tallinn* (2002) 3/4; *Znamia* (2002) 9; *Novyi mir* (2003) 6; I: http://www.stihi.ru/poems/2001/02/19-43.html

Vatutina, Mariya (1968, Moscow)

A: *Deviat izmerenii*; B: *Moskovskie stikhi* (1995); *Chetvertyi Rim* (2000); P: *Novyi mir* (2000) 5, (2001) 3, (2003) 1, (2004) 1; *Arion* (2001) 1; *Znamia* (2001) 10; *Ulov* 4; I: http://magazines.russ.ru/authors/v/vatutina/

Viazmitinova, Liudmila (1950, Moscow)

B: *Prostranstvo rosta* (1992); *Moneta* (1997)

Vinogradova, Nina (1958, Kharkov)

A: *Dikoe pole*; *Vremia Ch*; B: *Podokonnik* (1990); *Pamiat-machekha* (1997); *Solo-vei* (1997); *Svet klinom* (1997); *Naidenysh* (1998); *Antologiya egoizma* (1999); *Prosto sobaka* (2001); P: *Arion* (1995) 4, (1999) 3, (2000) 3; *Znamia* (1998) 10; *Ulov* 3; ©*oyuz pisatelei* (2000) 2, (2003) 5; *Rodomysl* (2001) 2; I: http://sp-issues.narod.ru/vinogradova/; http://kharkov.vbelous.net/iambus/vinograd.htm; http://sp-issues.narod.ru/vinogradova/index.htm

Vinogradova, Tatyana (1965, Moscow)

A: *Vremia Ch*; *Samoe vygodnoe zaniatie*; B: *Lotosy: Zoloto: Son* (1996); *Bogdanovo* (2003); *Kamennoe derevo* (2003); P: *Arion* (1998) 1; *Istoki* (2000) 8

Virta, Marina (Moscow)

A: *Grazhdane nochi*; B: *Snezhnaya subbota* (1986)

Vishnevskaya, Yana (1970, Kiev/Moscow)

P: *Vavilon* 1; I: http://www.vavilon.ru/metatext/vavilon1/vishnevskaya.html

Vitukhnovskaya, Alina (1973, Moscow)

B: *Detskaya kniga mertvykh* (1995), *Sobaka Pavlova* (1996); P: *Arion* (1995) 4; *Literaturnaya gazeta*, 4 October 1995; *Novyi mir* (1996) 5; *Remissionery*; I: http://alien.ush.ru/

Vladimirova, Liya (1938, Israel)

A: *Antologiya sovremennoi russkoi poezii tretei volny emigratsii*; B: *Sviaz vremen* (1975); *Pora predchuvstvii* (1978); *Sneg i pesok* (1982); *Stikhotvoreniya* (1988); *Stikhotvoreniya* (1990); *Sviaz vremen* (1990); P: *22* 6, 10, 20, 28, 37; *Kontinent* (1983) 37; *Vremia i my* 46, 73, 85; *Laterna Magica*; *Russkaya mysl*, 1 February 1991; *Ierusalimskii zhurnal* 8

*Vlasova, Ekaterina (1976, Cheliabinsk)

   A: *Antologiya: Sovremennaya uralskaya poeziya (1997–2003)*; B: *Malenkii Vishnu*
   (1998); P: *Uralskaya nov'* (2000) 2; *Nesovremennye zapiski* 3; E: *Russian Women*
   Poets

Volchenko, Viktoriya (1964, Moscow)

   A: *Vremia Ch*; B: *Stikhi* (1998); P: *GF* (1992) 17

*Voltskaya, Tatyana (1960, St. Petersburg)

   B: *Dve krovi* (1989); *Svitki* (1990); *Strela* (1994); *Ten* (1998); *Tsikada* (2002);
   P: *Molodoi Leningrad* 89; *Druzhba narodov* (1992) 8, (1994) 2, (1996) 1, (1997) 12,
   (2000) 2, (2001) 9; *Neva* (1993) 12; *Znamia* (1994) 12, (1996) 1, (1998) 3, (2001) 2;
   Novyi mir (1995) 12, (1998) 11, (2001) 5, (2002) 7; *Zvezda* (1995) 5, (1996) 2, (1997) 2,
   (1998) 5, (1999) 5, (2000) 3, (2001) 3, (2003) 11; *Oktiabr* (1996) 2; *Grani* 182; *Arion*
   (1997) 3; *Zolotoi vek* (1999) 13; *Postscriptum* 4, 6, 8, 10; E: *Russian Women Poets*;
   I: http://poetry.liter.net/voltskaya.html; http://magazines.russ.ru/authors/v/
   voltskaya/

Vorobeva, Evgeniya (1973, Moscow)

   P: *Arion* (2000) 2; *Kreshchatik* 16; *Solo* 21; *Iz arkhiva "Novoi literaturnoi gazety"*;
   Okrestnosti 3, 4; I: http://www.guelman.ru/slava/texts/vorob.htm

Voznesenskaya, Yuliya (1940, Leningrad/Munich)

   A: *The Blue Lagoon Anthology*, 5B; P: *Grani* 108, 111–112; *Tretya volna* (1979) 6;
   Vestnik 128; *Mariya* (1981) 1; E: *Reference Guide to Russian Literature*

Yagodintseva, Nina (1962, Cheliabinsk)

   A: *Sovremennaya uralskaya poeziya*; *Antologiya: Sovremennaya uralskaya*
   poeziya (1997–2003); B: *Idushchii nochyu* (1991); *Pered nebom* (1992); *Amarillis*
   (1997); *Na vysote meteli* (2000); *Techenye donnykh trav* (2002); P: *Uralskaya*
   nov' (2000) 8; *Ural* (2001) 2; I: http://magazines.russ.ru/urnov/2003/16/
   yag.html

Yamakova, Nailia (1982, St. Petersburg)

   P: *Arion* (2003) 4; *Vavilon* 10; I: http://www.litera.ru/slova/yamakova/; http://
   nailya-13.narod.ru/

Yarbusova, Francheska (1942, Alma-Ata/Moscow)

   A: *Antologiya russkogo verlibra*

Yusupova, Lidiya (1964, St. Petersburg/Canada)

   B: *Irasaliml* (1995); P: *Triton* 2

Yuzvak, Yana (1979, Almaty/Moscow)

   B: *Sogliadatai peremen* (2001); I: http://www.kastopravda.ru/verse/uzvak/yana
   .htm

Zagotova, Svetlana (1956, Donetsk)

   A: *Antologiya russkogo verlibra*; B: *Empiricheskie epizody* (1993); *S mirom po moriu*
   (1999); P: *Oktiabr* (1999) 8; *Soty* 5; I: http://www.loyola.h1.ru/skriptori/zag/
   zag1.shtml

Zakharova, Inna (Kharkov)

   B: *Triptikh* (1991)

Zalogina, Olga (St. Petersburg)

   B: *Stikhi* (1994); *Pesnia ognia* (1997); I: http://zhurnal.lib.ru/z/zalogina_o_b/

*Zelenina, Galina (1978, Moscow); now publishes under the name *Gila Loran*
  A: Deviat izmerenii; *Vremia Ch*; *B: Zh* (2000); *Voila* (2004); *P: Vavilon* 7, 8, 9;
  Solnechnoe spletenie 12/13, 18/19, 22/23; *Chernym po belomu*; *Anatomiya angela*;
  RISK 4; *Ulov* 4; *I:* http://www.vavilon.ru/texts/zeleninao.html; http://www
  .plexus.org.il/autors/zelenina.htm
Zima (Bolycheva), Natalya (1974, Barnaul)
  B: Vozdukhoplavatel Veter (1999)
*Zinger, Gali-Dana (1962, Leningrad/Jerusalem)
  A: Skopus-2; *Orientatsiya na mestnosti*; *Antologiya "Dvoetochiya"*; *B: Sbornik* (1992);
  Adel Kilka: Iz. 1985 (1993); *Osazhdennyi Yarusarim* (2002); *P: Narod i zemlia* (1989) 8;
  22 (1990) 74, (1992) 85, (1999) 108; *Obitaemyi ostrov* (1990) 1; *Targum* (1990) 1;
  Dvoetochie (1994) 1 and 3, (1995) 5; *Kamera khraneniya* (1994) 4; *Mnogotochie* (1999)
  4; *Solnechnoe spletenie* (1999) 8, (2000) 12/13, (2001) 18/19, (2003) 24/25; *Arion*
  (2000) 3, (2001) 2; *Stetoskop* (2000) 26; *I:* http://www.vavilon.ru/texts/zingero.
  html; http://a-kobrinsky.tripod.com/zinger/; http://www.plexus.org.il/dana
  .html; http://www.thedrunkenboat.com/singerview.html
Zinoveva, Liubov (Moscow/USA)
  P: GF (1993) 11
Znamenskaya, Irina (1951, St. Petersburg)
  A: Poryv; *Molodaya poeziya 89*; *Pozdnie peterburzhtsy*; *I vsiakie*; *Strofy veka*;
  B: Obrashchayus na ty (1989); *Glaz vopiyushchego* (1997); *P: Den poezii* (Leningrad,
  1989); *Molodoi Leningrad 89*; *Petropol* II (1990); *Postscriptum* 7; *Vestnik Evropy*
  (2002–2003) 7/8; *E: 20th-Century Russian Poetry*; *Dictionary of Russian Women
  Writers*
*Zondberg, Olga (1972, Moscow)
  A: Deviat izmerenii; *B: Kniga priznanii* (1997); *P: Vavilon* 1, 4, 8; *Ural* (1997) 1; *Arion*
  (1998) 2, (1999) 1; *Chernym po belomu*; *Kreshchatik* 10; *Okrestnosti* 3; *I:* http://
  www.vavilon.ru/texts/prim/zondbergo.html
Zubova, Liudmila (1946, St. Petersburg)
  P: Novyi zhurnal 195; *E: Russian Women Poets*; *I:* http://www.utoronto.ca/slavic/
  tsq/012002/zubova.html

THE POETS

Editorial Note
We are grateful to the poets themselves and to our correspondents for supplying biographical details. The disparity in length of these entries is due to the uneven availability of information and does not reflect value judgments. It seemed to us preferable, under the circumstances, to print what we had or could elicit rather than to impose a uniformity of length on these entries.

Izabella (Bella) Akhmadulina was born in Moscow in 1937. She is of partly Tatar descent. Akhmadulina came to prominence as one of the "New Wave" poets of the so-called Thaw period, after Stalin's death, being at one time married to Evtushenko. Her first collection appeared in 1962. Akhmadulina was awarded the State Prize for Literature in 1989. She was one of very few poets able to preserve her independence in the Soviet period. As Brodsky put it: "Her imagery derives from within vision as much as it does from sound, and the latter dictates to her more than she sometimes anticipates. In other words, the lyricism of her poetry is largely the lyricism of the Russian language itself" ("Why Russian Poets?" *Vogue* 167, no. 7 [July 1977]: 112). Akhmadulina's poetry has been translated into all European languages. She lives in Moscow with her husband, the artist Boris Messerer. Readers are also referred to *The Poetic Craft of Bella Akhmadulina* by Sonia Ketchian (1993).

Polina Barskova was born in 1976 in Leningrad. Since 1998 she has been a graduate student at the University of California, Berkeley. Barskova has published several collections of poetry, her first at the age of fifteen: *Christmas* (1991). The same year, she won the first All-Russian young poets contest, sponsored by Vavilon (its earliest major project). Another four collections followed, the last two being *Evridei and Orfika* (perhaps translatable as *Everydaeus and Orphica*) and *Arias*. Barskova writes: "I write poetry only in Russian and I write a lot. I study and relate to the world around me in English and carry in my head smatterings of Latin and Greek, French and Czech. I am seriously interested in film. At this time, on my desk is lying a book by Bakhtin, probably the main hero of my future (*EBZh* [God permitting] as Tolstoy said) dissertation."

Tatyana Bek was born in Moscow in 1949, into the family of the celebrated writer Aleksandr Bek. She graduated from Moscow State University's Department of Journalism and has worked as a bibliographer and editor. At present she teaches a poetry seminar at the Gorky Literary Institute in Moscow. Bek is a contributor to *Voprosy literatury* and *Obshchaya gazeta*. She has received prizes awarded by the journals *Znamia* and *Zvezda* and is the recipient of the All-Russian Golden Gong Award. The author of six collections of poetry, Bek died in 2005.

Natalya Belchenko was born in Kiev (Kyïv), Ukraine, in 1973. She has published three collections of poetry, and her work has appeared in numerous periodicals. Her poetry has been translated into German and French. In 2000 Belchenko received a grant for young poets from East Europe. She received a diploma in philology from Kiev National University and a grant for young poets, the Hubert-Burda Stipend 2000.

Larisa Berezovchuk was born in Kiev, Ukraine, in 1948. She is a graduate of the Kiev Conservatory Department of History and has completed graduate studies at the Leningrad Institute of Theatre, Music, and Cinematography. Berezovchuk has taught in the Kiev Theatrical Institute. She has been writing poetry since 1990. After the Chernobyl disaster, she moved to St. Petersburg, where she still lives. Berezovchuk is also the author of a number of articles on Aleksandr Gornon and other contemporary Russian poets such as Arkady Dragomoshchenko.

Marina Boroditskaya was born in Moscow in 1954. She graduated from the Moscow Institute of Foreign Languages and works as a guide, translator, and teacher of English. She has published in magazines since 1978 but is probably better known as a translator of English (and French) poetry, including John Donne, Robert Burns, G. K. Chesterton, and Rudyard Kipling. Boroditskaya is the author of many books for children. Her own first poetry collection was published in 1994. The third collection appeared in 2002. She works for Radio Russia and lives in Moscow.

Ekaterina Boyarskikh was born in 1976. She lives in Irkutsk. She is a graduate of the Philology Department of Irkutsk University, specializing in the history of the Russian language. She is a winner of the national Debiut Prize for 2000 for her text "Echo of Women."

Zinaida Bykova lives in Chernovtsy (Chernivtsy), Ukraine. She has published one collection of poetry, *Nezrimye ptitsy* (Invisible birds, 2000), and has contributed to *Znamia, Arion*, and *Druzhba narodov*. She is a retired schoolteacher of Russian language and literature; while she has written poetry for many years, only in the last seven to eight years have her poems been appearing in Moscow periodicals.

Svetlana Dengina was born in 1968 in Kuibyshev (now Samara). She graduated from Kuibyshev University and has published one collection of poetry. She lives in Samara.

Regina Derieva was born in Odessa in 1949. She lived for several years in Karaganda and emigrated to Israel in 1991. She now lives in Sweden. Her poetry has been translated into Swedish, French, Italian, Arabic, English, and other languages. She has published ten collections of poetry in Russian and three in English, including *The Inland Sea* (1998), from which the present selection has been taken. Brodsky has written of her poetry: "The real author is poetry itself. It is nearer to you than your pen is to paper" (*Zvezda* 5 [2000]: 62–63).

Marina Dolia was born in Kiev in 1951. She writes of herself: "Her family is a genetic product of Kiev at the beginning of the twentieth century. She absorbed a puritanical stoicism and humility in the face of the inevitable. Her wisdom, such as it is, is simply what has survived from the old generation. As for poetry, she was first inspired by the ballads of Vasily Zhukovsky. Her first mentor, so to speak, was Innokenty Annensky. Born at the beginning of the 50s, she was automatically marginalized. She graduated from Kiev University's Department of Mathematical Linguistics and was interested in cybernetics as well as theater. Brodsky's poetry became for her a model for overcoming the fear of being. Her distinguishing features are that she is an eternal student, a good friend to her friends, and capable of total empathy."

Irina Ermakova was born in 1951 in Crimea. She graduated from the Moscow Institute of Transport Engineering, specializing in bridges and tunnels. For twelve years she worked as a designer. At present she is freelancing as a literary editor and translator as well as adapting stories for radio. She has published in *Literaturnaya gazeta, Arion, Oktiabr, Druzhba narodov,* and other periodicals and is the author of four collections of poetry: *Provintsiya* (Province, 1991); Vinogradnik (Vineyard, 1994); *Stekliannyi sharik* (Glass sphere, 1998), and *Kolybelnaya dlia Odisseya* (Lullaby for Odysseus, 2002).

Galina Ermoshina was born in the Samara region in 1962. She is a graduate of the Kuibyshev Institute of Culture and works as a librarian. She lives in Samara. Ermoshina has published three collections of poetry and was awarded a prize at the Moscow Prose-Poetry Festival in 1999. She translates contemporary American poetry and reviews contemporary Russian and foreign literature for various Moscow and Internet periodicals.

Zoya Ezrokhi was born in Leningrad in 1946 and graduated from the Technological Institute. She has written poetry from the age of four. Her poetry, especially on the subject of cats, has appeared in many magazines and anthologies. Her most important collection, *Just in Case,* was published in 2002.

Elena Fanailova was born in 1962 in the Voronezh district. She has practiced as a doctor and taught at Voronezh University. She is the author of four poetry collections and of a theatrical novel with Aleksandr Anashevich. She was awarded the Andrey Bely Prize in 1999. Fanailova is the Moscow correspondent of Radio Liberty.

Nina Gabrielian was born in 1953 and lives in Moscow. She is a graduate of the Moscow Institute of Foreign Languages. She writes prose and criticism as well as poetry and also translates contemporary and classical poetry of the East. From 1994 to 1997, Gabrielian was chief editor of the feminist journal *Preobrazhenie* (Transformation). From 1996 to 1998 she was an editor of the bulletin *Zhenshchina i kultura* (Woman and culture). She now directs an education program for women, the Independent Women's Forum.

Mariya Galina was born in Tver in 1958. Her childhood and adolescence were spent in Odessa. She is by training a biologist. Her first publication was in *Yunost* in 1991. In 2000–2001 she was a regular columnist ("Poetry Nonstop") for *Literaturnaya gazeta.* Dmitry Kuzmin writes: "Mariya Galina's poetry is distinguished by its range, from Church Slavonic to the terminology of science, with an intermixture of Yiddish and Ukrainian. She recreates the unique and virtually lost social dialect of the Russian-Jewish intelligentsia of Ukraine, the only example of this in modern Russian poetry" (*Literaturnaya zhizn Moskvy,* 21 November 2000).

Dina Gatina, poet, prose writer, and artist, was born in 1981. She lives in the city of Engels (Saratov region). Gatina was the 2002 winner of the Debiut Prize, for which she had been short-listed in 2001.

Anna Glazova was born in Dubna, Moscow region, in 1973. She was educated at the Moscow Architectural Institute and the Berlin Technische Universität as well as the University of Illinois and Northwestern University, Chicago, where she is a doctoral student in comparative literary studies. Her work is to be found on various websites, and she has participated in the Franz Kafka scholarly project and the on-line journals *Speaking in Tongues* and *Text.only*. Her first collection, *Pust' i voda* (Let there be water too), was published in Moscow in 2002.

Linor Goralik was born in Dnepropetrovsk in 1975. From 1989 to 2001 she lived in Israel, where she graduated from Beer Sheva University. She now lives in Moscow, where she works as an Internet journalist. Goralik contributes regularly to *Profil* and *Russkii zhurnal* as well as other business and cultural magazines. She has published several collections of short prose, and she translates from English and Hebrew.

Natalya Gorbanevskaya was born in Moscow in 1936. Expelled from Moscow Univer-sity, she graduated from the Philology Department of Leningrad University. She was arrested in 1968 for protesting against the Soviet-led invasion of Czechoslo-vakia. Gorbanevskaya now lives in Paris and works for the paper *Russkaya mysl*, for which she has regularly written on topical themes. She also regularly publishes poetry collections. A selection of her early work, translated by Daniel Weissbort, was published by Carcanet in 1972. Although she has been typecast as a "political poet," Gorbanevskaya's voice is, in fact, one of the most distinct voices of con-temporary Russian poetry, combining a folk-inspired modernism with narrative clarity.

Anna Gorenko (Karpa) (1972–1999) was born in Bendery, Ukraine. In her youth she often visited Leningrad, to which there are many references in her poetry. In 1989 she emigrated to Israel, living in Tel Aviv and Jerusalem. Two collections of her poetry were published in Israel soon after her death, and in 2003 a revised selection of poems was published in Moscow under the title *Prazdnik nespelogo khleba* (Festival of unripe grain).

Nina Gorlanova was born in a village in the Perm district in 1947. She is a graduate of Perm State University and the author of two books of prose. Her work has appeared in several journals, including *Daugava, Avrora, Oktiabr*, and *Ural*. She lives in Perm.

Faina Grimberg was born in 1951 in Akmolinsk, Kazakhstan. She graduated in philol-ogy from Tashkent University, specializing in Balkan history. She is the author of several wide-circulation books on Russian history. Besides over twenty novels, Grimberg has also written plays and articles and has translated from English, Bul-garian, Greek, and other languages. She has published three collections of poems, including, most recently, *Liubovnaya Andreeva khrestomatiya* (The Andreeva love reader, 2002). She lives in Moscow.

Elena Ignatova was born in Leningrad in 1947. She writes prose as well as poetry. Her poetry has appeared in samizdat and from 1975 in Russian publications abroad. A book was published in Paris in 1976, and another in Leningrad in 1989. In 1992 *Nebesnoe zarevo* (Celestial glow) was published in Jerusalem. Ignatova's poetry has appeared widely in Russian and foreign periodicals and is represented in several anthologies of twentieth-century Russian poetry. In 1997 *Zapiski o Peterburge* (Notes on Petersburg), on the history of the city from the eighteenth to twentieth centuries, was published in St. Petersburg; a revised and expanded edition was published in 2003.

Nina Iskrenko was born in 1951 and graduated in physics from Moscow State Univer-sity. She was a leading underground poet in Moscow until her untimely death from cancer in 1995. Her performances and participation in various artistic "happenings" made her a central figure in the alternative culture of late Soviet and early post-Soviet Russia. Her poems are distinguished by a bold mix of themes, from the political and prosaic to the frankly sexual, and of tones, from the audacity of informal conversation to philosophical strivings after the sublime. Her early "Hymn to Polystylistics" stands as a manifesto of this self-conscious amalgamation. Iskrenko carefully divided her work into volumes, which have continued to appear since her death.

Olga Ivanova was born in Moscow in 1965 and is a graduate of the Gorky Literary Institute. Her first publication was in *Novyi mir* in 1988. She has also published in *Kontinent* and other periodicals, occasionally under the pseudonym Polina Ivanova. Ivanova has published four collections, most significantly the recent *Oda ulitse* (Ode to the street, 2001).

Svetlana Ivanova was born in Leningrad in 1965 and is a graduate of the Art School and the Gorky Literary Institute in Moscow. She is an artist and critic as well as a poet. Ivanova has published three collections of poetry, and her work has appeared in many periodicals, especially *Zvezda* and *Arion*. She has also edited an anthology of Russian émigré poetry, *Russian Atlantis*. Ivanova lives in Moscow.

Inna Kabysh was born in Moscow in 1963. She studied at the Pedagogical Institute and has worked as a schoolteacher. Her poetry has appeared in *Znamia*, *Druzhba narodov*, and *Novyi mir*. Her first individual collection was published in 1994.

Katia Kapovich was born in Kishinev in 1960. She lives and teaches in Cambridge, Massachusetts. Her first book, *Day of the Angel and Night*, was published in Israel in 1992; the poems published here, written in the 90s, come from that book. She also writes fluently in English. Kapovich is the author of four collections of Russian poetry and the recipient of the Library of Congress Literary Award for her collection *Gogol in Rome* (2004).

Svetlana Kekova was born in Sakhalin in 1951. She lives in Saratov and was trained as a philologist. Among her influences is the early poetry of Nikolay Zabolotsky. Kekova teaches in the Pedagogical Institute and has been widely published in all leading journals. She is not a modish poet. Her serious and even solemn relationship to her own life contrasts sharply with that daring which, in epidemic proportions, characterizes the work of so many contemporary writers. She is the recipient of several literary awards, including the Moscow-Transit Prize for the best poet living in the provinces.

Marina Khagen was born in 1974 and lives in Cheliabinsk. She graduated from Cheliabinsk State University as a mathematician and programmer. Khagen writes haiku and free verse. In 1998 she won the first Russian Haiku Contest, organized by the Japanese embassy in Moscow. Her poems have appeared in the Russian haiku magazine *Triton*. She has published one haiku collection, *Shades of Reflections* (2001).

Olga Khvostova was born in 1965 in Maili–Sai Sai, Oshsk region. She lived for a while in Dushanbe. Khvostova trained as a teacher of Russian language and literature. She has published poetry in a Dushanbe periodical and also in London. In 1990 she moved to Gulkevichi, in the Krasnodarsk region. She works wherever she can.

Mariya Kildibekova was born in Moscow in 1976. A graduate of the Moscow Literary Institute, she lived for several years in Yemen and Libya. Her poetry has been published in a number of magazines, including *Arion*. She has worked as a journalist.

Nina Kossman was born in Moscow in 1959 and emigrated to the United States in 1973. She lives in New York. A bilingual Russian-American poet, she has published two books of poetry in Russian, *Pereboi* (Syncopated rhythms, 1990) and *Po pravuyu ruku sna* (To the right of a dream, 1996), and a collection of short stories about her Moscow childhood, *Behind the Border* (1994). Her work has been translated into several languages. Her fiction won a UNESCO/PEN Short Story Award in 1995. Kossman has translated two books of Marina Tsvetaeva's poetry and is the editor of *Gods and Mortals: Modern Poems on Classical Myths* (2001). Two of her plays have been produced in New York City.

Elena Kostyleva was born in 1977 in Moscow. Her first collection was published in 2001. Her work has appeared in periodicals such *as Mitin Zhurnal* and *Vavilon* and has been short-listed for the national Debiut Prize for young writers.

Irina Kovaleva trained as a philologist and is a professor in the Department of Classics, Moscow State University. She has published over eighty articles on ancient and modern Greek literature and Russian literature as well as translations from ancient and modern languages (George Seferis, Miltos Sahtouris, and Odysseus Elytis into Russian; Brodsky and Sedakova into Greek). Kovaleva has written commentaries on works of classical authors published in Russian and edited Joseph Brodsky's *Kentavry: Antichnye siuzhety* (Centaurs: Classical subjects, 2001). She has published three collections of her own poetry.

Ella Krylova was born in Moscow in 1967. Her first publication was in *Znamia* in 1991. Her work has also appeared in *Druzhba narodov, Zvezda, Yunost*, and other Russian periodicals in France and the USA. She has published seven collections of poetry. Since 1993, Krylova has lived in St. Petersburg.

Marina Kudimova was born in Tambov in 1953 and graduated from Tambov Pedagogical Institute. She was influenced by Tsvetaeva, and her work began appearing in *Novyi mir* and *Znamia* after Glasnost. Kudimova is the author of three poetry collections. She lives outside Moscow.

Inna Kulishova was born in Tbilisi in 1969. She graduated from Tbilisi University. Her thesis, on Joseph Brodsky, was completed in 1998. Kulishova has been writing since the age of six. She has published one collection.

Yuliya Kunina was born in Moscow in 1966. She is a graduate of the Philology Department of Moscow State University. Her first book appeared in 1991. In addition to scholarly articles, Kunina has published translations of seventeenth-century English poetry. Her own poetry has been published in many journals and anthologies. The poets to whom she feels closest are Khodasevich and Derzhavin. She is working on a doctorate on translation theory at New York University.

Inga Kuznetsova was born in the village of Chernomorsk, Krasnodar region, in 1974 and was brought up in the Moscow region. She graduated from Moscow State University as a journalist and works as an editor at *Voprosy literatury*. Her work has appeared in *Arion, Novyi mir, Novaya yunost*, and *Volga*. She has published one collection, *Sny sinitsy* (Dreams of a tomtit) and lives in Moscow.

Evgeniya Lavut was born in Moscow in 1972 and graduated in Romance and Germanic languages from Moscow State University. She has published two collections of poetry.

Elena Lazutkina was born in Eisk, Krasnodar region, in 1975. She studied at the St. Petersburg Institute of Film and Television. Lazutkina lives in Moscow and hands out flyers in the street about foreign-language teaching.

Inna Lisnianskaya was born in Baku in 1928. Her first publication was in 1948, and her first collection of poetry appeared in 1957. In 1960 Lisnianskaya moved to Moscow. She published several more books. After her participation in the *Metropol* almanac in 1979, her books were published only abroad (France and the USA). In recent years several more collections have appeared. Lisnianskaya's work is regularly published in all the leading Russian literary periodicals. She was married to the late Semyon Lipkin, a celebrated poet, and their relationship is the subject of her recent poetry collection *V prigorode Sodoma* (In the suburbs of Sodom, 2002).

Sveta Litvak was born in Kovrov in 1959. She is a graduate of the Ivanovo Art Institute. In Moscow she was employed in the Soviet Army Theater as a scene-painter. Her work has appeared in a number of exhibitions of young artists, and in 1999 she had a one-person show. In 1996, with Nikolay Baitov, Litvak founded a literary club for the performance of poetry. She has published three collections, as well as a prose book, *My Journey to the East* (1998). She is a regular contributor to *Znamia* and *Arion*.

Mara Malanova was born in Leningrad in 1970. She graduated from the Russian State University of Humanities. Until the age of twenty, Malanova lived in Ulan-Ude (Buriatiya). Her favorite poet is T. S. Eliot, and her major influences are Mandelstam, Brodsky, and Sedakova. Her first collection, *Express*, appeared in 2002. "Morning" was first published in *Absinthe: New European Writing*.

Kseniya Marennikova was born in Kaliningrad in 1981. Since 1996 she has lived in Moscow. She graduated from the Department of Economics of the Moscow Aviation Institute. She works in public relations. Her main publications have been on the Internet (selected texts can be found on her own website, http://maren.pisem.net/. Marennikova has been published in the almanac *Vavilon*.

Olga Martynova was born in Siberia in 1962. She grew up in Leningrad and graduated from the Leningrad Pedagogical Institute. Since 1991 she has lived in Germany with her husband, the poet and playwright Oleg Yurev. Martynova has published three poetry collections in Russian and one in German and has written numerous critical essays and reviews for the German press. In 2000 she was awarded the Hubert Burda Prize.

Irina Mashinskaya was born in Moscow in 1958 and graduated from Moscow State University. Since 1991 she has lived in America, where she teaches mathematics in high school. She has published four collections, and her work has appeared in many Russian and American journals. Mashinskaya translates contemporary American poetry and won the "Russkaya Amerika" Prize in 2001. Her most recent collection, *Poems* (2001), was nominated for the Apollon Grigoriev Award.

Larisa Miller was born in 1940. She is a graduate of the Moscow Institute of Foreign Languages. Her first collection appeared in 1977, but her poetry has been in print since the mid 60s. She has published eight books of prose and poetry. Miller lives in Moscow.

Tatyana Milova was born in the Moscow region in 1965 and graduated in journalism and philosophy from Moscow State University. She has worked as an editor, night watchwoman, and boiler-person. Her first collection of poetry, *Nachalniku khora* (To the leader of the chorus, 1998), was awarded the International Tivoli Prize (1999). Her work has appeared in *Novyi mir*, *Yunost*, and *Arion* and has been translated into English and Italian.

Stella Morotskaya was born in Nizhnii Novgorod (then Gorkii) in 1962 and was educated at Moscow State University. She now lives in Moscow and works as a magazine editor. She has been publishing her poetry since 1991, including the collections *Metodika svobodnogo poleta* (Methodology of free flight, 1993) and *Vse 33 i drugie* (All 33 and others, 2001). Poems and essays have appeared in *Arion*, *Druzhba narodov*, *Novoe literaturnoe obozrenie*, *Zolotoi vek*, and other publications. Her work has been translated into six languages. She was a prize-winner at both the first and second Moscow festivals of free verse (1991 and 1992).

Raisa Moroz was born in Primorye in 1949 and graduated in engineering. She has lived and worked in Vladivostok and Moscow and is now working in South Korea as director of a company. Her poetry has been published in various journals in the far eastern and central regions of Russia.

Negar was born in Baku in 1975. She graduated in philology from Baku University and is fluent in four languages: Russian, Azeri, Turkish, and English. In 2000, in Baku, she published her first book of poetry in Russian, which includes poems from her teenaged years and early twenties. In 2001 she became the youngest member of the Azerbaijan Union of Writers. Since 2000 Negar has made her home in London. Her first book in England, *On Wings over the Horizon*, was translated by Richard McKane. In 2001 this volume was awarded the Azerbaijan Academy's National Public Prize.

Olesia Nikolaeva was born in Moscow in 1955. She started writing poetry at the age of seven, prose at the age of sixteen, and began to publish at the same age. She is a graduate of Moscow's Gorky Literary Institute, where she teaches a course in the history of Russian religious thought. Her first collection, *The Garden of Miracles* (1980), was followed by several collections of poetry and prose. She has been widely published, especially in *Arion*, *Znamia*, and *Novyi mir*, and has participated in a number of international festivals. In 1998 she was awarded the Töpfer Prize.

Rea Nikonova (Anna Tarshis) was born in Eisk in 1942 and grew up in Sverdlovsk, where she studied music, returning to Eisk in 1975. From there she emigrated to Germany in 1998. She and her husband, Sergey Sigey, produced the multimedia samizdat journal *Transponans* (36 issues, 1979–1987). Perhaps the premier avant-garde poet of Russia, she has invented and writes in an enormous variety of forms and styles, ranging from gesture poems and elaborately gridded texts to short lyrics and *zaum*. She has compiled a multivolume *System*, which attempts to survey and exemplify all possible kinds of poetry.

Vera Pavlova was born in Moscow in 1963. She graduated from the Schnittke College of Music and the Gnesin Academy, specializing in the history of music. Until the age of eighteen, she studied to become a composer. She has also worked as a guide in the Chaliapin Museum and published essays on music. For about ten years Pavlova sang in a church choir. Her first collection appeared in 1997, followed by no fewer than five other collections, the last containing 800 poems, written over a period of eighteen years. Pavlova's celebrity dates from the appearance in the paper *Segodnia* of no fewer than 72 poems (with a postscript by Boris Kuzminsky), which gave rise to the rumor that she was a literary hoax. Her poetry was published in many papers and most of the major journals. Pavlova also directs "Zodiak," a literary workshop for children. She has been awarded the Apollon Grigoriev Prize.

Aleksandra Petrova was born in Leningrad in 1964 and lived for a while in Israel. She is now living in Rome. She writes: "My biography is short for the moment: two books, two changes of country, two daughters. I studied in Tartu, and for me this is important." Her first book, *Liniya otryva* (Tearing-off line), is rich in urban-based elegies. As Stephanie Sandler comments, there is an improvisatory quality in Petrova's poetry, although her verse draws very much on the tradition, for instance, of Pushkin's *Eugene Onegin*. Her field of references, too, is wide, ranging from roller-blades to Dostoevsky's Smerdiakov! Recently the Milan-based journal *Poezia* dedicated eleven pages to her poetry, translated into Italian.

Liudmila Petrushevskaya was born in 1938 and attended Moscow University. She worked as a journalist from 1961 to 1970 and has also worked as a radio reporter, teacher, editor, and translator (from Polish). She came to prominence during the Gorbachev years, when her uncompromising depictions of the seamier side of life began to be published. She was short-listed for the Russian Booker Prize for her dark family saga, *The Time: Night* (1992). Best known, of course, for her prose and drama, Petrushevskaya is also well known in the world of cinema. She took to poetry comparatively late. Her "Karamzin: Village Diary," which also shows her preoccupation with monologue, self-absorption, and isolation, appeared in *Novyi mir* in 1994, and a full version was published in St. Petersburg in 2000.

Olga Postnikova was born in Evdakovo, Voronezh region, in 1943. She lives in Moscow and is a graduate of the Moscow Institute of Chemical Technology. She has worked as a restorer of old buildings and churches. She is the grand-daughter of a Russian priest who perished in the camps. Postnikova has been published in many magazines and anthologies, including *Novyi mir* and *Znamia*. A collection of poetry, *Stikhi* (Verses), appeared in 1993. In 1994 she was awarded the Töpfer Prize. Her novel *Roman na dva golosa* (Novel for two voices) was nominated for the Russian Booker Prize in 2001.

Irina Ratushinskaya was born in Odessa in 1954. She graduated from Odessa University and taught at the Odessa Pedagogical Institute. In 1976 Ratushinskaya was arrested for dissident activity and sentenced to seven years in a strict-regime prison. A collection of poems was published in 1984 by International PEN, with an introduction by Joseph Brodsky. This helped to focus attention on her case. She was released in 1986 and left for England, where her poetry was published by Bloodaxe. She returned to Russia in 2001. Her poetry has been translated into many European languages, and she has published numerous collections of poetry and prose, including a chronicle of her prison ordeal. Ratushinskaya has won many international awards.

Tatyana Retivova was born in New York in 1954 and studied poetry at the University of Montana with Richard Hugo and then at the University of Michigan with Joseph Brodsky. She writes poetry in both English and Russian and has been living in Ukraine for over seven years.

Tatyana Rizdvenko was born in Moscow in 1969 and graduated in graphic arts from the Moscow Pedagogical Institute. She taught art and composition in a drama college. Rizdvenko works in advertising. She has published two collections, and her poems have appeared in *Oktiabr, Znamia,* and *Druzhba narodov.*

Olga Sedakova was born in Moscow in 1949. Her work first appeared in print when she was eleven. Sedakova is a polyglot translator (Eliot, Pound, Hardy, Claudel, Rilke, Petrarch, Horace, and Dante) and a celebrated essayist. In the late 80s her poetry appeared in unofficial journals in Moscow and Leningrad. She is perhaps the leading confessional Christian poet writing in Russian today. Sedakova enjoys the distinction of having been the only Russian poet-in-residence at a British University (Keele). She is the first and, so far, only poet to receive the Vatican Prize for Literature, awarded in 1999. She was awarded the Solzhenitsyn Prize in 2003.

Evelina Shats was born in Odessa and has lived and worked in Italy for many years. She writes poems in Italian and Russian. An artist and performer, essayist, journalist and critic, and theater director, she has published widely in Italy, Russia, and elsewhere. She has been a regular contributor to *Corriere della Sera* as well as to TV and radio shows. Shats is vice-president of the International Consortium for Art Masterpieces (strategies and new technologies for culture) in Moscow. She has exhibited object-books, limited editions, visual poems, and conceptual works.

Tatyana Shcherbina was born in Moscow in 1954. She is a graduate of Moscow State University. Five collections appeared in samizdat, as well as a novel. In 1989 she represented alternative ("second") literature at the Poetry International in Rotterdam, where she met Joseph Brodsky and Derek Walcott. In 1989 Shcherbina's poems began to be published in the official Soviet press. She worked for Radio Liberty in Munich in 1991 and in Paris from 1992 to 1997. Shcherbina speaks fluent French, writes poems in French as well as Russian, and has translated a number of French poets into Russian. In 1994 she was awarded a scholarship by the French minister of culture. Her own poetry has been widely translated. She returned to Russia in 1997 and now lives in Moscow; in 2001 she became deputy editor of the journal *Vestnik Evropy* (European messenger). Her first English collection, *The Score of the Game,* translated by J. Kates, appeared in the USA in 2003.

Irina Shostakovskaya was born in Moscow in 1978 and came to public attention as early as 1994, when she received an award at the All-Russian Young Poets Competition. Since 1997, her poetry and prose has appeared widely. She has published two collections.

Elena Shvarts has long been acknowledged as one of the most important poets in contemporary Russia. She is a prolific, compelling poet who mixes the skepticism of postmodern sensibilities with the haunted primitivism of ancient Slavic folk belief. Her work emerged from the Petersburg artistic underground of late

Soviet Russia, and she continues to explore its themes of marginalization, poverty, and commitment to authentic, dangerous utterance. She was awarded the Solzhenitsyn Prize in 2005. Her poems translated here by Stephanie Sandler pay tribute to and memorialize her mother, Dina Shvarts, who died in 1998.

Natalya Starodubtseva was born in 1979. Her work has appeared in *Vavilon, Ural, RISK,* and *Uralskaya nov'*. In 2001 she received the Debiut Prize. Starodubtseva lives in Nizhnii Tagil (Ural region), where she teaches Russian language and literature in a night school for prisoners.

Mariya Stepanova was born in Moscow in 1972 and has written poetry since childhood. Her first publication was in *Yunost* in 1988. Stepanova is published regularly in *Znamia*. She has published three collections of poetry. She was short-listed for the Andrey Bely Prize in 2002.

Darya Sukhovey was born in Leningrad in 1977 and graduated from St. Petersburg University. She is a poet and literary curator of the Internet project "The St. Petersburg Literary Guide," providing information about literary life in St. Petersburg. Sukhovey is the author of two poetry collections.

Olga Sulchinskaya was born in Moscow in 1966. She graduated from Moscow State University and has published poems in *Arion, Znamia,* and *Novyi mir* as well as a chapbook of poems.

Elena Suntsova was born in Nizhnii Tagil in 1976. She studied at St. Petersburg University, 1995–2001, graduating in journalism. She works as a columnist of cultural events for the journal *Maksimalist,* in Nizhnii Tagil. Suntsova has published one collection, and a second is due shortly. Her work has appeared in *Vavilon, Uralskaya nov',* and *Ural*.

Vitalina Tkhorzhevskaya was born in Sverdlovsk in 1971. Her first poems appeared in samizdat and in the journal *Ural*. Since then, she has published four collections of poetry, most recently *Smirennyi gnev* (Meek wrath, 1997). She lives and works in Ekaterinburg.

Yana Tokareva was born in Moscow in 1976. Graduating in history and literature from the Russian State University for Humanities, she has taught English at the same university and works as a translator of contemporary English and Italian literature and literary theory. Original poems, prose, and translations have been published in *Vavilon, Avtornik, Okrestnosti,* and other literary periodicals, as well as on the Internet. In 2001 Tokareva was short-listed for the Debiut Prize.

Elena Vasileva was born in Vladivostok in 1964 and graduated in geophysics. She works for the Vladivostok television station and edits the almanac *Seraya loshad* (Gray horse). Vasileva has published one collection of poetry, and her work has appeared in several anthologies and journals.

Ekaterina Vlasova was born in Zlatoust in 1976. She has published poetry in *Uralskaya nov'* and *Nesovremennye zapiski*. A collection of her poetry appeared in 1998. She now lives in Cheliabinsk.

Tatyana Voltskaya was born in Leningrad and graduated from the Krupskaya Institute of Culture. She is the author of three collections of poetry and of critical essays, which have appeared in many leading journals. Her poetry has been translated into English, Italian, Dutch, Swedish, and Finnish. Voltskaya began working as a journalist in 1987–1988 on Petersburg (at that time still Leningrad) Radio, with programs on early twentieth century Russian philosophers, journals, contemporary writers, and poets. Since 2000 she has been a correspondent of Radio Liberty.

Galina Zelenina was born in 1978 in Moscow. She graduated from the department of history and philology at the Russian State University for Humanities and completed postgraduate studies at the Judaica Center of Moscow State University. Since 1999 she has published prose and poetry in the journals *Vavilon* and *RISK* (Moscow) and *Solnechnoe spletenie* (Tel Aviv). She contributed to the poetry collection *Vremia Ch* (Ch time, poems connected with the theme of Chechen war) and to the collective project *Zh* (2000), involving four young poets (four small collections under the same title). In 2001 Zelenina was short-listed for the Debiut Prize. She lives in Moscow, frequently visiting Israel, and works as a teacher of and researcher on various Jewish themes (especially regarding gender).

Gali-Dana Zinger was born in Leningrad in 1962 and graduated from the Institute of Theater, Music, and Cinematography. Since 1988, she has lived in Jerusalem, Israel. She edited the journal *IO* (1994–1995) and now edits *Dvoetochie*. She has published three collections in Russian and several in Hebrew. Her work has appeared widely and has won many awards, including Poeziya 2000 for a first collection of poetry in Hebrew.

Olga Zondberg was born in Moscow in 1972 and graduated in chemistry from Moscow State University. She now works as a manager in a public-relations firm. Since 1990 Zondberg has been one of the key figures in the Union of Young Writers "Vavilon" and has published her poetry and prose in the journals *Vavilon*, *Ural*, *Ulov*, and others. She is the author of a collection of poetry, *Kniga priznanii* (A book of confessions, 1997), and two collections of prose, *Zimniaya kampaniya nulevogo goda* (Winter campaign of the year zero, 2000) and *Ochen spokoinyi rasskaz* (A very peaceful story, 2003). Zondberg lives in Moscow.

THE TRANSLATORS

Christopher Arkell is the chief shareholder in the *London Magazine*. He also owns the *London Miscellany* and writes occasional pieces on current affairs for the *European Journal*. He has published translations, done in collaboration with Eugene Dubnov, of other Russian poets, including Pushkin.

Kevin Carey is a poet and translator. He was educated at Williams College, Massachusetts, and at Georgetown University, Washington. For some years Carey has been a member of the U.S. diplomatic corps. For the last ten years he has worked in Jerusalem.

Vitaly Chernetsky was born in 1970 in Odessa, Ukraine. He has a doctorate in comparative literature (University of Pennsylvania, 1996) and teaches in the Slavic Department at Columbia University. He has co-edited the anthology *Crossing Centuries: The New Generation in Russian Poetry* (2000). His translations from Russian and Ukrainian have appeared in *Bald Ego*, *boundary 2*, *Five Fingers Review*, *PEN International*, and *Two Lines*, among other publications, and in the anthologies *Out of the Blue: Russia's Hidden Gay Literature* (1997) and *A Hundred Years of Youth: Twentieth-Century Ukrainian Poetry* (2000).

Jenefer Coates taught literary translation at Middlesex University and also works as a translator, writer, and editor. Until recently she co-edited *In Other Words*, the journal of the Translators Association. She is writing a book on Vladimir Nabokov and translation.

Maura Dooley has edited *Making for Planet Alice: New Women Poets* (1997). *The Honey Gatherers: A Book of Love Poems* was published in 2003. She is the author of the non-fiction book *How Novelists Work* (2000). Her latest collection, *Sound Barrier: Poems 1982–2002* (2003), draws on several collections, two of which were Poetry Book Society Recommendations and one of which was short-listed for the T. S. Eliot Prize.

Terence Dooley has published original work in many magazines and journals, most recently the *Swansea Review* and *Smiths Knoll*. He translates widely from Spanish, Italian, and French and has just completed a verse translation of Paul Valéry's *Le jeune parque*.

Yury Drobyshev was born in Leningrad and graduated from the Naval Engineering Academy. He emigrated to Britain in 1978. He has contributed to the anthology *The Poetry of Perestroika* (1989) as well as to the Irina Ratushinskaya collection *Pencil Letter* (1988) and, with Carol Rumens, to *Evgeny Rein: Selected Poems* (2001).

Ruth Fainlight recently published her twelfth collection of poems, *Burning Wire*. The title poem of her previous book, *Sugar-Paper Blue* (short-listed for the 1998 Whitbread Poetry Award), is based on a visit to Leningrad in 1965 and the shock of discovering that the footsteps she could hear in the flat above were those of Anna Ahkmatova. Collections of her poems have been published in Portuguese, French, and Spanish translation, and she has published translations from the same languages.

Elaine Feinstein is a poet and novelist. In 1980 she was made a Fellow of the Royal Society of Literature. In 1990 she received a Cholmondeley Award for Poetry and was given an Honorary D.Lit. from the University of Leicester. Her versions of Marina Tsvetaeva have remained in print since 1970. Her most recent books of poems are *Daylight* (1997), a Poetry Book Society Recommendation, and *Gold* (2000). Her fourteenth novel, *Dark Inheritance*, and her biography *Ted Hughes: The Life of a Poet* were published in 2001. Her *Collected Poems and Translations*, a Poetry Book Society Special Commendation, was published in 2002.

Roy Fisher was born in 1930 in Handsworth, Birmingham. A poet and jazz piano-player, he has worked as a school and college teacher. He retired as senior lecturer in American Studies from Keele University in 1982. He is now a freelance writer and lives in Derbyshire. Fisher is the author of several collections of poetry, including *Poems, 1955–1987* (1988), and *The Dow Low Drop: New and Selected Poems* (1996). He was recently appointed poet laureate emeritus of his native city, Birmingham.

Peter France, who recently retired from a chair in French at Edinburgh University, has translated *An Anthology of Chuvash Poetry* (1991) and collections of poems by Gennady Aygi, Joseph Brodsky, Vladimir Mayakovsky, and (with Jon Stallworthy) Aleksandr Blok and Boris Pasternak. He is the author of *Poets of Modern Russia* (1982) and the editor of the *Oxford Guide to Literature in English Translation* (2000).

Gerald Janecek was born in New York in 1945. He is a professor of Russian at the University of Kentucky. He specializes in avant-garde Russian poetry and has written on and translated Andrey Bely, Russian Futurist poetry, and contemporary Russian poetry. He is the author of *The Look of Russian Poetry* (1984), *ZAUM: The Transrational Poetry of Russian Futurism* (1996), *Sight and Sound Entwined: Studies of the New Russian Poetry* (2000), and a number of articles on these subjects.

Chris Jones graduated in Russian Studies from Keele University, where he also worked on a dissertation on Joseph Brodsky's rhymes. He has translated many academic papers, some poetry, and an as yet unpublished novel by Dmitry Savitsky.

J. Kates is a poet and literary translator who lives in Fitzwilliam, New Hampshire. He is the editor of the Zephyr anthology *In the Grip of Strange Thoughts* (1999). Recently he published his own translation of Tatyana Shcherbina's collection of poems *The Score of the Game* (2003).

Catriona Kelly is reader in Russian at Oxford and tutorial fellow at New College. She has a large number of publications about Russian literature and cultural history, including, most recently, *Russian Literature: A Very Short Introduction* (2001). Published translations include work by various Russian poets and prose writers in her anthologies *Utopias: Russian Modernist Texts 1905–1940* (1999) and *An Anthology of Russian Women's Writing, 1777–1992* (1994) as well as novels by Leonid Borodin (1989) and Sergey Kaledin (1990) and poems by Elena Shvarts (in *Paradise*, 1993) and Olga Sedakova (in *The Silk of Time*, 1994).

Elizabeth Krizenesky, instructor of Russian at both Lawrence University and Fox Valley Technical College, Appleton, Wisconsin, has a B.A. from Ripon College in Ripon, Wisconsin. In addition to teaching, she both translates and interprets Russian. Her translation of Gorbanevskaya's poem was performed at an International Women's Day celebration at Lawrence University in 2002.

Dmitry Kuzmin was born in 1968 and graduated from Moscow Pedagogical University. He has published poetry since 1980 and also articles on contemporary literature, as well as translations of contemporary English, French, and Belorussian poetry. Kuzmin has won a number of prizes, including the Arion Prize (1996) and the Andrey Bely Prize (2002). He is best known as the founder of the Union of Young Writers, Vavilon (1989), and chief editor of the publishing house ARGO-RISK (1993). He runs the Avtornik literary club (founded in 1996) and has organized a number of literary festivals. Kuzmin edits several magazines, including *Vavilon*, *Triton*, and RISK (an almanac of gay literature).

Angela Livingstone is emeritus professor of Russian at Essex University and has written widely on Russian literature, translating Boris Pasternak, Marina Tsvetaeva (*The Rat-Catcher*, 1999) and, with Robert Chandler, works by Andrey Platonov (1999).

Alex Marshall was a Russian tutor, translator, and interpreter and lectured in Russian, German, and English Studies at Northbrook College, Worthing.

Fay Marshall is a widely published poet with two collections: *and* (1991) and *Mapping the Debris* (2000). She and her late husband, Alex, translated a large number of poems from Russian and German together.

Christopher Mattison studied Russian and received an MFA in translation from the University of Iowa. He is currently the managing editor of Zephyr Press and the co-director of Adventures in Poetry, in Boston.

James McGavran recently finished undergraduate studies at Kenyon College, Ohio, where he majored in modern languages and literatures. He will begin graduate school in Slavic literatures at Princeton University in 2002. He intends to focus on contemporary Russian poetry and translation.

Richard McKane's first book was *Selected Poems of Anna Akhmatova* (1969). He has co-translated, with Elizabeth McKane, the poetry of Osip Mandelstam, and his translation of Nikolay Gumilev was published as *The Pillar of Fire: Selected Poems* (1999). Among his numerous translations are selections by Leonid Aronzon and Olga Sedakova, as well as an anthology: *Ten Russian Poets: Surviving the Twentieth Century* (2003). His translations from Turkish (co-translated with Ruth Christie) are numerous. Since 1980 he has made his home in London, where he works as an interpreter and co-chairs the Pushkin Club. His own poetry has been published in Turkey with translations into Turkish. A selection of his poems on poetry along with translations was published as *Poet for Poet* (1998, 2001).

Alan Myers graduated in Russian from London University and studied at Moscow University, 1960–1961. He taught Russian and English for over twenty years, during which time he published reviews, translations, and educational articles and also worked as an interpreter for the British Council in Britain and the USSR. Since 1986 he has worked as a freelance literary translator, including mimetic rhymed versions of nineteenth-century Russian poetry, *An Age Ago* (1989). Major translations include Dostoevsky's *The Idiot* (1992) as well as Pushkin's *The Queen of Spades and Other Stories* (1997). Myers has translated poems and essays for Joseph Brodsky as well as the latter's two plays *Marbles* (1988) and *Democracy!* (1990). He was born in County Durham and is author of *Myers' Literary Guide: The North East* (1995, 1997) and co-author of *W. H. Auden: Pennine Poet* (1999).

Max Nemtsov writes: "Well, there's not much to say. I'm thirty-nine, born in Vladivostok, currently live in Moscow, a freelance translator/editor, am responsible for the *Speaking in Tongues* web publication (http://spintongues.msk.ru/)."

Robert Reid is reader in modern languages (Russian) at Keele University. He has written and edited many books and articles on Romanticism and is co-editor of *Essays in Poetics*, the journal of the British Neo-Formalist Circle, to which he has also regularly contributed translations of modern Russian poetry. He has translated Russian poetry for various other collections and anthologies, including work by Brodsky, Prigov, and Sedakova.

Carol Rumens has published eleven collections of poetry, a novel, short stories, and literary journalism and has edited several anthologies. With Yury Drobyshev she has contributed translations from the Russian to several publications, including *Evgeny Rein: Selected Poems* (2002) and *After Pushkin* (1999). Recent poetry books include *Best China Sky* (1995) and *Holding Pattern* (1998). Based in Belfast for some years, she has held several residencies and currently teaches at the University of Bangor, North Wales.

Stephanie Sandler is a scholar of modern Russian poetry and of the Pushkin period, with a special interest in women's writing. Her publications include *Distant Pleasures: Alexander Pushkin and the Writing of Exile* (1989) and several edited collections, including *Sexuality and the Body in Russian Culture* (with Jane T. Costlow and Judith Vowles, 1993) and *Rereading Russian Poetry* (1999). She is professor of Slavic languages and literatures at Harvard University.

Jason Schneiderman was educated at the University of Maryland, New York University, and the Herzen Institute (St. Petersburg, Russia). His poems have appeared in *The Penguin Book of the Sonnet* and other places. His essays have appeared in *Frigate*. He teaches creative writing at Hofstra (New York) and lives in New York City.

Steven Seymour is a freelance simultaneous interpreter of Russian, currently based in New York.

Alan Shaw has published translations of Pushkin (*Mozart and Salieri*) and Aleksandr Griboedov. His own poems have appeared in *Grand Street* and *Partisan Review*. He also writes drama, music, and essays. Currently he is living in New York.

Dennis Silk (1928–1998) was born in London and after 1955 lived in Jerusalem. His collections of poetry include *Punished Land* (1980), *Hold Fast* (1984), *Catwalk and Overpass* (1990), and *William the Wonder-Kid: Plays, Puppet Plays, and Theater Writings* (1996).

Nika Skandiaka (Anna Khazin) was born in Moscow and raised in the United States. Her translations have appeared in *Modern Poetry in Translation*, *Absinthe: New Writing from Europe*, and the online magazine *Speaking in Tongues* (www.spintongues.com).

Derek Walcott, poet and playwright, was awarded the Nobel Prize for Literature in 1992. His epic poem *Omeros* appeared in 1990. Born in Castries, St. Lucia, in 1930, Walcott divides his time between St. Lucia and New York. Apart from Pavlova's and Shcherbina's works, he has produced translations of some other poetry, notably work by his close friend Joseph Brodsky.

INDEX TO TITLES